How To Stop Existing And Start Living

Secrets Of Successful Living, Making & Saving Money

How To Stop Existing And Start Living

Secrets Of Successful Living, Making & Saving Money

Vince Stanzione

First Success Publishing

Published by
First Success Publishing Limited
Exchange House
494 Midsummer Boulevard
Central Milton Keynes
MK9 2EA
U.K.

Email: Info@firstsuccess.com

First edition published in Great Britain 1997
Second edition published in 1999
Third edition published in 2000
ISBN 0-95-307750-0

British Library Cataloguing in Publication Data.
A catalogue record for this book is available from the
British Library.

Acknowledgements

Many authors write long acknowledgements which most readers including me, don't really care about. They mention lots of names of people who have helped them produce the book, they mention their friends, parents, wife/husband, children and even their dog, however, they never acknowledge the most important person in the world, and that is the reader and buyer of the book, after all, if it wasn't for the readers who invest their time and money in reading and buying books, then the publishing world wouldn't exist. So my acknowledgement and true thanks is to you the reader and buyer of this book.

The only other acknowledgement is a legal one, which is that the Author and the Publisher acknowledges all trademarks mentioned in this book. The author also gives credit to any named individual and any quote of theirs that has been used. The author also acknowledges the excellent work provided by Chelsey Baker in proof reading and checking this book.

> **NOTE:** The Author and the Publisher have taken the utmost care and effort to check the information and advice in this book, nevertheless, with a book as comprehensive as this one and the fact that things do change, the Author and the Publisher cannot be responsible for any loss that you may suffer as a result of any omission or inaccuracy.

Contents

Contents

CHAPTER 1

Introduction

As far as I am aware we only live once, at least on this planet, therefore, don't you think that you should reach out and get everything that you really want out of life?

If you can truly say that you are happy with the quality of your life, the amount of money you earn, and your relationship with your partner and others, then read no further, I congratulate you and would be interested to learn your secrets.

If, however, you are one of the millions that hate getting up in the morning and going to a dead end job to earn a meagre wage, only to find that your pay cheque has run out when there is still 25 days in the month to go, then read on.

This book has been written for everyone that wants to increase their income, reduce their out-goings and to increase their standard of living.

The book is divided into 3 sections:

❶ This is about yourself, your goals, your fears, your past, your state of mind and how to start taking control of your life and living every day to its fullest potential.

❷ Making Money. I will reveal to you my secrets on how money is made and how you can copy tried and tested formulas that will make you as much money as you want and deserve. I'll also explain how to get a pay rise and start earning what you are truly worth.

❸ Saving Money. Smart people are not only good at making money they're also good at saving money and buying everything at the lowest possible price. Whether you are buying a car, a toaster, a designer dress or the latest hi-fi, I will reveal to you how to buy at the lowest price.

There is a better way of life

I don't know what your current position is, however, I can guess that you are working on a low wage or so called acceptable wage, have debts, average relationship, plodding along and you are not sure what the future will hold for you. You feel that life is passing you by and although you know you should be doing better, you just seem to be stuck in a rut and living an average life-style.

Well the good news is that there is a better life, you can increase your income, pay off debts and most importantly increase your quality of life and gain self-confidence and respect. You genuinely "can have everything in the world that you really want."

It's easy for you to say

I can tell you truthfully, however bad your situation is, whether you are in debt, having personal difficulties, totally demoralised, addicted to drugs/alcohol or worse, I can guarantee you that I have been in a worse position or I know someone who has.

I want you to remember this forever:

"You may be crying and upset because you haven't any shoes, and that's terrible, however, spare a thought for the person next to you, he hasn't any feet and that's truly disastrous."

And that's your first lesson, it may look bad but believe me it could be worse.

If you stop reading this book now and don't read any further, then this one piece of information is worth more than what you paid for the book.

Only you can change your life for the better

You are in charge of your life. Everything that's happened to you in the past, your successes, your failures and the problems you may be currently going through, were brought about by your actions in one shape or form. I know the truth hurts and it's easy for us all to blame other people for our failures, problems and shortcomings. How many times do you hear people say, "It's my boss's fault," "It's my wife's fault," "If only I was older/younger," or "It's the government's fault..."

Well the fact is that you are in charge of your life, you're the driver of the train and you can either choose to drive the train around the world on a rich, fulfilling and rewarding journey or you can choose to leave the train standing at the station, with the wheel rusting away and the engine ceasing up.

You choose! 95% of the population, including dare I say YOU, are at the station. If you believe in safety in numbers then carry on, go with the flow, stick with the masses. If, however, you know deep down that there is more to life and you want to join the 5% then let this book help you to get the train going. Now I'm not saying that you will go flying out of the station at 100 m.p.h., but we can at least start to pull away and even if we only start at 1 mile per hour, that's more than the other 95% that are travelling at 0 m.p.h. isn't it?

You see, if you told me that you wanted to be rich, give up smoking, alcohol, drugs or get into shape etc. I could help you, I could encourage you, give you books to read, audio tapes etc. but unless you really want to do it, then it's pointless, only you can make it happen, I guarantee that if you want something badly enough, then with the help of this book you can have it.

Some years ago a baseball manager, Tommy Lasorda said, "There are those that watch things happen, those who wonder what happened and those that make things happen." You need to become a player to win in life, being a spectator and watching the world go by just isn't any fun. Others may be content to exist and get by being a statistic on a government chart, but I know that you are not satisfied with being just a number, you want to do better than this.

I'm very unlucky

I come from a background that believes you make your own luck. If you work 14 hours a day, it's amazing how lucky you will become. And that's a fact, luck is determined by our own efforts, the blood, sweat and tears that we put into life.

I'm sorry, I do not believe that luck has anything to do with whether Jupiter is in Mars, or it's the Chinese year of the rat which means it's my lucky year or that my horoscope in the daily down-market newspaper says that today will be good for finances.

What about lottery winners? That's great, I'm pleased for them, but if you are going to waste the rest of your life hoping for a quick fix, then I think you've got a problem. The odds are stacked against you and even if you did win the lottery, don't think that will be the end of your problems, because it won't be.

You make your own luck in this world and I don't like the term "opportunity knocks," I have found in 99% of cases it doesn't. I went out and searched high and low for the opportunities, so if you are sitting at home waiting for the door bell to ring expecting "opportunities" to be standing outside, I am sorry to disappoint you.

I hear you say, "What about the 1% when opportunity does knock on the door?" or in most cases lands through the letterbox, well what normally happens is that either no one's at home because they are down the local store buying a lottery ticket, they don't bother answering the door because their favourite depressing soap is on TV, or if they do drag themselves to the door, they'll slam the door shut on opportunity because they won't recognise it or they won't believe it.

And that's the way it is, then when they sit back down they'll say, "I never get any lucky breaks or opportunities in life."

CHAPTER 2

Getting Started

The first thing to understand is that getting out of your current position will take effort, perseverance and time. Most people spend 20 to 30 years messing up their lives, they over-eat, over-drink, don't save for the future, don't learn any new skills, let their minds cease up and then one day they decide that they want a new life and they expect to sort all of their problems out with a magic pill or by reading a book within a few hours! Get real, success and riches come to those that do something to earn it.

The old Chinese proverb "A journey of a million miles begins with one step," is very true in these circumstances. It's also important to remember that a steady amount of effort is far better than a short burst and then nothing. It is a fact that the only way to lose weight is by a steady diet and not a get slim quick regime.

Making money and increasing the quality of your life will be similar to being on a diet, you'll have high points and low points, but the key is to keep going and don't give up.

Tiny steps lead to massive leaps

Success normally comes not from one big change or action, it comes from lots of small successes, which when put together make a big success. Remember this as you work through the book, steps that may seem stupid, pointless and have no meaning on their own will combine to make massive leaps forward in your life.

Imagine a brick, a brick on its own is not very exciting, stylish or useful, yet when thousands or millions of bricks are put together we have amazing buildings, churches, houses and hospitals etc.

You often hear pop stars and TV celebrities being called "an over-night success," well the truth is that there is no such thing and I know many stars are deeply offended by being called "an over-night success." Just because a star has recently come into the spotlight, doesn't mean that they've just sprung out of nowhere, many TV stars had already spent many years working in theatre, TV commercials and small background parts before they landed their big part. This is a great example of the small successes leading to a big success.

Can you go the extra mile?

If you answer this question truthfully at the moment, the answer will be "No" however, with some time and the help of this book we can and we must change that answer to "Yes."

If you look at life's winners, whether they are a great business person, sports person or show business celebrity, one of their strongest attributes will be their ability to go the extra mile.

Imagine you are a salesman or an aspiring model looking to be discovered, you've been out all day knocking on doors without any success, it's getting late, you're tired, do you give up and go home or do you try those extra few doors?

Successful inventors are very good at going the extra mile. Many top inventors and scientists have died in their pursuit of perfection.

Many items that we use everyday that are best sellers were at one time or the other called "stupid," "useless" or "it will never catch on." Now imagine if that inventor had given up because he had been rejected. Do you know that many top selling bands like the Beatles and U2 were turned down by many big record labels? The Beatles were told that they were losers and would never last, well we all know what happened to them!

I've recently been researching explorers or more importantly failed explorations and I've noticed that almost without fail, as soon as one failed attempt is finished they are already planing their next attempt. These people do not give up do they?

When you go the extra mile and you will, you will stand out and shine. Today most people try to get by with the minimum amount of work or effort, that's why when someone goes the extra mile, especially in the service industry, it really stands out. I'll talk more about this later.

Now let's go back to you, as you read this book you will be asked to put various plans into action, you will be asked to change the way you act and think. Now just like an inventor you will come up against resistance from your so called friends, family and people you meet every day. They will think you are mad, stupid and they will advise you to give up and when things are not working out they will tell you those famous words "I told you it wouldn't work."

Please learn to ignore these people as they will destroy you. Stick to the plans outlined in this book and I guarantee that you will have the last laugh. A famous newspaper advert from the 1950's had the headline "They all laughed when I sat at the piano, but when I started to play..."

You see people may laugh at you and put you down today, but when you drive past them in your new shiny Ferrari and they are standing at the bus stop, I guarantee that you will be laughing louder.

Breaking free from your comfort zone

The only thing that is holding you back from success and happiness is you or should I say the old you, as you are now making a change for the better. You see, you are currently living in your comfort zone, this is what most people call normal or acceptable, i.e. you get up, you commute to work, you work, you commute home, you eat, watch TV, sleep and then start all over again. At weekends you do what you can with the meagre pay you receive including, buying a lottery ticket. What a waste of a life, yet millions of people are living or should I say existing like this as you read this book.

Here's a quote by Denis Waitley:

I go to work, I earn my bread,

I watch TV and go to bed,

Sunrise, sunset - year to year,

Before I know it winter's here.

I know that this may sound harsh, but if you are truly honest with yourself, you will agree with me that that's what life is like for 95% of the population, possibly including yourself. Go to a train station and see people running around like headless chickens. Look at the way they dress, their postures and their facial expressions. You can feel and smell the stress and pollution in the air. Is this the way you want to live?

Of course not! So why are you? Simply because you don't know that there's a better way and you have accepted that this is your life. The other big factor holding you back is fear of failure, embarrassment and change.

I truly believe that the majority of people are so busy trying to earn a living to get by, that they have lost all hope in life and inspiration to be a millionaire. They have accepted that where they are today is the best they can do and they don't have any dreams, goals or desires. They have accepted that this is "happy."

You see, you have been brainwashed by your parents, friends, teachers, the media, your boss, that it's OK to get by and live like this.

Well I am here to set you loose, break you free from a mediocre life-style. You can and will do better than you are doing today. I want you to be unhappy with your current position. It's time for you to change and to act. I want you to dream, I want you to reach up for the stars. Today is the first day of your new life.

> **"When you reach out for the stars, you may not quite get one, but you won't come up with a handful of mud either."**
>
> **Leo Burnett**

Why I really want you to succeed

You may think, "Why is this guy trying to help me?" Well firstly, you've paid by purchasing this book, which helps in a small way towards my wealth and secondly, I've done very well over the last few years and it's my way of giving something back. If I can show you how to avoid just a few of the mistakes that I've made, then I feel I've done a good thing.

The other reason I am willing to disclose my secrets is that when you become successful it will not affect me in any negative way, in fact your success will help me become more successful because the chances are you'll tell others about this book and you will probably buy other books and videos from me. So it's a, you win I win partnership. I really do want you to succeed and be happy, in fact I could be the only one that does.

I'm sure there will be times when it seems that it's you against the rest of the world, well remember that I will be on your side, so that's two against the rest of the world, which may sound like we are outnumbered, but we can do it can't we?

Before we get started I want to apologise in advance if I come across arrogant, rude or harsh in any of the following text. I need to shake you loose of all the negative thoughts that are inside you and I need to fire you into action and this may require a kick in the rear!

I would also like to point out that I am the most un-sexist person you will ever meet, I want everyone to be a success whether they are a man, woman, black, Asian, green, pink or whatever, so when I state "Him," "He" or "Man" etc. it could equally be "Her," "She" or "Woman" etc.

We're here to learn not have fun

If I had a pound for every time I was told "We're here to learn not have fun" when I was at school I would be a billionaire! I'm sure you know what I'm talking about, you probably still remember Mrs Parker your maths teacher telling you the same thing, or if you went to a Convent school (like me), it would have been Sister Mary Michael.

When I went to work (for a real company) it was the same again "You're here to work, not to mess around," you no doubt get the same.

Well I'm here to rebel. I can tell you that you can learn, work and have fun, in fact I believe that if it's fun, it gets done. I've tried my best to remember this throughout the book and keep the text informative but fun. I've thrown a few pieces of humour in and I hope this helps. Let's give you a little something to start you chuckling:

☺

It's amazing that what we say or write doesn't always come out how we meant it to, here are a few apparently true quotes that were written on motor insurance claims forms or statements made to the police:

"Coming home, I drove into the wrong house and collided with a tree I don't have!"

"I had been driving my car for 40 years when I fell asleep at the wheel and had an accident!"

And here's my favourite, apparently given to the police:

"The guy was all over the road. I had to swerve a number of times before I finally managed to hit him!"

I hope you are smiling, at least a little.

The quicker that the "learning and working can be fun" mentality gets into our schools and work-places, the quicker we'll have smarter children and a better work-force.

So let's get started on our journey...

CHAPTER 3

Let's talk about you

This section of the book will talk about the most important person in the world, that's you. You see, unless we can get you in the right frame of mind, then it's pointless discussing making money or saving money. Many of the techniques discussed in the next sections will only work once we have made you stronger and outlined your goals, wants and needs.

DO NOT SKIP THIS SECTION

If you skip this section you are guaranteed to fail at saving and making money. Yes, you are eager to start, but we need to build you up, just as if we were building an office block, we need strong foundations and a plan to build from.

Q. How much do you think you are worth?

a) 1 million pounds

b) 10 million pounds

c) 100 million pounds

Now, before you answer this question let me make you an offer. Let's imagine that I am a body broker, I buy and sell body parts such as, eyes, legs and hearts etc. Now imagine that I come and see you and I offer you 10 million pounds for your eyes and another 10 million pounds for your legs. Would you sell me your eyes and legs? The answer I'm sure is NO, you'll slam the door shut on me and tell me to get lost.

So how much are you worth? The answer is you are priceless, you are unique and you are smarter than any super computer. Your brain is the most powerful computer in the world. Even with great new technology and modern micro chips these computers cannot compete with your brain. Your biggest asset is that you are unique, you are the original one and only. Of the 6 billion people who currently inhabit the earth, there never has been, nor will there ever be, another YOU.

You are truly an incredibly sophisticated creation. Let me tell you a few facts about yourself:

- Your body has the capability to repair itself continually at the rate of 2 billion cells per day. (Don't you wish that dent in your car could do that!)
- 98% of all the atoms in your body change in less than one year.

More specifically, you change:

- Your skin about every 20 days
- Your stomach about once a month
- All of your brain cells every year
- Your skeleton once every three months

Just think, by the time you've finished reading this book you will be a new person, both in mind and body, so if you wanted a new start, then here it is.

A few other facts about yourself:

- Your brain has limitless capacity to store and process information

- You have about 600 muscles
- You have about 200 bones
- You have about 20 square feet of skin
- Your heart beats about 100,000 times per day
- Your kidneys will remove 1 million gallons of waste products from your blood by the time you are 70 years of age.

The most expensive, rarest, beautiful and precious asset that you will ever own is not a painting, piece of jewellery or anything else, it's YOU.

Now I want to teach you an important lesson in SELF-CONFIDENCE and SELF-ESTEEM. You must develop high self-confidence and self-esteem, regardless of your past failures or current difficulties, you must believe in yourself.

If you do not believe in yourself, then you will never be able to convince anyone else to believe in you. I've worked in finance and banking in the past and have turned down many business loans for the simple reason that the applicant just didn't prove to me that he believed in the project himself, you see banks often lend on the strength of the individual's character and enthusiasm in many cases, and unless you show that you are 100% committed and believe in yourself, then don't expect the bank to back you.

The next time someone tries to put you down or the next time that you criticise or feel sorry for yourself, remember how valuable and precious you are.

Write this down on a piece of paper in big letters and read it over a few times:

The most expensive, rarest, beautiful and most precious asset that I will ever own is ME.

Feeling better? Good, you should do, feeling positive about yourself inspires the confidence and respect that you must have and deserve.

The aim of this section is to make you:

A) Start feeling successful

B) Act as if you are already successful

The combination of A+B will = You will be successful

It's time for some surgery

No, I don't mean cosmetic surgery, I mean surgery from within, changing the way you look and feel about yourself, and life in general.

Let's start with the way you act and present yourself to others, whether it's in person or on the telephone. Here are some important qualities that you need to brush up on and improve:

A smile

A smile can get you a long way. You can even hear a smile on the telephone. If you ask for something with a smile, there's a far better chance of getting it than if you look glum and grumpy. Smiling is a positive statement about yourself, it gives others confidence in you and implies success. The great thing about a smile is that it is internationally known, I can't speak Japanese but if I walked into a room of Japanese businessmen that couldn't speak English, I could still smile and they would understand me, wouldn't they?

I recently heard about a telesales company that has put mirrors on their staff's desks, so that they could see their facial expressions while they were on the phone selling, apparently sales figures are soaring!

A warm, rich tone to your voice

The way you speak can give you a very big advantage or disadvantage. Now I'm not saying that you should try to speak like the Queen, that would be false. (Unless of course, you are the Queen and in which case I apologise your Majesty.) I also do not believe that you should try and change your accent, what I do recommend is:

Try to speak clearly, do not cut words short and do not speak too fast as this shows nervousness, at the same time speaking very slowly can be annoying and very boring.

To be able to speak in public is a very desirable asset, like everything it takes practice and courage. You could practice important everyday phrases in front of a mirror or with a tape recorder/video camera.

There are many books, audio tapes and videos that are dedicated to this subject and it could be wise to invest in one, or take one out from the library. You may also consider enrolling in a course or evening class on public speaking, as this is a very good way to build up practice and confidence. One day you could become very successful and you may even appear on television or be heard on the radio and your public speaking skills will really help you.

As well as speaking in public it is important to be able to use the telephone effectively, whether you are booking a reservation for a hotel or trying to sell something, your telephone manner is very important.

I've sold hundreds of thousands of pounds worth of products over the phone, ranging from computer software, to stocks and shares and the best tip I can give you is to stand up or walk a few paces while you are on the phone. Trust me, it makes a difference, you may need to get a cheap extension cable which are available from stores like Tandy or Radio Shack.

There's a lot of skill to using the telephone effectively, most of us are not taught any telephone skills and I would strongly recommend that you get hold of a free booklet, published by British Telecom called "Talkworks tm, How to get more out of life through better conversations." Tel: 0800 800 808 for your copy.

Enthusiasm in what you request

This is self-explanatory, don't sound unsure or timid (even if you really are), ask for the product/service you require with enthusiasm. It works.

Good eye contact

I always think that people who cannot look you in the eye are shifty and are hiding something. Maintaining good eye contact is an easy thing to do with some practice.

A firm handshake

In this day and age where we have videophones, faxes and E-mail, it is easy to forget about a handshake. There will be times when you will be introduced to someone for the first time and a firm handshake will make a good first impression. Whether you are male or female, you should not be afraid of a handshake.

Sincerity and interest in others

This is a very important quality and will make a big difference in whether you get what you want or not. During everyday life you will come across people who can make a big difference to the quality of your life. People such as hotel desk clerks, airline check-in staff, waiters, office clerks and sales staff, to name a few.

In the saving money section, we will go into how these people can make the difference between you flying in the worst seat in economy class or flying in the best seat in first class, so take note.

You see, most of us will treat the "little" people with no respect or dignity. When checking into a hotel, picking up a car etc. try to show some interest in the person on the other side, don't be false, but look cheerful and ask a few questions. I normally find a question such as "It looks busy/quiet today," or "Your working late/early today," work quite well as a starting point.

Why bother? Well firstly, it is courteous to your fellow human being and secondly, if the clerk can offer an upgrade, newer car or a way to save money, who do you think they will give it to? The guy who looks friendly and takes an interest in them, or the guy that treats them like a nobody or like they are invisible?

Every time you meet someone or you talk to someone on the phone, you have the opportunity to sell yourself and you have the opportunity to be liked or disliked and although it is a fact that you will not get on, or be liked by 100% of the population, you can try and beat the averages.

A purposeful posture - standing tall and a manner which communicates an expectation that you deserve and expect to get what you request

I've read a few times that taller people get further ahead and this may have some truth, however, I believe that a purposeful posture is more important than your height. Walking tall, not slouching in chairs etc. helps your appearance to others, it will also help you to speak more clearly and prevent back pains later on in life.

Ensure that your head is up high and that your eyes are looking straight ahead or up. It is impossible to feel good if you are constantly looking down.

A good posture, energetic movements, a bounce in your step and a good smile instantly give you an air of success and what does it cost you? Absolutely nothing! If you feel depressed, put on a smile, change your posture and I guarantee that you will start to feel happy. Be proud, walk like a peacock with its feathers spread out, not all scrunched up and looking down.

Let's summarise

If you sit or stand slouched, speak softly with a slow and boring tone, then you are going to have a hard job convincing anyone that you are successful and that they should be dealing with you. It is important to put the points discussed into practice as soon as possible, even if your financial position has not changed yet at this stage, you will start to feel better.

I don't know about you, but I like to deal with colourful people, by this I mean people who are happy, they smile and they are enthusiastic, both in their movements and their voice tones. If I am going to spend money in a shop or take on an employee, then this is the person that I want, I don't want a dull, boring and depressing person who acts like they are made out of wood.

As I've already said, giving out the right impression, standing tall, with a smile etc. is easy to do and it costs you nothing. If you've ever said to yourself "They're not very helpful," or "They don't look happy." Have you ever thought that it could be you, giving off the wrong impression? I've found that smiling is contagious, you smile at someone and in most cases they smile back at you, you look grumpy and they'll look grumpy at you, it's a bit like a mirror. Try it out and see what I mean.

Listening

If you hadn't already noticed, you have two ears, one on each side of your head, yet you only have one mouth but most people spend more time talking than listening, when really they should listen twice as often as they speak! Being a good listener will help you immensely, both in your personal and business life. I've made a great deal of money from ideas that came to me by listening to people. I regularly listen to talk radio, where people phone in and give their opinions and concerns, by listening I can get a good idea of what people are interested in and what they are concerned about, I would then develop something to fill that need.

Most people like to talk about themselves, a lot of people divulge many trade secrets by talking too much. I've watched people mess up sales which were already in the bag, if they had only stopped talking, instead they go on and on and say something they shouldn't and before you know it, they've talked themselves out of the sale. When I was in telephone sales I would always get off the phone as soon as possible, once the client had said, "Yes."

If you become an active listener, you will find that this will become a very good asset. I've met people who have said that they'd really enjoyed my company and that we'd had an interesting conversation, but the amazing fact was that I had only spoken a few words during the whole meeting, but they hadn't even noticed, people really do like to talk about themselves, so let them.

On the point of listening, wherever possible, let the other person finish before you butt in or try and pre-empt what they are going to say. Firstly, it's annoying for the other person and secondly, you can do yourself a lot of damage by pre-empting what they were going to say, wrongly.

Think before you speak, I know there are times in all of our lives when we come out with words that we live to regret later. Remember to think twice, before you speak once!

Dressing for success

I believe that you should never judge someone by the way they dress, especially in this day and age, however, most "normal" companies still believe that if you wear a suit and tie you are successful, yet if you wear jeans and trainers you are a loser and haven't any money.

You really need to dress to suit the occasion and the person you are meeting, take into account the person's age and the type of business they are in.

Before I go on to dress, remember that the way you carry yourself and your posture will make you look better, you can have the most expensive, tailored suit in the world, but if you don't stand or sit correctly it will look terrible.

The right dress code for men

The classic business uniform for a man is still a good suit, a good shirt, preferably white (no stripes, or shirts with a different coloured collar to the body) and a sensible coloured tie, not over the top (avoid Mickey Mouse ties for sensible meetings), but not boring or grey and a good pair of comfortable leather shoes which are clean.

Grooming

You should have clean hair and be well shaved, if you have a beard or moustache then make sure it is clean and tidy.

Good skin

Most men spend little or no time looking after their skin, a good complexion is important for men. There are now many products made for men such as, cleansers and moisturisers, start including them in your daily routine and if you get stuck on what to buy, ask your wife or girlfriend for help.

The right dress code for women

Although women have more options and can be a bit more adventurous with colours, I still think that a good suit is the best bet. Dress smart, but not overly sexy as this will intimidate both men and women.

Grooming

Hair should be neat and clean, and should not cover the eye or cause you to keep sweeping it away. Although colouring your hair is acceptable these days, you must ensure that the colour is well maintained and done professionally.

Make-up

Make-up is an essential part of everyday life for most women, however, I believe that more women should take advice, read books or attend a course on how to apply make up effectively and to suit their face and skin. I also believe that like clothes, make-up should be varied to suit the occasion.

It's the way you apply make-up that makes the difference, not whether it is a top designer brand or a budget brand.

Perfumes/aftershaves

I don't believe there is a problem with perfume or aftershave, however, it must NOT be too overpowering, remember that less is more.

Summary to dress appearance

It is important to "look the part" with the correct dress and appearance for the correct occasion, dress how you think the other person would expect you to look.

Inside feelings

We've discussed our outside appearance, however, what about the inner voice we all have? The silent words that we all say to ourselves produce feelings. These can be positive, happy and life-enhancing, or negative, unhappy and detrimental to us.

Just like we need to project the right external voice, we also need to have the right internal voice. As you read this do you hear a whiny, sleepy, apologetic voice or do you hear a rich, strong energetic voice?

If you have just read this paragraph sitting slouched in a chair and your inner voice sounded as though it was sleepy and lacked energy, then we have a problem!

Let's try a test. Read the previous paragraph but sit back in your chair with your head up, read the paragraph silently to yourself in a strong voice with energy. Feel excited about what you are learning, you should be after all, your life is changing for the better.

Happy music makes happy people

Until recently I had never realised how important music and the sounds that surround us are. Music can truly change your mood. If you don't believe me, try listening to a morbid, slow song and then listen to a fast, up beat song, it makes a difference doesn't it?

CHAPTER 4

What do you want out of your life?

Unless you really know what you want to achieve, you will never get it. Excuse me for being blunt, but the biggest reason why you are getting nowhere in life is not the fact that you are unlucky, disadvantaged, black, Japanese or whatever, it is the fact that you have never sat down and been honest with yourself and laid out your goals and ambitions.

Imagine going into a travel agent and saying, "Send me somewhere!" The agent would say, "Where do you want to go?" and you say, "A really nice place, you know, a place where I can be happy, a place I can have an important job, a beautiful wife, some nice kids, a really great place." Could a travel agent help you? Of course not! No one can help you until you tell them exactly where you want to go and what you want.

What DO you want? I suppose you want lots of money and a good life! That is not a specific goal, that's what idiots say every week when they spend their money on the lottery. You have to be far more specific than that. Even if you believe in yourself, success is impossible without specific, well-defined goals.

I have asked hundreds of people, "What do you want out of life?" and very rarely do I ever get an answer and even when I do, it's something like "I want to be happy." Most people just don't know what they want and that's why they don't get anywhere. Before you read this book I would be amazed if you had already made out a written goals sheet, I would guess that 99% of the population do not have well-defined or written goals.

I didn't have any specific goals, I had ideas and vague generalities, but not any goals and I didn't get anywhere. Until I developed specific, well defined goals, I could not succeed. When I made specific goals, which I wrote down, then I started to succeed.

Your road map to success

If you wanted to drive from London to Edinburgh, would you just get in your car and drive in any direction? Or would you plan out a journey, get a map and think about where you are going?

You see, that's how life is for most people they are on the road to nowhere, they're not sure where they are going, in most cases they are travelling in the wrong direction and then they wonder why they never get anywhere.

Until you map out your life, you will never achieve anything. You need to know what direction you are travelling in, why you are travelling in that direction and what you are going to find along the way. Setting goals and mapping out your life is the foundation to success. Now this may sound tedious and boring, but in fact it is very exciting, it's your chance to write down anything and everything that you want out of your life, it's like writing a letter to Father Christmas and as long as you are good and you do whatever it takes to succeed, you are guaranteed to get everything on your wish list and a bit extra.

Where will you be 5 or 10 years from now?

At this point you probably can't answer this question, the chances are you couldn't tell me where you will be by the end of this year, but after working through the next section you will be able to answer this question with laser precision, you will also be able to answer the question in a positive format, for example, "I will own my own business," not "I don't want to be on the scrap heap!"

The following two charts are very important to your success. FILL THEM OUT. Don't pass them over and say, "I'll do that later" or "I don't need goals." If you don't fill them out you will never succeed.

I suggest that you get a piece of paper, pen and a ruler and then copy out this chart in your own handwriting and fill in the blanks. Think hard about your answers, this is not a game!

Chart 1 - I NEED

This chart is really what you need right now. Imagine that I met you today with an open cheque book and offered to take care of all your immediate needs. List the things you need such as:

Suggestions:

> Bills paid
>
> Rent or mortgage paid
>
> Insurance
>
> Clothing
>
> Medical Insurance
>
> Car running costs
>
> Food

Chart 2 - I WANT

In this list you should list out specifically what you want in your life. This list is very personal to you, after all, not everyone will want a Ferrari!

Suggestions:

Rolls Royce/Ferrari F40/Porsche 911 *

£400,000 house/apartment in...*

One year trip around the world

£500,000 in the bank

A gold Rolex watch

A Chanel suit

A certain piece of antique furniture/painting

To have an American Express Platinum Card

To stay in the world's leading hotels

To eat at a top restaurant

To own a racehorse

* Note: Specific wants - state the actual location of your dream home i.e. London or Los Angeles. You can even state the street name i.e. £400,000 home on Baker Street, London. State the amount of bedrooms, tennis courts, gardens, swimmingpools. Describe the house as if you already own it or are about to buy it today. If your want is a car, then state the model and colour of the car, i.e. red Ferrari F40, with Alpine stereo/cd and air-conditioning etc.

As well as material items you should also list wants such as, to find a new partner, to improve my relationship, to get into better shape. These characteristics or attributes are intangible and are sometimes harder to list. Use the list that follows to help you.

Next to each quality circle a number. If you have the
quality, circle 3 if you don't have the quality and don't want
to have the quality, circle 2 if you don't have the quality
but really want the quality, circle 1

To be more assertive	1	2	3
To be more friendly	1	2	3
The ability to finish what I start	1	2	3
To stop wasting time	1	2	3
To be a leader	1	2	3
To improve my relationship with my spouse	1	2	3
To be in good health	1	2	3
To be enthusiastic	1	2	3
To be admired by others	1	2	3
To organise ideas better	1	2	3
To feel less guilty	1	2	3
To be more considerate	1	2	3
To admit being wrong	1	2	3
To speak well	1	2	3
To be interested in others	1	2	3
To stop putting things off	1	2	3
To have a good sense of humour	1	2	3
To try new things	1	2	3
To face problems with courage	1	2	3
To not blame others for my errors	1	2	3
To be ambitious	1	2	3
To take pride in my work	1	2	3
To have a good memory	1	2	3

Feel free to add anything else you wish to this list.

Once you have completed this list you can add all the
qualities that you want and have circled with a 1, to your
Want List.

Important notes on goals

1. The list of goals is for your use and benefit only. Be honest with yourself and don't write things down for the sake of it or because it will sound good if someone else reads it.

2. Make sure you really want the goal. When you wrote that goal down it should have been with passion and excitement, not as if it was a chore. Every item you have asked for will have to be earned and unless you really want it, you won't be able to have it. Now I'm not limiting you, ask for everything you truly want, but get ready to give something back.

3. Make sure your goal was positive, for example, "I want a new £400,000 house," NOT "I want to get out of this awful studio flat!" Always keep your mind fixed on the qualities and possessions you want, never what you don't want.

4. Is the goal high enough. Set your goals high, for example, if you are currently earning £10,000 a year, don't set your goal to earn £11,000 or £12,000, set it at £40,000. You may be afraid to write down a high goal for fear of failing and that's understandable, however, you must get what you deserve. Reach out and reach up, aim for the peak of the mountain. If you really want the goal, you will achieve it. Don't be a little dreamer, because that's all you will achieve - little success, think big, it's the only way.

5. Make sure your goals are realistic and I don't mean limiting yourself. If you want to earn £500,000 next year running your own business, then that's fine and is a realistic goal, I've done it so it is possible. An unrealistic goal is to make £500,000 by gambling or winning the lottery. You might as well set a goal that you want to walk on water!

6. Make sure your goals do not clash. If you want to live in a £400,000 house, your income goal needs to be at a level to support that. If you want to own a private jet, then you are going to need money for landing fees, fuel etc.

7. Your goals should be a base not a maximum. Let me explain, when I was in stockbroking we would have sales allocations i.e. to place 500,000 shares in ABC plc during the next 7 days. Let me add that we would earn commission on these transactions and if we sold more than the allocation, we would earn extra commission. Now many brokers would sell their allocation within the first 3 or 4 days and sit back and relax for the next few days, others would do totally the opposite and place their allocation within the last 2 days, either way most met their required target, however, very few exceeded this amount. You see, the target had been seen as a base as well as a maximum. Now if the base target had been set at 750,000, I'm sure this would have been achieved as well.

8. Set time limits to achieve your goals, be optimistic, but do not set insane goals, i.e. making a million in the next 48 hours. I've found that setting a time frame has helped me greatly, for example, to buy a new, red Ferrari F40 in cash, within the next 6 to 9 months.

Fine tune your Goal List

Study and revise your list until you have everything down that you want, both materialistic and on a personal quality level. You must have certain personal qualities, i.e. self-confidence, self-respect and the ability to follow through and finish what you start etc. to achieve other materialistic goals.

Re-write your Goal List in the current tense - I am, I have, I own:

I now want you to write a new Goal List as if you already have them. For example:

If you listed that you wanted self-confidence, the ability to follow through and finish what you start, have more energy and to own a private jet, then your list should state:

I am self-confident, I enjoy meeting new challenges and people

I do follow through and finish what I start

It's the year 2010 and I own a private jet

It's the year 2001 and I have found my perfect partner

I have energy and determination

Summary

If you have used this section correctly you should now have a list of your goals, both materialistic and personal qualities, written in the current accomplished format. Make sure they are full and specific goals.

How is this list going to help me?

Well when I asked you earlier in the book what you wanted out of life, you probably couldn't answer the question, not specifically. When I asked where you would be in 5 or 10 years time, you probably stumbled, now you have a positive list of what you want to achieve and a time frame in which to do it in.

So where do we go now?

The next section is going to explain how you are going to put this list into action. For the moment, put your lists to one side and remember, these are your personal lists, don't show them to anyone.

A quick note at this stage, remember what I said at the start of the book about a "journey of a million miles begins with one step," well we are now going through those steps, so bear with me as you work through the book, it will become clearer and the jigsaw pieces will start to fall into place.

CHAPTER 5

How to re-programme your mind for success

If you can imagine that your brain is a video cassette, when you were born it was blank, you didn't know anything, you couldn't read or write etc. As a child you would be taught wrong from right and you would be taught what is acceptable and what is not.

The new information which has been taught to you, is stored on the cassette in your brain. Every time a teacher or your parent gave you positive or negative comments they would then be recorded on to the cassette.

Now the problem with the cassette in your head is that it contains a lot of negative information. Let me give you some examples of negative comments that your teachers and parents would have said:

"You never do anything right."

"You're always so clumsy."

"You'll never learn anything."

"Your stupid."

"You'll never be as good/nice/clever as your brother/sister."

"You're always lying, making mistakes, getting it wrong."

I'm sure that many of these sound familiar, these suggestions together with other childhood mistakes, such as breaking things, spilling things and upsetting people are all stored on our cassette, which in fact is our subconscious mind. Other factors that are stored include, rejection and punishment i.e. "Don't get your shoes dirty or you won't get any sweets," you get your shoes dirty and you therefore have a negative experience.

The big factor that is holding you and most people back is FEAR. Fear is a hindering force and a buried force, you could say it sits at the back of your mind. Fear has come from our childhood programming. Let me give you an example:

Imagine that you were at school and the teacher asks a questions, you think you know the answer and you put your hand up and answer incorrectly. The teacher then says, "That's a stupid answer" or " No that's the silliest answer I've ever heard" and everyone in the class laughs at you. Now, next time a question is asked are you going to put your hand up? No way, there's the FEAR of failure and embarrassment.

No doubt you've had similar experiences and the chances are that you still remember them today.

If you are told that you're stupid hundreds of times as a child, you will believe it, which in turn gives you a negative self-image. You see, the subconscious part of the mind is non-critical, it is very powerful but has no regard for logic or questioning. The subconscious mind accepts everything you feed it as reality, you become what you think you are. Now when we are young the mind will accept what it is told as fact, because our conscious mind had not grown or matured yet.

Examples of the power of your mind

Example 1

If you were four years old and I told you that the first six letters of the alphabet were B,N,D,G,L,Z, you would not doubt me!

Example 2

There are many teenage girls who suffer from Anorexia. They have convinced their mind that they are fat, even when in reality they are dangerously thin.

Example 3

I was an overweight child, this came from watching my parents overeating and thinking that this was normal. Overeating disorders are in nearly all cases mind related.

I remember a saying about a Catholic priest, it went something like, "Give me a Protestant four year old child and I will convert him into a Catholic for life."

What has this got to do with where I am today?

Simply put, that cassette is still in your head and those childhood recordings are still ruling your activities today!

We need to record over those old negative messages with new positive suggestions, we need to clean out your head of all your past mistakes and fears and replace them with happy, positive and constructive thoughts.

What shall I use?

Well if you've followed this book correctly you should have a positive list of goals.

That's the list you're going to record on to the cassette in your mind and now you can understand what the list making was all about. You see, just as the negative messages in your head are holding you back, the positive messages will push you forward and help you.

A Positive Mental Attitude is the key to unlocking the success, energy, goodness, creativity, power and everything else that is locked up inside you.

Dwelling on past failures, negative experiences, problems and shortcomings etc. have no place in your new life, there is no reason for you to carry this unwanted, useless, heavy baggage around with you.

Declarations

You now need to put your lists into action and start feeding it in to your mind. Your list should consist of all the materialistic items you really want and all of the personal qualities you might need to acquire them.

Morning Declarations

Every morning without fail upon awakening, you must read out your list of goals as prepared in their positive, accomplished format. Read out loud if possible, if not read silently but move your lips.

Read out your goals with conviction, belief and enthusiasm, don't just read them out for the sake of it. You can say, "I am happy, I am happy, I am happy..." hundreds of times, but if you don't add enthusiasm and belief, then it's not going to work.

As well as reading, you need to visualise your goals. See yourself driving the car, opening the door to your new house/office. If you have a fear which you need to overcome, i.e. going for a job interview, imagine that you are in the office and you are calm and in control of the situation.

If you find that photos or brochures help you to visualise, then use them. Request a brochure on your dream car etc.

Let your mind wonder with the new positive thoughts.

Night-time Declarations

Every night however late, before you go to bed, read your goals again and visualise your success.

I have found the night-time declarations to be very positive and I suggest that you read out your goals, as per the morning session and then with your eyes closed, visualise your goals and success. Ensure that you are relaxed and are totally committed.

I've recently been using relaxation sound tapes to help in this process. These tapes have relaxing music or natural sounds, such as the ocean or rain.

Remember that your goals should be in their accomplished format, i.e. you have already obtained the goal, you already have your dream house etc.

Now you may say, "I don't have my dream house, I'm really living in a bed-sit" well yes, that is where you are today, but you are not going to be there forever, by programming your subconscious mind now, we are preparing you for the future, so we are not really lying to our subconscious mind we are telling the truth, just a little earlier than in reality.

Waking up to a bright day

When you wake up in the morning do you start the day by saying, "Oh no, not another day," or even stronger words! The fact that you have been fortunate enough to survive another day is a gift, not a tragedy. Look out of the window and see a bright sunny day (if that makes you feel better), even though it may be dull. Every day when you wake up, stretch out, put your arms in the air and say, "YES" and "Today is a good day and it's getting better." Now even if the day doesn't turn out to be your best, you started the day the right way and I assure you that your day turned out better than if you had started the day by saying, "Today is a bad day."

By the way, there is no such thing as "getting out on the wrong side of the bed," is there?

Is a sunny day a good day and a rainy day a bad one?

Well it's all down to your perceptions and your needs. There are certain parts of the world where a rainy day is a happy day, because they desperately need water for their crops and animals.

Starting the day on the right note

As we've already mentioned, it is important to review your daily goals in the morning. I also think it is very important for you to have something for breakfast. A fruit juice, coffee/tea, breakfast cereal helps to set your body up for the day.

Try to allow time for breakfast, to review your goals and your daily schedule etc.

Feed your brain with positive information and feed your body with nutritious food in the morning, which will give you energy for the day ahead. Yes, it means getting up earlier, but it's worth it. You can train yourself to wake up earlier over a period of time. For example:

If you normally wake up at 8.00am and have to be out by 8.30am, then try waking up at 7.50am for the first week, 7.40am for the second week etc. until you wake up at the optimum time that allows you to have breakfast, review your goals and prepare for the day ahead.

Preparing the night before

Here's a tip, when I am catching an early morning plane, I prepare everything the night before such as, having all the clothes I need to wear laid out or ready on clothes hangers. My tickets, passport, money and bags are packed and ready at the front door.

I always make sure that I have a check list, i.e. to water the plants, switch on the light timers etc. I then tick off each point as it's done. A good idea is to take the list with you, so that if you ask yourself, "Did I put the burglar alarm on?" you can then check your list and see that it has been ticked off and therefore put your mind at rest.

How to turn a 7 day week into an 8 day week

Carrying on with what we've just said, imagine if you were to wake up roughly 1 hour earlier than you do now, over the week that's an extra 7 hours, which is almost an average working day, just think that one hour of less sleep a day will give you an extra 365 hours of time over a year, time that you can use to read, have fun, exercise or do anything you want to.

Now I'm not saying that you should give up sleeping, we all need sleep, it is an important part of our life and our body and skin need the repair time, but there is no excuse for oversleeping. If you were to sleep for 15 hours a day, you would not become more intelligent or beautiful than if you only had slept for 9 hours a day.

Why I hate people who lie-in

I know many people who enjoy staying in bed until 11am or later at the weekends, my argument is that what benefits do you get? (By the way I mean sleeping!) If you are one of these people then I have to say that it is a total waste of time. Time is one of the rarest commodities that we have, I hate to tell you but none of us are getting any younger and once today is over, that's it, you can't bring it back again. I hate to sound morbid, but I can't guarantee how long you are going to live for, I certainly don't know if there is life after death.

Don't you think that you should jump out of bed every day and enjoy your life? If you honestly think that there is nothing better to do in the world than sleep, then you've got a big problem which needs to be sorted out.

A common reason for people oversleeping is that they don't want to get up, they feel that life has dealt them a bad hand and there is nothing worth getting up for. It's also a fact that people who don't enjoy their work tend to oversleep, anyone with children will know that many children wake up at the crack of dawn on a Saturday and Sunday, yet on a school day you have to drag them out of bed!

Some people sleep to try and forget, they think that sleeping is the easy way out, however, this is not a solution as your problems will still be there when you wake up in the morning.

Margaret Thatcher, the great British Prime Minister and Iron Lady, claims that she would only ever sleep 5 to 6 hours a day at the most. My grandmother in Italy, who is 77 years old and still going strong, gets up at 5am every day, by 8.00am she has cleaned the house, done the shopping and made the day's dinner, it puts us all to shame.

Now I know everyone is different, but be honest, do you really need 12 hours of sleep? I don't think so. If you are an over-sleeper, think about why you are doing it.

Imagine if I told you that tomorrow would be the last day of your life, would you lie-in, or would you be out there doing everything possible?

NOTE: Resist the temptation to sleep in at weekends, it really messes up your body clock and your sleep patterns, get up at the same time every day, you'll feel better.

Going to bed satisfied

As we've previously mentioned, your night-time declarations are very important, every night however late, before you go to bed, read your goals again and visualise your success.

Reflect on the day, focus on the positive points and congratulate yourself on your good work. As for the negative factors, reflect on them and ask yourself what you have learnt from the experience and what you can do differently next time.

Learn a new piece of information every day

When you go to bed and you are in your review mode, ask yourself what new piece of information you have learned that day, make a point to learn at least one new piece of information a day.

Summary to setting goals, visualising and your subconscious mind

I know there are people who will say, "Day-dreamers, what a load of rubbish/mumbo-jumbo," or words to this effect.

My answer to these people, which may include you at this stage, is what do you have to lose? You have everything to gain and nothing to lose, except a little of your time. Give yourself a chance, it's worked for me and thousands of others. Notice that I said, "give yourself a chance," of course I want you to succeed and I want you to put these tasks into action, but I am not the loser if you don't, YOU ARE!

How does visualising and using your subconscious mind work?

Well, to be totally honest I've never wasted too much time looking into why it works, except I can tell you that it has for me. I presume that you use an electronic calculator and you believe the results it produces, but do you understand how the calculator works? I doubt it!

All I can say is that many of the things I have visualised and fed into my subconscious mind have become reality, and yes, I did think in the early days that it could be just a coincidence, but after a while there were just too many coincidences. Some of the goals and the things that I had visualised have turned into reality, almost exactly as I had visualised them or written them down in my goals.

Before I used positive thinking, I would worry about a problem or visualise something going wrong and yes, that's exactly what happened in real life.

Here is my non-scientific explanation of how goals and visualising works. First of all, it's not the fairies that make it happen, it's you, what happens is that you take certain actions that lead to the programmed goal, even though you do not always consciously know you're doing it.

Here's an example, have you ever driven your car on a long journey and then arrived at your destination, but you are not quite sure how you got there? It's like you were in a trance for part of the journey or on auto pilot.

I recently read about Roger Bannister, the first man who on the 6th May 1954 ran a mile in 3:59:4 and broke the then world record of under 4 minutes, which had always been considered impossible. He claims that he ran the race hundreds of times in his head, then it happened in reality.

How people in sport train their minds

When you see a great sportsman or woman win a gold medal, a boxing match or a motor racing championship etc. you will be aware that they have spent days, months and even years practising their sport and building up their physical strength, but do you know that they all practice mental exercises to build up their minds? Some sportsmen now even use various spiritual chants. Have you ever seen a weightlifter lifting a heavy weight? Notice how they make noises as they lift the weight, it is their mind working that is giving them the extra strength.

Some years ago there was a big uproar about how certain countries from the Far East were doing extremely well in the Olympics. These teams were breaking many records and although everyone thought they were on drugs or using special running shoes, it was concluded that there was no wrong doing and I believe that these athletes had perfected the art of "mind over matter" to such a high level that the competition just couldn't compete.

I've already mentioned how the four minute mile was run in the mind, hundreds of times before it was run in reality, but one of the most amazing acts of mind over matter happened in 1994, when George Foreman reclaimed the heavyweight boxing championship.

For those that don't know anything about boxing, George was 45 years of age which is very old in boxing and he had been out of the ring for over 10 years. Before the fight he didn't look in very good shape and there was no hiding his age, the odds were totally against him, yet he won. I believe his mind won him back the championship.

Never, never, underestimate the power of the mind. A Positive Mental Attitude is one of the biggest factors that will help you to lead a rich, healthy and successful life, start using it TODAY, it's there to be used. We can all have a Positive Mental Attitude, it's FREE and you already own it, you probably just need to release it.

On the subject of George Foreman, never let anyone tell you that you are too old, you are only as old as you feel, age is no reason to put anything off.

The late George Burns, the American funny-man was going strong at over 100 years old, when he was asked about dying he said, "I haven't got time to die I'm booked."

Are you saying that I just think about it and it happens?

No, certainly not, positive thinking without any action is just like reading a cookery book without putting it into practice, you need to DO SOMETHING. Towards the end of the book I will explain more about achieving non-financial goals and the making money and saving money sections will address the financial goals. What I can truthfully say is that a combination of the positive thinking, goal making, visualising and taking action, has been the formula for success that I have used and many others use every day.

Setting new goals and keeping the momentum going

After you have set your goals, you should be ready to add new ones as you begin to achieve your previous ones. Life is a journey and although there will be times when you will want to stop and admire the view, I have found that the most rewarding and exciting time in my life is when I am working towards a goal. When I've finished a project I tend to pause and review it and then I start looking at the next project. I find that I really enjoy the run up to making a major purchase, as much as I actually like the purchase. For instance, if I am buying a new car I really enjoy the looking, the research and the negotiating as much as the actual purchase.

As you grow older and become more successful you will think of different goals, for example, you may decide to buy a yacht and sail around the world when you are older, but you probably have no desire to do that now.

There will always be new goals and adventures, anyone who thinks that they've done everything in life is very mistaken.

☺

Hate getting up in the morning!

Mum was trying to get Dave out of bed. After her third attempt, she got angry and shouted, "Dave, get up right now, or you'll be late for school."

Dave protested, "I don't want to go to school. The kids pick on me, they give me a hard time, and they laugh at me, why should I go to school?"

"Two good reasons," answered Mum. "First, you are 47 years old; and second, you are the Headmaster!"

CHAPTER 6

Making decisions, dealing with problems and taking action

Earlier in this book I mentioned that everything that happens, whether it be good or bad, comes from an action that we have previously taken. The decisions that you make or in some cases don't make, shape your life both in the short-term and long-term.

In life you will be faced with many choices and our aim is to make more right decisions than wrong ones. We must also realise that the right long-term decision will not always be the easiest one in the short-term, there are times when you have to endure the short-term pain to receive the long-term gain.

How many times have you said, "If only I'd listened to" or "If only I'd left earlier" or "If only I'd invested in XYZ" or "I knew I should have?" Well here are some techniques that will help you to make more of the right decisions.

The Ben Franklin method

I learnt this method of decision making some years ago and I really think that you can use it to.

Let's say that you've been offered a job in Germany and you need to make the right decision whether to take the job or not. You would get a piece of paper and write down the question at the top. Draw a line down the middle and head one column "Benefits/Yes/For" and head the other column "Disadvantages/No/Against."

Now put your positive head on and write down all of the advantages underneath the benefits column, such as better pay etc. and then put on your negative head and write down all of the disadvantages under the disadvantages column, such as losing contact with friends etc.

Take your time and think hard, this exercise is for your benefit, be truthful with yourself and get it all out of your system.

Now once you have finished, look at all the advantages and weigh them up against the disadvantages. Your decision is made for you. You can enhance the system by adding a value to each point i.e. Money = 10, losing contact with friends = 8.

Example:

Should I take up the new job in Germany?

For	Against
Better Pay (10)	New surroundings (7)
Better conditions (10)	Losing contact with friends (8)
Better opportunities for promotion (8)	New language (7)
Chance to make a fresh start (6)	
Total for = 34	**Total against = 22**

The coin method

Here is another way to help you make your mind up, it's tossing a coin with a difference. The difference is that it doesn't matter which way the coin lands.

Let me explain, before you think that I am totally mad. You have no doubt had to make a decision where you sort of knew what you should do, but you were not quite sure.

Take for example, "I'm going to invest in XYZ company," but I'm still not 100% sure, so I would say "heads" invest, "tails" don't invest, now here's the important part, when you toss the coin which side are you really hoping for? What's your inside feeling? Say for instance that I felt I didn't want to invest when I was tossing the coin, and "heads" came up, I would not invest even though the coin said invest.

It's a way of letting your true inside feelings out, try it.

The sleep on it method

You must of heard people say, "I need to go and sleep on it" before they make a decision, well here is a way to do it effectively. Before you go to bed write down the question, problem or decision and think out the options, now tell yourself that you need to have the decision by tomorrow at 1pm or whatever time, drift off to sleep thinking about your options and decisions.

When tomorrow comes, ask yourself the question and see what comes into your mind and in most cases that's the right decision.

The flow chart method

This method is a way of using logic to make a decision. You write down the problem or question and then you make a chart with all the possible outcomes that you can think of. It's like asking lots of "what ifs."

Once you have made the decision

The NO decision

After using one or maybe all of the above methods to make a decision and the decision is "NO," then no it is, move on to the next thing, you've made your decision, whether it turns out to be the right or wrong decision, you have tried your best and thought out the decision carefully. Don't waste your energy looking back and saying, "If only" or "I should have..." turning back the clock is one thing that we can't do, however, we can look forward.

I know that it is sometimes very hard to say "NO" especially in personal matters, how many people are in unhappy or abusive relationships? Yet they just can't say "NO" and get out. I'll discuss personal relationships later on in the book.

The YES decision

After using one or maybe all of the above methods to make a decision and the decision is "YES," then you should put all of your doubts and negative feelings to one side and TAKE ACTION. You've made your decision, whether it turns out to be the right or wrong decision, you have tried your best and thought out the decision carefully. You must do everything in your power to help that decision become the right one. If negative thoughts such as, "I'm not sure if I should have done this" come into your mind, then quickly block them out and remind yourself of all the positive things that made you make the decision, i.e. the better pay, better conditions etc.

Taking action

Making the decision was hard, but taking action and sticking with it is even harder. Unless you take action, your decision is worthless. Unless you make the call, write the letter, call a meeting or whatever, then nothing will ever happen.

Once you have made the decision, then without fail you should put it into action as soon as possible. The reason I say as soon as possible and not immediately, is because I know that there will be times when by stalling the action for a short while you can gain. For example, if you have made the decision to leave your current employer for a new one, you may need to talk to your clients first and persuade them to join you at the new company.

I know that it's a vulnerable time between making the decision and taking the action, your mind will be doing overtime, your stomach will be churning and you will be very anxious.

See the section on doing it now if you are stuck.

Once you have taken the initial action you will normally feel better.

Whether it is a decision to resign, to end an arrangement, to move to a new country, to announce that you are an alcoholic, to announce that you are gay, to start a new business, to tell your partner that you have been having an affair or to take a trip around the world, once you have come out and made the announcement, then you will feel better. The saying, "a weight off your shoulders" has some truth.

Whatever the reaction to your action or announcement, once you've made it there is no turning back. Now depending on your action or announcement, you will cause a "storm," there could be crying, screaming, shouting, swearing and more, however, once you have got over the initial storm, you can then move on to the calm.

What is holding you back from taking action?

The main thing that holds most people back from taking action is the "what will happen?" question. The FEAR of the unknown, you see in most cases, however bad your current position is, it is easier to do nothing than to take action and possibly FAIL.

The question you must ask yourself is "What do I have to gain from taking this action?" and "What do I have to lose by not taking this action?"

If you have more to gain than lose, you MUST take action and go for it. If your current position is bad and possibly getting worse, then what do you have to lose? If you've hit rock bottom, then there's only one way to go and that is up.

Remember what I said at the start of this book about "this is the only life you have," you have to take opportunities, stick your neck out, take some risks, go against the flow and most importantly take a stand and claim your piece of the pie.

How never to fail at anything again

I have the best system ever invented for you never to fail at anything again. The simple way is to never do anything. Stay in bed all day, don't take risks, don't take any opportunities etc. and as long as your roof doesn't cave in, then you should be OK.

Let's not kid ourselves, you will FAIL at one time or another, I've failed, everyone's failed. When you see a famous and successful film/pop star or politician on TV, you see their success, but what you don't see is all the work and failures that are behind that success.

When you watch a TV programme or film do you think that it was shot all in one go, with no edits or mistakes? The truth is that there were many mistakes, missed lines and retakes etc. The average film shoots about 1 hour of footage for every 5 minutes shown.

One of the smartest self-made businesswomen in the last few years has to be MADONNA. You may not like her style, music or films, however, you must respect her perseverance and success. She doesn't ever give up, she makes a film and it flops, then she starts again. She has written hundreds of songs, many of them are successful but not all of them. I recently watched a biography on Madonna which showed that even though she was broke and hadn't achieved any success, she acted as though she was already a superstar. In her mind she had already visualised what was going to happen in reality. Madonna definitely knew what she wanted and did whatever she had to do to achieve her goals.

In an interview with the late actor Cary Grant, he was asked how he went from nowhere to being a world recognised actor who had class and was well spoken. His answer was "I started to act like the person I wanted to be and eventually I became that person."

Dealing with failure

We have all experienced failures in our life and we will experience many more in our time, however, failures can be managed and the negative effects can be reduced, in fact most failures can be turned into a learning lesson.

A story that has been told many times bears repeating to emphasise this important point. Thomas Edison, while trying to build a light bulb, was being interviewed. The young reporter said, "Mr Edison, how does it feel to have failed 10,000 times?" Astonished and perplexed, Edison replied, "I have not failed 10,000 times. I have successfully found 10,000 ways that will not work and I am 10,000 times closer to finding a formula that will work."

So take note from this story if you go to a job interview and the outcome is not successful, this does not mean that you have failed, you have successfully proven that the interview did not work, see the difference?

You see, I believe that everything we do has a result, it could be a positive or negative result, but there is always an outcome or result and we can and MUST learn from these results. Making mistakes is acceptable, however, continually making the same mistake over and over again is not.

Another point on mistakes and failing, it seems that the people who make the most mistakes, including ME, are the ones that are DOING SOMETHING. When I worked for a bank years ago, I remember that I would make quite a few mistakes and I would have quite a few queries on the transactions I did, it then came to me that the reason I was getting more queries and apparently making more mistakes was because I was in fact DOING THE MOST WORK, in fact I was doing 3 deals to everyone else's 1 deal, so when the volume was taken into account I was actually making less mistakes than everyone else.

So remember, if you don't want to make any mistakes you can just sit around and do little or nothing, but you won't get anywhere, however, if you work hard and want to be successful, the chances are you'll also make more mistakes and have more failures.

Getting a second chance - people have short memories

For most things in life you will always get a second chance and in most cases a third and a fourth. It's amazing how short people's memories are and how they just forgive and forget. If you don't believe me then think about this:

How do political parties get re-elected after all the mess ups they make? It's simple, as long as they can avoid making too many mistakes in the run up to the election and as long as they make some good promises, they are home and dry, people will forget about all the scandals, tax increases and spending cuts.

Here's another example:

How many food scares can you remember? There have been scares about eggs, meat, diet soft drinks, food additives, pesticides and many others. Now when a scare hits, sales drop and people stop buying the product, the scare is all over the newspapers and on televisions, but what happens after 6 or 12 months? Sales come back because people forget!

And that's the way it is, scandals and scares come and go, today it's some famous actor, tomorrow it's a well known politician.

So back to you, if you mess something up you should reapply, re-sit the exam or try again. If you are interested in working for a women's magazine and you get turned down by one title, go and apply to another and when you've been turned down by all of them, then start all over again and by that time the first one who turned you down will have forgotten you and the chances are the personnel officer has changed!

At this point let me give you a tip:

If you attend an interview and you are turned down for the job, you'll receive the standard, short, rejection letter. Now for whatever reason something didn't go right. Most people will now drop that company, however, why not write back or phone them and explain that you really think you are the right person for the job and you would like a second chance.

Believe me, most people don't do this and you will find in most cases that the company will find your persistence impressive and they will give you the benefit of the doubt and ask you back. This tip can work if you are selling a product or asking for start-up capital for a business etc.

I recently read about a self-made millionaire called Dan Pena, he was turned down nearly 200 times by different banks. He finally got the financing he needed and is now worth around $250 million. Now most people would have given up at being turned down 6, 12, or definitely 50 times, but he didn't did he?

On the subject of failures, did you know that Colonel Sanders, the Kentucky Fried Chicken inventor, started at the age of 66 flat broke with just his chicken recipe? He was turned down by over 2,000 restaurants before finally getting his recipe accepted. Look at the chain now, there is a KFC nearly everywhere.

Dealing with rejection

Here is one dilemma that I'm sure everyone reading this book has had, it is asking a boy or girl out for a date. As a youth or even as an adult, what in reality is such a simple task becomes an impossible problem.

Well the simple answer is this, if you don't ask you don't get, unless you ask the question, you will never know where you stand. Now if you ask the question and the answer is "Yes," you've got the date of your dreams and if you ask and the answer is "No," you now know where you stand and although you may feel rejected today, you'll get over it and at least you've tried. Remember, just because it is "No" today, doesn't mean it can't be "Yes" tomorrow.

I am using dating as an example because it has happened to most of us at some time or the other, but it could be any other subject.

Here's another point on the dating subject, I have concluded that there are many famous, rich, good-looking men and women who do not have partners and spend many of their nights alone and here's why:

Because if someone in our opinion is better looking than us, we automatically think that they will never go out with us for reasons such as, "I'm only a..." or "I'm fat/short/ugly etc."

Well you'll be amazed what can happen if you ask or try. You see, if you aim high and it doesn't work out, you have room to come down, but if you aim low and you succeed you will always be asking, "what if..."

Now I need to be careful here and I don't want to get into too much hot water, but I hope you can understand my point. Remember that "the grass is not always greener on the other side." A good example is that everything always looks better on TV, doesn't it? But unless you experience it for yourself you'll never know.

Why you don't need horoscopes, tarot cards or clairvoyants

I've noticed a worrying trend lately which is that more women and men are looking for guidance, hope and a miracle cure from horoscopes, tarot card readings and clairvoyants.

It seems that what may appear to be a bit of fun can actually become very addictive and a controlling factor in many people's lives. Only you know if you find yourself looking to these sources for guidance, there are many people who will genuinely not do something because their horoscope says that it's a bad time for money or moving house.

Let's get real. It is your actions and decisions that will shape your life and will lead to your success or failure. It can be tempting in turbulent and restless times to seek guidance from horoscopes and psychic readings, however, on the whole you are wasting your time and money. Your goals and your lifelong plan should be your inspiration. Positive thinking and your own self-confidence is what will see you through the good and bad times.

If you want to know what is going to happen in the future, then ask yourself. Visualise what you want to happen in the future, don't take advice from someone who doesn't really know you, the answer to your problem is not in the stars, it's inside you.

I have nothing against horoscopes, which I personally don't read, but I truly believe that it is not healthy for you to live your life on the basis of someone else's suggestions, when really you should control your own future. As you become more successful, confident and feel in control of your life, I guarantee you that you will never look at a horoscope column again.

Focusing on the positive

By simply changing your focus, you can change the outcome of an event. Let me give you an example:

Imagine that you are driving in your car, all of a sudden you lose control of the car and you are heading straight for a wall, now if you keep focusing on the wall, the chances are you are going to hit it, however, if you can focus on another object, you will steer towards that and reduce your chances of hitting the wall.

This may sound far fetched, but ask any professional racing car driver and I guarantee you that they know and use this technique.

If you put more energy into focusing on a negative outcome the chances are that's what is going to happen.

Congratulations you're a loser

If you constantly focus on a negative outcome then you will become an expert at losing. For example, have you ever said:

"I knew I was not going to find a parking space."

"I knew I was not going to make a sale."

"I knew she was going to say no."

Don't become famous for being a loser, become famous for being a winner. You should certainly not congratulate yourself for predicting a negative outcome, when the chances are you turned it into a negative outcome when you could just have easily made the outcome positive.

It's harder today to be a success

I hear people say, "If only it was the 1970's or the 1980's, I could have made money, there were more opportunities in those days." What a load of rubbish, if they were in the 1970's or the 1980's, they would probably say, "Oh if only it was the 1950's or the 1960's."

The fact is this, firstly, unless you have a time machine you cannot go back and secondly, there is no better time to make money or seize opportunities, than today.

Negative losers console themselves with "back in the good old days," but the only person they are fooling is themselves. Even when economies are booming there are still many companies that go broke and when the world is in a deep recession, there are plenty of companies that continue to do very well. I made all of my money during so called recessions. One day I was queuing up at my bank waiting to pay my cheques in, when I overheard two so called businessmen talking behind me saying how bad business was, how the recession was terrible and everything in the world was wrong, yet here's me, a 20 year old at the time, in front of them paying in thousands of pounds in cheques with a big smile.

Life is what you make it.

Beating yourself up has no positive effect

When something goes wrong, you mess up, an outcome is not as expected or you receive bad news, how do you deal with it? I found that I would mentally beat myself up, constantly blame myself and generally get down. Now even though I was to blame, I found that there were no positive effects by constantly beating myself up, in fact it makes you feel worse. Yes, you should accept responsibility for your life, but at the same time you need to forgive yourself and move onwards.

Let me give you an example, say you were reversing your car out of the garage and you hit something and dented your car, now you can curse and tell yourself that you should have been more careful and how stupid you are, but you could do this for a whole year and the dent would not miraculously fix itself would it?

Another example is, if you spill your coffee over your computer keyboard, you can feel as bad as you want to, but the coffee won't clear itself up will it?

I've now learnt to get over mistakes and accidents etc. as quickly as possible and focus straight away on sorting the mess out and moving on.

Your success file

This is something quite unique and although very simple, can have a very big effect. I am realistic enough to realise that in everyone's life there will be times when everything seems to be going wrong, you receive bad news and you generally feel that you are fighting a losing battle. This is where your success file comes in.

What is a success file?

It's simple, a file, shoe box or hopefully a very big box which has all your positive documents, photos, certificates, music and anything else that you are proud of in it.

Now some people are going to say, "I've never achieved anything," well I don't believe that, everyone has had some success in their life, even if it was winning the egg and spoon race at school or anything that you may class as trivial.

Dig deep, it could be school reports, medals, trophies, certificates of achievement or copies of any licences you hold. (If you have a driving licence then you passed a test, which is an achievement.)

You can also include, happy photographs, a cartoon strip that you like, a picture of your favourite film/pop star, their autographs, a book of your favourite jokes/quotes, a newspaper clipping or what about tickets from when you went to see your favourite sports team win?

If all else fails, copy out your favourite parts from this book that make you feel good, you must have some, I hope! Don't put anything in the file/box that will make you feel nostalgic or sad, I don't think a photo of an ex-partner would be a very good idea or a photo of your dream car which you once owned, but had to sell.

The idea of this file/box is to help you out of any troubled times by showing you what you have achieved and showing you happy things, it is a way to distract you from the current problem and help you to realise that you are a WINNER.

It is all to easy to brush away past successes and remember only the current problems, this will hopefully help you to remember your successes.

Now I don't recommend that with every little problem you have you rush for the file, you should be strong enough to get through most things, the success file/box is for emergencies only, I truly hope that you will never need to use it. Dwelling on your success file/box will mean that you will never move forward, your aim is to constantly be able to add to that success file/box.

CHAPTER 7

Your worst enemy & your best friend

I would like to introduce you to two people you've known for years, in fact all of your life, they are your worst enemy and your best friend, who are these people? Well it's YOU, these little people live inside your head and you may think that you have friends and family who are supportive and helpful, but at the end of the day it's those two little people inside you that count, they are with you every day, 24 hours a day and they will be with you for the rest of your life, so you had better get used to them and start communication with them.

What you need to do is allow for your best friend to grow and develop and you need your worst enemy to shrink and sit at the back of your mind. Your worst enemy will never die, he/she will always be there ready to come and see you, especially if you are going through a low point.

Developing your best friend

Your best friend wants you to be happy, he/she likes it when you get something right, you achieve success or you learn new information etc. Your best friend likes to hear positive thoughts, stories, happy music and funny films. Your best friend also likes to smile and laugh out loud when you do.

To keep your best friend alive you must continue to build up your relationship, you need to treat them well and in return they will treat you well. Your best friend knows that things don't always go right, but it also knows that any problem, challenge or set back is only temporary and can be overcome.

YOU MUST FEED AND WATER YOUR BEST FRIEND, let them grow.

Getting rid of your worst enemy

Your worst enemy likes to see you suffering, it laughs at you when you make a mistake or things go wrong, it likes drugs, alcohol, cigarettes and other nasty habits. Your worst enemy likes sad sombre music, violent and sad films, your worst enemy doesn't like laughing and hates seeing you try to achieve anything. Your worst enemy is out of shape and does not believe in reading books and further education.

YOU MUST STARVE YOUR WORST ENEMY, they need to shrink and go away, there is no place for them in your life.

Summary

You may think that this is all a little crazy, "I don't have a best friend and a worst enemy living inside my head," OK then, who do you think your inner voice is? When you read a book or think of something, who's that voice inside your head? You decide whether it is your friend or enemy.

I believe that we can all be our best friend or our worst enemy, no one can hold you down or push you forward, but yourself.

Learning to love yourself

Unless you can learn to be at ease with your own mind and body, then success is going to be a very, very steep hill to climb.

We all seem to be unhappy with something about ourselves, either we are too short, too tall, too fat, too thin, have a big nose, big ears or even big hands. As well as the physical features we may also be unhappy with other areas such as, I'm shy, I'm bad at maths, I talk too much and so on...

Even the so called "supermodels" are unhappy with parts of their body.

So how can we overcome our insecurities, fears and so called failings? Well the first thing is to write them down, list out what you don't like about yourself and then analyse what you can do about it. Also be totally objective, are your ears really that big? (By the way I read that people with big ears live longer!)

Once you've openly analysed the list, I think you can cross off most of the items, you should also cross them out in your mind, by physically scrubbing out the item on the piece of paper, this will reinforce your mind.

As for the remaining shortcomings, what can you do about them? Now for physical problems like weight, we can of course do something and if this is making you so unhappy and insecure, then you must do something about it. I'll talk about diet and exercise later.

As for height, I believe that everyone who thinks they are too short can increase their height through exercise and improving their posture, as we have already mentioned.

Of course, other parts of our body in this acceptable day and age of cosmetic surgery, can for a price be improved, however, I would strongly recommend that you think very hard before going to the length of having cosmetic surgery. I also think it is important to realise that after any surgery, you may still feel inferior and unhappy with yourself. It is quite common for people to start having an item of cosmetic surgery done, then they become unhappy with something else and they get this done and so on, before you know it thousands of pounds have been spent and in many cases people are still finding faults with themselves.

I have already mentioned this and I will continue to mention it over and over again, the MIND is really where it all starts, it's our perception, if you constantly keep thinking that you are shy or that your nose is too big, then the mind will believe that.

You really have to learn to believe in your own body and mind. You must start to love yourself, many shortcomings are in the mind and can be eliminated by positive mental programming. Other shortcomings can be overcome by attending training courses, for instance public speaking, shyness, fear of flying etc. A healthy life-style and good eating can help weight and posture problems and for general well-being, associating yourself with winners and other positively programmed people will help you immensely.

As for cosmetic surgery think hard, if you are so unhappy about a physical part of your body, then you may wish to go down this route. I believe that cosmetic surgery does have its place, especially for rectifying birth defects, major skin problems or scaring after an accident etc., however, I feel that if you have to have cosmetic surgery for vanity reasons, then there is a deeper problem inside your mind that needs to be addressed first.

Stop worrying today

Worrying is one of the most negative factors that has affected my life, I was a master at worrying. If there was a degree in worrying, then I would have it. I don't know why I did it, it certainly didn't make me feel any better. Over the years I have learnt to reduce my worrying as I have proven to myself, time after time that what I worry about just never happens. I can't say that I've stopped worrying completely, however, I have learnt to channel my energy into taking care of legitimate worries, rather than worrying about anything and everything.

Here are some of the things that I would worry about:

1. Things that are very unlikely to ever happen

As I've already said, worrying about things that might never happen can really make you feel bad and wear you out. The energy, pain and effort that I have put into worrying about things that never happened is just not worth it. Worrying is like visualising failure instead of success, put your efforts into visualising "success" not failure.

2. Things that have already happened

Worrying about things that have already happened is a pointless exercise, it will not change the outcome and it doesn't make you feel better. I would carry negative thoughts over to the next day, where as now I close that worry off and start fresh the next day.

3. Worries about health that were in my mind

I've woken up a few times in the middle of the night and convinced myself that I was dying, when clearly it was all in my mind. Another worry of mine would be if I had read an article about an illness, I would then start to worry that I had the illness. Now thanks to positive mental programming and a healthy diet, my health worries are minimal.

4. Miscellaneous minor worries

These worries would tend to come into my mind after reading an article or receiving a salesletter, telling me that I could be at risk from XYZ or that I need XYZ. Many adverts are written to play on our worries, a headline that made me worry was "What will you do when the IRS seizes your assets?" the advert was of course selling a tax planning book.

5. Legitimate worries

Legitimate worries are where our efforts should be placed,

normally legitimate worries are only about 5 to 10% of all worries. A legitimate worry is something that you can control or take action on. If you have planned an outdoor wedding tomorrow it is pointless worrying about the weather, because if it rains with all the will in the world, you cannot make it stop, but you can take action to set up tents etc. to minimise the damage.

Another worry could be starting a new job tomorrow, will I like it? What will the new people be like? Will they like me? And so it goes on. Well the answer is, you are going to find out tomorrow, you can stay up all night and worry, but it's not going to change things, you are better off pushing your worries to the back of your mind and concentrating on getting a good night's sleep.

Use the positive thinking techniques to overcome your worrying, visualise yourself walking into the new office, shaking hands with your new work-mates etc. Change your focus to the positive changes such as, a bigger pay cheque, new company car, better prospects, new goals and challenges.

Blast out the negative thoughts and worries with happy and positive thoughts.

Tips to help you deal with worries

1. Define your worry. If it helps write it down. Let's take the example of the outdoor wedding and you are worried about the weather.

2. Ask yourself what you can do to change the worry or reduce the worry. If there is nothing you can do, then stop worrying. Kill the worry and work on your next one.

3. If there is something that you can do, then draw an action plan, you hopefully won't need it. In the case of the wedding, be ready to move indoors or hire tents etc.

4. Ask yourself if there is a way to eliminate the problem that's causing the worry, could the wedding be held indoors? Then weather permitting, the photos etc. can be taken outdoors.

Why worry?

There are only two things to worry about; either you are well or you are sick.

If you are well, then you have nothing to worry about.

If you are sick, there are only two things to worry about; either you will get well or you will die.

If you get well, there is nothing to worry about.

If you die, either you will go to heaven or you will go to hell.

If you go to heaven, there is nothing to worry about.

If you go to hell, you will be so busy shaking hands with friends, you will not have time to worry.

I don't know who wrote the above, but I thought it was worth including in the book, as it makes me laugh when I read it.

Summary on worrying

Concentrate on legitimate worries, throw all other worries out of your mind. Use whatever techniques you need to blast the worries out of your head, you don't have time to carry them around. I speak from experience, worrying about things that might never happen would make me feel ill and it would stop me from getting on with my life and achieving success.

The chances are that worrying is causing you unnecessary strains and could be a big factor which is holding you back. Try programming your mind with a daily declaration such as, "I am in control of my life and I don't have any worries."

Finally, I thought you'd be interested to know what the top 10 fears and worries are for most people:

1. Public speaking (People are terrified about speaking in front of a group.)

2. Heights

3. Insects and bugs

4. Financial problems

5. Deep water

6. Sickness and ill health

7. Death (I personally thought this would have been higher up on the list.)

8. Flying

9. Loneliness

10. Dogs

What I find hard to believe is that with the exception of number 7, we can do something about all of the other fears, also be honest, how likely are you to come into contact with insects and bugs? And if you do, compare their size to you, they are the ones that should be terrified!

The past is history and the future is where to look to

Past failures, past traumatic relationships and generally any negative past events, seem to be the biggest problem which stops many people from moving on and getting ahead.

Now I don't want to sound uncaring and I understand that people suffer from very painful divorces, loss of a loved one and losses due to a failed business to name a few, however, the past is one thing that I cannot help you with in this book, what has already happened is history, but I can help you to look forward to the future and it is the hope and belief of the brighter things ahead that should move you upwards and onwards. Many people dwell on ifs and whys, however, wallowing and torturing yourself over the past has no positive effect. Channel your energies and focus on the future, because you can do something about tomorrow, but you can't do anything about yesterday.

☺

Making decisions

A man went for a job as a railway signal controller, the job involved making sure the various trains were spaced out and were on the right tracks.

The personnel officer asked the man to tell how he would react in various circumstances, "What would you do if the 8.46 was travelling southbound and the 8.50 was travelling northbound?" the man answered "That's easy, I would switch the south rail over and change the signal," very good answered the personnel officer, he then went on to ask a few more questions, which the man answered perfectly.

The personnel officer then asked one final question, "If the 4.40 to London is on the Southbound track, the 3.54 is on the Southbound track and the 4.01 Express is on the Southbound track, what would you do?

The man stopped for a while and then answered, "I'd phone up my wife and get her to come over as soon as possible," the personnel officer asked, "Why would you do that?" the man answered, "Because my wife has never seen a train crash before!"

CHAPTER **8**

Magic words or tragic words?

The old saying "sticks and stones will break my bones but words will never hurt" is a little misleading. Words have amazing powers, both positive and negative. Words both in the written form and in the spoken form can change the way we feel and act. Words can make us laugh, cry, be co-operative or make us buy a product. They can also cause hurt feelings, anger and irritation.

Spoken words have extra power because you have the added factor of the voice tone, emotion and the way the words are said.

Remember that our mind is talking all day, our inner voice as you read this book has around 50,000 thoughts everyday. Now if 95% of those thoughts are negative we are really beating ourselves up, however, if we can change those thoughts to 95% positive, we will really give ourselves a big advantage and you will feel charged up from within.

At this point let me ask you to do something for me, from this day onwards I would like you to remember that "If you can't say something nice about someone, don't say anything at all." If you can't do this and you are going to say something bad about someone, then have the courage to say it to their face.

When I worked for a big company the rumour mill worked overtime, in fact that's what most people did all day long, gossip, start rumours and generally bad mouth people, in fact they would try to drag me into these stupid conversations, they would tell me about Joe down the corridor, and this and that, but I would stay out of any gossip or rumours, because even then I knew that those who talked about others to me, talked about me to others, it is a fact.

Don't get involved in these type of conversations, rise above them and I guarantee you that you will gain more respect.

Tragic words

I want you to say goodbye to these words and these kind of phrases. These words are for losers, not a winner like you!

- ☹ "I know I'm going to miss the bus." (Yeah, say that and I'm sure you will.)
- ☹ "It's not my day today." (Keep telling yourself this and YES, you'll have a bad day.)
- ☹ "I wish I was still in bed." (Great, waste your life away, there are millions of sick people that will swap your life for their death bed.)
- ☹ "I'm scared of computers." (I've never been beaten up or hit by my computer!)
- ☹ "I can't understand..." (It could be that you don't want to understand.)
- ☹ "He's always picking on me."
- ☹ "I knew this was a bad idea."

Words to erase from your life:

Doom, low self-esteem, pessimism, defeat, gloom, misery, negativity, anger, failure, malice, bitterness, ignorance, anxiety, hatred and losing.

Magic words

☺ "Today is a good day and it's getting better."

☺ "I am excited and I look forward to this new challenge."

☺ "I can fix this problem."

☺ "There's a better way to do this."

☺ "I will do whatever it takes to be successful."

☺ "Past mistakes and failings are history, future successes and achievements are present."

Words to add to your life and to use as replacements for the tragic words:

Positive, energetic, valuable, sharp, bright, praised, brilliant, excellent, appreciated, winner, dynamic, resilient, intelligent, success, achiever, happy and exciting.

Listening to sceptics, self-doubt and taking advice

Many people have said to me, "You don't want to do that, you want to do this," or "It will never work," or "I think you should..." and "Somebody has already done that."

Sceptics are all around us, they instantly look for the flaws in a scheme, they don't believe in anything, even when you show them hard evidence, they still convince themselves that they are right and everyone else is wrong. In one of my businesses I showed various commission cheques that people had earned from acting as agents for my company. These cheques ranged from £2,000 up to £6,000. In my literature I showed copies of the cheques and an extract from my bank statement showing that the cheques had been cleared through my bank account.

One day a gentleman called me and just would not and could not believe that people could earn these amounts, even though there was 100% proof, he just wouldn't take it in.

You see, just because he couldn't do it, he didn't believe that anyone else could do it either.

Now I'm not saying that you should be an unrealistic optimist, we are living in turbulent times and regrettably everyone isn't as honest and truthful as they should be, but please don't become a 100% sceptic, otherwise you will never do anything.

Taking advice

Let's say that you've decided you are going to start your own business, you've done your research and you are very excited about the project. Because you are so excited about the project, you decide to tell your so called friends, family and anyone else that will listen. You will present your case and you will normally say, "What do you think Jane/John?"

Now here's where the problems start:

The chances are that however nice your friends and family are, they are negatively programmed, I doubt very much if they have ever thought about buying a book like this one and in most cases they have no experience in business or about the subject that you are asking advice on.

You see, if you ask for an opinion or advice, you need to qualify the person who is giving you the advice. Let's say that John's reply is, "I don't know if that will catch on." You need to ask John for a full explanation of why he doesn't think that it will work and here is the important question to ask "Have you ever run your own business John?" or "Do you know about XYZ John?"

Now if John is working on a minimum wage in a factory, then I would not take much notice of his answer, whether it is positive (which I doubt) or negative. If John is running his own business which seems to be quite successful, in the same or similar field, then I would listen and take note of every word he says.

How I give advice

If someone asks me for advice I will always be careful before I answer or make any negative observations. I know from personal experience how people can put doubts into your mind which can lead to you abandoning a project that could have been successful. I would listen and look carefully at the proposal and in most cases I would not give an instant opinion, I would normally go away and do some of my own research and fact finding. Only after this and based on my own judgement, would I then pass on my opinion. If it is something that I don't think I can advise on, then I will say so.

If a good friend asks you for advice, think hard before you give it. I believe that many great ideas and businesses have been abandoned, because of people giving advice which is not based on any facts. At the same time if you can save a lot of trouble and money by accepting someone's unbiased and objective advice, then take it, it may hurt in the short-term, but it will save you the heartache, time and money in the long run.

In the past people have approached me about entering the same business that I was in, as they had seen me do well at it and it looked easy from the outside. Now even though they could have been going into competition with me, I still gave them objective and truthful advice and in most cases I told them what the business was really like, some people took the advice and stayed out, but others gave it a try and failed miserably.

Professional advice

Taking professional advice can sometimes be worse than not taking any advice at all, again I speak from experience. There are thousands of Lawyers, Bankers and Accountants etc. and regrettably there are many bad and average ones amongst them.

Now for some reason, when people take on a professional adviser they think that they are released from their obligations or they don't have to worry about anything. Well GET REAL, if you take on an accountant and for any reason there is a problem with your tax return or your accounts, do you think that the accountant is going to get into trouble? I don't think so, it's YOU. In the U.K. if your limited company accounts are filed late, it's not your accountant that gets fined, it's you. And if you receive bad legal advice, do you think that you will find a solicitor to sue another solicitor!

So taking professional advice is not the answer to all your problems, you've got to have some trust and with research and by asking the right questions, you can find a half decent adviser. Remember, don't let your guard down and never give the adviser 100% control of anything. An adviser should be able to prove themselves and over time trust can be built up.

Another point to remember about solicitors, accountants and bankers etc. is that they are only human and they make mistakes. They have bad days, they have matrimonial problems, they have health problems and they have financial problems. (Yes, bank managers and accountants have bills and debts too!) You must also remember that circumstances change, I've had two good bank managers who regrettably left the bank, one got transferred and the other one died.

So to summarise, should you take professional advice and advice from friends and family? The answer is "yes," seek the advice, but qualify the person who is giving you the advice. Listen to their views carefully and if there is any truth in what they say, then you should act on the advice, however, if it is just their opinion, then stick with your own feelings.

As for professional advice, you will no doubt need the services of an accountant, solicitor or banker etc. at some time, but remember that they work for you, not the other way round and whatever advice they give you, the final decision is yours. No solicitor can make you plead guilty if you want to plead innocent and do remember that you are the one who ends up with the legal outcome, whether it be a judgment, a fine or even ending up in jail, YES, IT'S YOU, your solicitor goes home!

"I am now in your capable hands and I will leave it with you." If you ever say words along these lines, either in your head or out loud to any adviser, then you are heading for trouble.

I won't bore you with the full details, but when I was around 13 years old, while all the other kids were out playing, I was making money. I wrote a computer game and was starting to buy and sell computer software, in those days the information was stored on audio cassettes. Now I knew the potential of the market and although I did make quite a bit of money, remember £200 is a lot of money when you're 13 years old and everyone else has a paper-round, I knew there was more potential in buying and selling software, my problem was at that age it was hard to get people to trust and take you seriously. Anyway, I presented my case to my father for assistance, however, he shot the whole business down, totally demoralised me and I dumped the project. Please don't let anyone do the same to you.

Taking responsibility for your life

I want to be happy

When I ask people what they want out of life, the common answer is "I want to be happy." I then ask them to explain and define happiness, and in all cases they pause for a while and then cannot define it.

Happiness is a state of mind, it's in your head or in most cases it is defined by advertising agencies that are trying to sell you something. Although most adverts don't say, "This will make you happy" directly, that's what the advert is suggesting. Most adverts fall into the same categories which are, the product will make you happy, it will make you sexy, look good or feel great.

One thing that I have realised is that what one person calls a happy place, someone else will call hell. Some people think that living in a penthouse flat in London or Manhattan is happiness, others think that living in the middle of nowhere on a farm is happiness. Some people think that the ideal holiday is sun-bathing on an unspoilt desert island, others think that it is living it up and shopping in New York.

Think about actual things that make you really happy and be honest, don't just say lots of money, as money alone will not make you completely happy. On the subject of money, what is money? It's pieces of paper, or a piece of plastic which is then settled by pieces of paper. Money itself isn't very exciting unless you are into collecting bank notes. No, it's not the actual money, it's what the money can be exchanged for, like a Rolex watch or a designer suit that makes you excited.

How to make yourself happy at any time

The easiest way to make yourself feel happy at any time, is to change your focus and think of a time when you were happy, either as a child or an adult. Even if you've had a rough life like me, there must have been times in the past when you have been happy. Think back as hard as you can, feel excited, remember how you felt, remember the sights and sounds and put all your focus on happy times.

I've used this technique successfully to help me out of tough spots. With some practice you can call up the good times and focus on the positive, not the negative, give it a try!

Accepting praise and taking criticism

It seems that most people today are very quick to criticise or complain, however, they very rarely give out any praise or complements, even when they are due. I also find that many people give out praise and criticism in the same sentence. Has your boss ever said, "That report is very good but you need to...?" You probably forget about the second of praise and all you remember is the criticism.

I try wherever possible, to thank people who provide me with a good service and pay them a sincere complement. I was recently on an airline and the cabin crew were excellent, on leaving the aircraft I made sure that I thanked them and told them that they were very good at what they did.

Accepting criticism

Nobody is perfect and I am definitely not perfect. I try to improve every day and I am in search of perfection, however, I have not reached this status. Now if someone phoned me up or wrote me a letter advising me that I had done something wrong, or I was failing in some area, I would take notice, I would look at how I can improve or rectify the matter. If the criticism was genuine then I would take notice and act, however, if it was someone just trying to pick holes, then I wouldn't take any action and I would try to get the negative thought out of my mind.

You know deep down if a criticism is justified or not

Now I know many people who when you advise them of a problem or a failing, the first think they do is go all defensive and say, "No I don't" or they laugh it off. Some people automatically apologise, but they still don't do anything to rectify the problem.

If someone points out a justified criticism, act on it and take action to solve the problem and eliminate it, that way no one else can criticise you for the same mistake. It is very fashionable for companies to ask their customers, "Are we providing a good service or have we messed up?" Now this is very good, listening to customers is a way to learn and even if you don't like what they tell you, by making the changes, you'll benefit in the long run, you see for every one person that complains, there's another 100 that are not happy with the service, but don't complain.

A problem with companies that ask for your views and

complaints, is that they don't always act on your suggestion or complaint. What is the point of asking, if you are not going to take any notice? Around 3 years ago I made a complaint to a very big airline, advising them of a problem, I didn't even get an acknowledgement for the complaint form I filled in. I travelled using this airline again and they still hadn't fixed the problem.

To summarise

You should give praise when it is due, you should also accept praise when it is due. When people used to comment about my good work I would say, "Oh it's nothing, it only took a few minutes." I make sure that I don't say that any more, because you are robbing yourself of the praise, accept the praise and let it sink into your subconscious mind, it's very good for you.

As for criticism, if it's valid accept it and act, if it's not reject it.

Asking questions makes you more successful

For most of us as children, we learned by asking questions. Listen to a child and hear how many times they ask questions or say "Why." Now for some reason when we become adults we start to ask less questions, it could be because we may have come across the "don't ask questions just do it" attitude.

My view is that brighter children are the ones who ask more questions and as long as they have a good teacher or parent who takes the time to answer the questions, the child will be very smart and beat the averages.

As an adult we should continue asking questions, we should ask ourselves questions such as "Is there a better route?" or "Can I do this a better way?"

We should ask our partners or loved ones questions, I know it may be embarrassing, but all the top love making therapists say that asking your partner questions leads to better love making!

We should also ask our customers questions. For example, "Do you prefer black or red?" or "Which day do you prefer to shop on?"

Many new products are developed by asking questions or by answering the "why" statement. Take for example the Polaroid instant camera, you take your picture, the picture pops out from the bottom of the camera and within a minute you can see it.

Well I read that the camera was invented as a result of a child's "Why" question. After taking a photo of a child with a normal camera the child wanted to see the photo right away, which was fair enough, she couldn't understand why she had to wait for the film to be finished and for it to be processed.

Later that day, thinking about the child's "why wait" question the inventor sat down and started to work on the Polaroid instant camera, which went on to be a massive seller, all this from a child's "Why" question.

If you work in a sales environment you should already know that if someone asks you a valid question, they are an interested buyer.

To summarise

Asking questions is a good way to learn and taking notice of "WHY" is very important. Both in business and on a personal level, asking questions gives us a chance to see if we are doing something right or wrong.

CHAPTER **9**

Associate yourself with eagles and not with chickens or turkeys!

I know people who will always look to others who are not doing as well as them, but they will never look up to someone that is doing better than them. They like to think that they have the best house or the best car in the street, well maybe they have, but if they go a mile down the road, their house or car would probably be the worst!

If you always look down or look at your equals, then you will never progress and in fact if you focus downwards, the chances are you'll start moving downwards.

Aim high, look up and try to do better, you need to soar like an eagle high in the sky, not run around like a chicken on the ground. Find yourself a role model, someone that you can relate to, try to associate yourself with people who are positive and winning at life, the people that you surround yourself with can help you or they can hold you back. Now I'm not saying that you should always be chasing the bigger and better deal, but realise your true potential.

Let me give you an example of good association and bad association:

Good association is WeightWatchers. If you are trying to lose weight on your own and you have little or no support from your family or friends, it can be very difficult. WeightWatchers get together groups of people who all have the same interest, losing weight. The group encourages others, it sets goals, it has past slimmers as role models and most people who visit WeightWatchers find that the meetings are very uplifting and they get motivation and inspiration from them.

Bad association is negative people and down-market pubs and night-clubs. You will find that very few people can give you positive aspirations in a down-market pub or club, in fact the chances are smoking, drinking and drugs will be all around you. Add in a negative so called friend or fellow patron and you're on the way down. However positive you are, if you spend enough time around depressing people, it is very hard to stay positive.

I've been out with depressing people who believed that life was terrible and everything was bad, and after a few hours I started to feel quite down, even though I was very happy before.

Now on the other hand I've met up with happy, positive people who were very interesting and they were really making something of their lives, when I met with these people I wanted time to stand still for me, they inspired me and I didn't want to leave.

You must have heard the saying "Birds of a feather flock together." Well who are you flocking with? Totally negative dead-beat people or positive, happy upbeat people?

Summary

Success does breed success, read about people who are doing well and ask yourself how you can do the same. Associate with people who are trying to solve the same problem that you have, such as losing weight, giving up alcohol or learning to speak in public etc. I think that you owe it to yourself to push as hard as you can and maximise your true potential.

Success is a journey and I've found that it is definitely better to travel than arrive.

A good friend gives as much as they take!

I'd like to carry on from what we've just said about good and bad associations and I want to warn you about "hangers-on" and people who will use you, I don't want you to become one of those people either.

What do I mean? Well do you have any so called friends or associates who you only ever hear from when they need a favour or those that you never hear from when they are happy, only when they need a shoulder to cry on? If you don't know anyone like this and you can honestly say that you don't do this on a regular basis, then that's excellent and you can skip the next bit, however, if you regularly experience so called friends who only call you during their hour of need, or if you are one of those people, then read on.

A good friendship and relationship is based on give and take, it is simply not on to only ask for favours and expect your friends to listen to your problems time after time, sure you may call on friends for assistance occasionally, but don't abuse their friendship. If you take something today then make sure that you give something back in the near future, be ready to ask about any problems that they may have or if there is anything that you can help with, it's only fair. Don't phone only when you are unhappy or need help, phone when you are happy and give something back, listen to what your friend has to say.

Some people look to God or go to church when a tragedy or a problem arises, they pray for forgiveness and for God to help them out of their problem, but how often do these people ever GIVE THANKS for happiness, health and prosperity? Very rarely, if ever.

I do not have any problems with people going to church and worshipping God, however, it is simply not on to just go when you want something.

Dealing with envy and jealousy

Imagine that I park my new Ferrari in front of your car, I step out and I am wearing an expensive suit, I have a Rolex watch on and I generally look happy and successful, now what will be your first honest thought? For most of us it would probably be, "What a lucky bastard, I wish I had a Ferrari," "He must be a drugs dealer," or "He probably won the lottery, I'll go and scratch it..."

And that's how most people think, in fact you may be thinking this now, but you must stop because envy and jealousy has only one loser and that's the person who has it.

Don't be angry or jealous of someone who is doing better than you, admire them, congratulate them, find out their secrets and copy them. (As long as they're not really a drugs dealer!) It is always better to imitate a successful man or woman rather than hate them.

I love to see successful people, why? Because they are rare and I can learn something from them, it also proves that success is achievable. As I am writing this it has occurred to me that one day you could become far richer than I am, you may appear on TV or write a book etc. in fact you may already be richer than me, but I don't envy you, I admire you and I want you to do better than me, if I didn't I would never have published this book and revealed my secrets to you. Nothing makes me happier than hearing success stories and if I have contributed to a bit of that success, then even better.

Working smarter not harder

This is a slogan which has become fashionable lately and I believe that if you work smarter and a bit harder, then you are on the way to the top. I'm not going to turn this into a science lesson, but you need to understand the meaning of "leverage," this is how a one man/woman company can beat a massive corporation.

Let me give you an example: You have 20 large heavy boxes to move, now you can work hard and pick them up individually or you can get a trolley and push them along. You would still have to move the boxes but it would be much easier to use a trolley, wouldn't it?

The next time you have a task or a problem to solve, think about the moving boxes example, is there anything you can use to help you "leverage" your powers? A computer can help you leverage your powers, you still need to tell it what to do, but for repetitive jobs it really can make your life easier and give you more time to concentrate on other tasks.

Hard workers who get nowhere

I've recently met some people who work very hard, they've worked hard for the last 25 years. Their business involves them working very early in the morning as well as late at night and every time I see them they look sleep starved. Now although they have achieved some limited success for the amount of effort and hours that they have worked, they are getting nowhere. The point that I am making is that working hard is important, but you also need to be smart. At the end of the day it is the results that count, not the fact that you've worked hard for 25 years. A few simple changes to their business could easily have improved their results. It's like a farmer still using a horse and plough, compared to a farmer using the latest tractor and latest farming technology.

Learning to adapt and changing direction

Most of us are very "set in our ways," we tend to do the same things over and over again. We live in changing times where there are new discoveries and inventions every day, many of which can make our life easier, but if we are not willing to learn about them or use them, then we are only letting ourselves down.

Here is an example:

You drive to work every day using the same road, one day I tell you that there is a new road which has now opened that will cut your journey time by 15 minutes. All you need to do is turn right a few miles on, instead of doing your normal left turn.

Now tomorrow, when it comes to your normal left turn, will you go straight for it or will you remember to stay on and take the next right? The chances are you'll take the normal left turn because that's what has been programmed in your mind and you've been doing it for years.

The only way that you will learn to take the new route is by sticking a note on the dashboard and thinking hard about your journey, after some weeks of pushing yourself to take the new route, you will find that it becomes natural and the new route will be easy to remember.

What's the point?

The point is, things change, just because something "has always been done that way," doesn't mean that there isn't a better way. You need to learn to break old habits and replace them with new ones, as and when they are required.

Let me give you another example, if you had to go and see a surgeon for a heart operation, who would you want to see, someone who qualified 50 years ago and has never done any further studying or kept up with the latest medical technology and trends or would you want to see someone who qualified 50 years ago, but reads all the medical journals, attends seminars and further training and knows all the latest medical techniques? I'm sure that like me, you would want the second one.

You see, if every surgeon did everything the way it was done 50 years ago, we would be in big trouble!

Working around problems

Earlier on I mentioned the people who were working very hard but getting nowhere, well looking back on it they are very similar to flies banging their heads against a window. I'm sure you've seen a fly doing this, they want to get out of the window but they just can't understand glass!

Well that's what many people are doing every day, they keep hitting themselves against the glass. The smart way to overcome the problem is to look for a way round the problem, if something is just not working, then take a step back and look again.

Here's an interesting quote I heard some time ago:

> **"Some people are so busy chopping wood, they don't have time to sharpen their axes!"**

And isn't that a fact, just by taking a few minutes to sharpen the axe, they would be able to cut more wood with less effort.

If you are out walking one day and there is an obstruction in your path, you don't keep hitting yourself against it or start building a tunnel, you step back and walk around it and that is what you need to do in everyday life. If you are at point X and you need to get to Z, there will no doubt be many obstructions and problems in between, but by learning to go around these obstructions, you will get to Z much quicker.

CHAPTER 10

Personal relationships

They say that "Behind a great man is a great woman," and vice versa. There is a lot of truth in this, however, we must also understand that a negative partner who does not share your goals and aspirations, can be your worst enemy. The fact that you have decided to better your life, increase your income, increase your knowledge or improve your appearance, may not be shared by your partner.

When I refer to partner, this could be somcone that you are married to or not, it is the person that you spend the most time with or the person you consider to be your significant other.

How can I tell whether my partner is on my side?

There is no simple way to answer this question, however, you do need to analyse how your partner reacts when you suggest something new, a change, a new business idea or further education etc. Do they always react in a negative and lethargic way or do they sit up, take note and give you constructive input?

If your partner is genuinely enthusiastic about your plans, your achievements, your goals and your success, then that's excellent, you have a partner who will help you get to the top and help you through any rough patches.

If your partner isn't very enthusiastic about your new plans and your new found success, then you have a problem that will only increase as you become more successful and wealthy.

The problem that can occur in relationships is when one partner starts to make positive changes, starts to increase their income, changes their circle of friends or starts to get into shape and the other partner gets left behind and starts to feel neglected, inferior or insecure.

A common problem for many men is if their wife or partner becomes more successful and earns more money than them, they get upset and feel insecure. I think it must have something to do with our ancestors and that the caveman must bring back the food!

How to deal with a lagging partner

There are probably 3 categories that your partner could fall into, which are:

100% They are very supportive, provide objective views and support your ideas, visions and goals. They are ready to come along with you on your journey and help you all the way, they trust your judgement and are willing to drop everything to be with you.

50% They are not particularly supportive, but not overly negative. With some coaxing they agree to help you, they try to be helpful but their heart is not really in it. They think that your goals and ambitions are OK, but they doubt that you will ever reach them.

0% They are totally unsupportive and negative. Any suggestions or new ideas are shot down immediately and faults are found. They are quick to remind you

of your past mistakes and that it is your fault that
both of your lives are in a mess. They are very set in
their ways and would always have to take advice
from their parents and family before they did
anything. They would never consider moving away
and losing close contact with their family and friends.

Now these are the extremes and many readers will find that
their partner is in-between, only you truthfully know.

How can you help your lagging partner?

Well a good start would be to give them a copy of this
book, you should also talk at length with your partner about
what you are aiming to achieve and why you are changing
your life. You then need to see if the lagging partner is
willing to make any changes to themselves, the theory is
that if one partner is starting to lead a richer life, the other
partner should be able to copy. Encourage the other partner
to try some of the new activities that you are taking part in,
if you are increasing your fitness level and you've joined a
health club, then bring your partner with you. I believe that
the lagging partner may need a kick start, but once they
understand the benefits they will be happy to follow you.

**What happens if my partner still doesn't want to come
forward with me?**

I would find it very hard to believe that your partner
however stubborn, does not see the benefits of improving
their life, especially if they can see that you are starting to
do well. Only you know if you've tried hard enough to get
the lagging partner motivated and to take more of an interest
in life.

If you are now at the point where you are still not getting
any support and you find that the negativeness is starting to
drain you, then a MAJOR DECISION has to be made. Now
before I go any further you need to see my section on
BALANCE and you need to ask yourself if you are being
fair to your partner, it's hard to expect their support if you

are totally neglecting them.

The major decision is this, you give up your goals, your ambitions and forget about the success you've started to achieve or do you be SELFISH, part company and carry on with your new life? You see, having a negative partner is worse than not having a partner at all. Having a negative partner is like running through a sticky surface, you are trying hard but it seems that you are just not moving.

Here's an example

YOU = ☺ ☺ ☺ ☺ ☺ ☺ ☺ ☺ ☺ ☺

NEGATIVE PARTNER = ☹ ☹ ☹ ☹ ☹ ☹ ☹ ☹ ☹ ☹

Taking the extreme, every time you add a ☺ your partner takes one away with a ☹ - the net result is then 0, so you are working hard but getting nowhere.

Summary on partners

On the whole I think that most partners are supportive because after all, if you start earning more money or start getting invited to nice places etc. the chances are that your partner is going to benefit anyway and although an average partner is not as good as a 100% partner, it is passable and you will probably be able to continue being together.

The big problem you face is if your partner falls in the below 50 to 0% bracket, only you will know this and be realistic when rating your partner, do try to help improve their self-esteem and show them the techniques that you have learnt and adopted, if however you genuinely know that you have done everything possible and they are miserable and in turn you are miserable, then the right solution for both of you is to part company.

Finding the right partner

It seems that finding the right partner or dating is becoming more and more complicated, however, it doesn't have to be this way.

What are you looking for in a partner?

This is where you have to be 100% open and honest with yourself, don't take any notice of what anyone else thinks or what magazines tell you, it is your life and if you are looking for a lifelong partner, then you must be happy with your decision. Family politics and generalisations tend to cloud relationships, for example "You can't go out with him, he's Chinese," "She's Jewish" or "They're a bad family."

You cannot live your life to keep other people happy, you have to DO WHAT YOU WANT and you need to define your ideal partner. I suggest you take a piece of paper and on one half you write ME and on the other half you write MY PERFECT PARTNER. Write down all your likes, interests and qualities on your side, also write down any dislikes. You now need to think hard of the qualities that you really want in your partner.

ME	MY PERFECT PARTNER
Generous	Supportive
Enjoy Travelling	Caring
Hard worker	Hard worker
Ambitious	Ambitious
Good sense of humour	Good sense of humour

Now I know you may want qualities like supermodel looks, to be a multimillionaire or a prince who lives in a castle, however, these qualities alone are not going to fulfil you for a lifetime, sure it will be exciting in the beginning, but just like eating your favourite food everyday for a month, you'll get bored with it. Look at some of the high profile Hollywood divorces, it looks as though they have everything, but if certain basic qualities are not there, then it will be a short-term and very shallow relationship.

A note about your prospective partner, it would be foolish to think that you would find every quality you have listed in a partner, however, if you can find as many as possible, then you are on the right track. You don't necessarily want your partner to be an exact mirror of yourself, it's good if your partner has some different qualities and interests that they can bring into the partnership.

Defining your ideal partner will help you to find them, if you wonder around not knowing what you want, you will never find the ideal partner because you don't know what you are really looking for. There are thousands of people out there saying, "I just can't find Mr or Mrs Right," but when you ask them to define Mr or Mrs Right, they can't.

Meeting your ideal partner

The first thing to remember is that if you sit indoors every night hoping that your right partner is going to knock on the door, then I hate to tell you but it doesn't work like that, you have to make opportunities, you have to meet people and I don't mean in down-market pubs or night-clubs.

Good ways to meet your ideal partner are by taking part in activities that you like on your own, if for example you like cookery, join an evening class or go on a course. If you like travelling, then go away on your own, sure it can be scary and a bit lonely, however, you'll be amazed how many people you can meet like this.

If you are uncomfortable or unsuccessful with this you should consider joining an Introduction Agency.

Introduction/dating agencies and up-market dinner parties

You are probably thinking, "I'm not joining one of those, they're for losers who haven't been able to find a partner."

Well let me tell you that these agencies have changed a great deal over the last few years, there are now many quality agencies who deal with people that are very successful in their lives, however, for whatever reason have not been able to find an ideal partner. If you are running your own business and working long hours, it can be very difficult to meet people. Many very attractive men and women are lonely, there are also some extremely rich people who are registered with introduction agencies.

By joining an agency it doesn't mean that you are a failure and that there is something wrong with you. Using a dating agency can be a very effective way to find a partner with the minimum amount of fuss. The agency can use the information you supply about yourself and your ideal partner requirements and MATCH them to other prospective partner seekers.

When you analyse the role of an agency it really makes sense and although a computer is not guaranteed to find you an ideal partner, it can at least help to lay a foundation of common interests.

Up-market dinner parties

These have become quite popular and they are advertised in quality magazines and Saturday newspapers in the personal sections, such as the Times and the Daily Telegraph.

Now if you are not willing to go to a dating agency, then this could be a softer option. The dinner parties are organised to bring professional and normally affluent people together in a social atmosphere, now even if you don't find your ideal partner, you haven't lost anything and in most cases you would have had a nice evening out and you may still make a few friends or contacts.

It is far easier to strike up a conversation and start a friendship in this type of environment, rather than going to a night-club or pub alone.

An old friend of mine has started to attend these type of dinner parties and although he has not found his ideal partner yet, he's having a great time and meeting many new and interesting people.

Summary to partners

Not everyone wants a long-term partner and of course that is their choice, many men and women find that they are far happier and more productive living a single life. Many people now live alone and they find that as long as they have their family and friends, they don't need a long-term partner and their life is full enough without one. As I've already mentioned, you are better off without a partner at all, than to have a bad partner.

If you do however find that being alone is not for you and that the lack of a long-term partner leaves a whole in your life and a sense of emptiness, then put your plans into action so that you can make opportunities to meet your ideal partner, and don't settle until you have found them. Don't be ashamed to join an introduction agency or to seek guidance from others.

Don't wait for pain to make you act

I've noticed that many people have to wait until something disastrous happens before they act, here's an example: How many people regularly go to the dentist for check-ups, compared to how many people rush to the dentist when they have a big problem or they are in PAIN?

You see how pain makes you act? It is a sad fact that although we all know that PREVENTION is BETTER than cure, many of us still let things happen and then hope that there is a cure for it.

Waiting for something to get worse is no way to run a successful life, thinking that the hole in the roof will cure itself is mad, the chances are the hole will get bigger and it will cost you more in the long run.

Learn to identify problems early, take actions wherever possible to PREVENT, rather than wasting your efforts on finding a CURE.

Now if you are looking to start a business, then you should be in the CURE business rather than the PREVEN-TION business, let me explain, how many people take vitamins or medicine to help prevent a cold? But how many people spend millions on cold cures? A lot more is spent on cure than prevention and I don't want to get into any moral arguments, but I believe that far more money and effort is going into finding a magic pill to cure AIDS, rather than working on a prevention campaign.

Look out for any early warning signs telling you that there could be something wrong, this could be your health, your personal life or your business. I see many bad business practices every day and if it were my business I would have stamped them out very early on, things like minor employee theft, bad security, computer passwords being written on pieces of paper and stuck on a VDU and confidential paperwork which is thrown away in the rubbish without shredding it first. These practices may not sound significant, but believe me they can blow up into problems that can sink a company.

Although I strongly believe in prevention, please don't confuse prevention with paranoia or constant worrying, certain things that are very unlikely to happen are not worth spending time or money preventing. For example, if your home is in the middle of nowhere and there has never been a terrorist bombing or an earthquake in the area, then I think it would be foolish to worry about buying insurance to cover terrorism and earthquakes.

CHAPTER 11

Getting it done now

As we've just mentioned, acting quickly to stop things from getting any worse makes real sense, you know when you should be doing something, yet before you know it, it's too late and it doesn't get done.

The simplest tool that I've found which helps me to get things done is a TO DO list. Simply write down the tasks that need to be done, either that day or week and you do not stop until they are done.

Now this is where people are going to say, "It's not that easy" and they will think of a hundred reasons to put things off, well who are they trying to kid? Most likely themselves because I don't believe any of their excuses, this is called procrastination and is a big factor why people just don't get anywhere.

A winner will find ways to get things done, a loser will find ways not to get things done. I have come across people who put so much effort into finding faults and ways not to get something done, yet if they had only put half of that energy into getting it done, it would have been!

Here are some common reasons that people say, which stops them from getting things done and here are my views:

1. Lack of time

This is a very common reason and it tends to be the biggest excuse used for not getting things done. First of all you can make time for anything, however, most people miraculously find the time to watch their favourite TV programme or to do what they like doing, yet they can't make the time to fix that leaking tap or mow the lawn etc., they say they just can't find the time!

The lack of time excuse is just that, it's an excuse not to do something.

2. Overwhelmed

I've seen people who are overwhelmed, they have good intentions and try to do lots at once, however, they normally end up doing nothing. They write very long TO DO lists, when what they should do is cut the tasks down into smaller chunks. It's like trying to eat a steak all at once, you need to cut it up.

Make realistic TO DO lists and deal with one task at a time, if it's a big task, then cut the task up. Deal only with that task and don't even think about or look at the TO DO list, until that task is finished and crossed off your list.

3. I don't like doing it

Regrettably in life there are many things we have to do that we don't like doing and putting it off will not make the problem go away. The way to see it is this, if it has to be done, get it done now and then you've got it over and done with. I find that it is better to do the worst jobs first and leave the best jobs until last, that way you've got something to look forward to.

As you become more successful you will be able to appoint others to do tasks that you don't particularly like. For example, I don't like bookkeeping, it is repetitive and I feel that I could use my time and talents elsewhere, so I pay a bookkeeper and I use the time I would spend bookkeeping in another area, which in turn makes enough money to pay the bookkeeper and a bit more.

4. It's not due yet

It's amazing how quick the due date comes around. Why not do it now? You'll have it over and done with and when the due date comes you will be ready, in fact why not score a few extra points and hand the work in early? Being one step ahead is never a bad thing, especially as things seem to change so quickly these days.

5. I just can't concentrate

Constant distractions do make tasks harder to finish, it is therefore your job to work around these distractions. If you're office is busy, then come in early or stay late when it is quieter, so that you can concentrate. Use whatever it takes to get the job done. When I worked in stockbroking I was on a dealing floor with over 150 other dealers screaming and yelling on the telephone, when the noise became unbearable I would take the phone and I would sit underneath my desk, so I had some sound proofing which helped me to hear myself and my client.

6. Hopefully the task will go away and I won't have to do it

There may be a 1 in a 1,000th chance that this could happen. For example, your boss dies so you don't need to submit the business plan on Monday or the research you need to compile is no longer required, because something has changed.

There's no way you can live your life like this, it's gambling and it is hoping for a miracle. Remember that you are in charge of your life and acting like a coward is not the right way forward.

Get it done!

7. I work best under pressure

This is an interesting reason and although it has some truth that many people only act when they are desperate or they are forced to, I don't believe that working like this all the time is good for the body or mind. If you prefer to work under pressure, then set yourself a strict time to have something done by, fool yourself into thinking that you have less time than you really have, this way the task will get done early and should any unforeseen circumstances arise, then you've got time to spare.

8. I need a cigarette or a stiff drink first

I hear this one normally before someone has to do an unpleasant task, like telling someone that they are fired or delivering other bad news and my view is that if you must have a cigarette or stiff drink (both of which are very bad habits that I do not believe in and which do not contribute to a successful life), deliver the news or do the task first and then reward yourself afterwards.

9. It's too late for today

This is a classic, used by lazy salespeople especially on a Friday afternoon. Let me tell you that I've done some excellent deals out of normal business hours. If you are selling a product and all of the other salespeople stop at 5.00pm on the dot and you make the call at 5.30pm or drop in at 5.30pm, you have more of a chance of getting through the door. You will also find that if the secretary has gone home, you have more of a chance to speak to the boss directly.

10. It's too early

This is the reverse of too late. Being the first caller of the day can get the deal done before anyone else. Again, many Directors come in earlier than their staff and you could get through directly. I've clinched deals early in the morning, where as if I had called a bit later the customer would have done something else. They say, "The early bird catches the worm!"

11. It might not work

You will only find out if you try and remember that if you start with a negative outlook, you are reducing your chances of making it work.

12. I meant to do it, but I keep forgetting

I'm sure! If I had been meaning to write your pay cheque but I kept forgetting, you would no doubt remind me. If you are genuinely forgetting something then write notes or ask people to remind you about it.

The chances are that you are forgetting because there is another reason deep down, you don't tend to forget things that you want to do.

13. I don't know how to do it

This is not a legitimate reason to put something off, you should seek advice, read the manual, call a technical help line or do whatever you need to do to learn how to do it. It's amazing how many tasks which may look complicated or boring can turn out to be simple and enjoyable.

14. If I do it now they'll just give me something else to do

I met someone recently who said this to me and after a brief discussion it was clear that he hated his job and was just coasting by. If you are saying similar things to yourself, then it is time to change jobs, you are not helping your employer and you are not working to your full potential.

15. I'll wait until after Christmas, the first of the month or the New Year etc.

I have found that without fail, there really is no time like the present. If you have genuinely decided to do something then start TODAY. Be honest with yourself, setting a delayed time to start something like a diet will not make any difference.

Improve your memory

A good memory is an asset which I'm sure you will agree with me is an essential part of success. A good memory helps us to obtain qualifications, popularity (remembering people's names is very impressive), a good memory helps in public speaking and almost all other areas of our lives.

Before I go any further, how do you rate your memory?

> **100%** - I remember everything, in fact I am thinking of applying to go on Mastermind!

> **50%** - I remember most things.

> **0%** - What was the question again?

Well let's put a myth to rest, for most healthy people we all have very good memories, unless we have suffered a genuine medical problem. As stated earlier in this book we all have amazing brains and memories, in fact we carry very sophisticated computers in our head.

How to improve your memory instantly

STOP SAYING THAT YOU HAVE A BAD MEMORY. If you think that you have a bad memory and you rated yourself less than 100%, then the problem is that you think you have a bad memory, which in turn has become reality. We have already discussed our subconscious mind and whatever is repeatedly suggested to the mind tends to become reality.

To improve your memory, use positive thinking and suggest to yourself repeatedly that your memory is excellent and it is improving every day.

Exercise your memory

I believe that the mind and in turn your memory is a muscle and unless you exercise it regularly it will go rusty, work your memory out, let me give you an example:

Next time you go shopping make a list, study it and then put it in your pocket. Now go about your shopping without referring to the list, let your memory work and trust your memory. Now as you approach the check-out, check the list and see how well you did. Keep up with this memory building exercise and eventually you won't even need a list.

A good tip to help you remember is to imagine yourself doing it before hand. For example, if you have onions and potatoes on your shopping list, imagine you're at the supermarket and you are picking them up.

You WILL remember

Don't use words like, I will try to remember, I should remember or I hope that I will remember, make a bold statement to yourself that YOU WILL remember.

Repetition

Repetition is still one of the best ways to learn and remember. Repeating information out loud has more effect than silently. It is also better to think about what you are repeating, rather than just saying it in parrot-fashion. Another tip is to repeat things for short regular intervals rather than repeating all in one session.

Remembering by association

This is a technique which is extensively used by waiters, casino card-counters and many others who have to remember and constantly recall information for a living. Here's how it works:

You basically link up the new information with something or someone you already know, so if you need to remember an onion, you can link that up with your bank manager, a potato your uncle Ted and a tomato with your sister and so on.

Now when you want to call up the information, think of the familiar name/person, then think again and the new information should come next and so on.

I suggest you look into learning more about how the memory works and how you can optimise yours. As already mentioned, you have an excellent memory, it's there but you may need to tune it up a little and with some practice you could even become the next international memory champion! In business it is very impressive when you meet someone and say "Yes, I remember you Mr Smith, how did that trade show in Germany go?"

Balance

One of the biggest problems that we all face in life is how to live the ideal balanced life. If you imagine a see-saw, you increase the weight on one side, that side goes down and the other side goes up, that's what life is like, if you spend too much time at work your personal and health side goes down.

I can safely say that for me true success has only come since I have been able to balance my work, financial, health and personal life. Only you know if you are neglecting your personal or health life, as I mention in the diet and exercise section, I certainly neglected my health life, I have now corrected this imbalance and the rewards are coming through.

For most of us the work and financial side always seems to be the big problem and it normally stems from the fact that most people spend more hours at work than anywhere else. In the making money section of this book I am going to tell you about a business that will allow you to spend more time with your children, family and loved ones and still make you more money than you are making now. I strongly believe that if you can balance your personal life, which includes your loved ones, your own mental state and your health life, then the work and financial life will be easier to manage.

Trying to make money with a poor mental state, traumatic personal relationship or poor health is going to be very difficult and my aim is to show you the easiest way to reach your goals.

Let's look at the things you need to balance:

Your mental health

By following this book and by further reading you will be on the way to sorting out your mental health. With your goals outlined, increased self-confidence, the use of positive thinking and all the other points we've outlined, you are on the way to keeping your mind in very good health.

Your physical health

We will discuss this at length in the next section. A balanced life includes a balanced diet, exercise and avoiding negative items like tobacco, alcohol and drugs.

Personal relationships

A happy relationship with your significant other and children if applicable, ensures that you start the day on the right note. Making time for family and friends should not be a chore, it should be enjoyable. Money cannot replace your family relationships. If you have young children and they grow up never seeing you, you are letting them down and yourself. You will find that children who don't see their parents when they are younger, tend to have very little respect for their parents as they grow older. Make time for your children and significant other, you can't expect to gain respect and trust if your wife/husband/girlfriend/boyfriend never sees you. You need to take a genuine interest in your partner, not come home and expect them to hear all of your problems. If you find that your partner is unsupportive, lethargic or uninspired, then it is very likely that you are causing these problems.

Marital disputes and affairs

I believe that most problems and affairs start because of neglect. The wife/husband feels that the other partner has lost interest in them and to rebel they start looking at another person. Some men/women have affairs for months, if not years and the other partner still doesn't notice. There is no way that can happen if you are spending time with your partner and taking an interest in their life.

Your work and financial life

Many of you are saying, "I'd love to spend time with my wife/children," and "I would love to go and have a regular work-out at the gym, but I don't have the time because I have to work to make money."

I understand that money is needed to support your family, but be honest here, could you not make a few hours a week to go to a gym? Could you not spare a few hours to spend time with your children and wife? No doubt you make the time to watch TV and go out with your friends after work!

Summary

I've had my life in and out of balance and it only takes a few simple steps to put your life back in balance. Only someone who has a balanced life can truly say that they are successful. A balanced life will certainly make you happier and as long as you can keep your personal, mental and physical health in good order, then you will find that the work and financial side will become easier.

CHAPTER 12

The food we eat and exercise

You may be thinking, "What has exercise and the food we eat got to do with making money and becoming successful?" Well I can tell you from experience that eating the right foods and exercising really helps. I've made some real discoveries that I would like to share with you.

First of all, let me tell you that I have spent most of my life in an overweight state and I've never been one to take part in any regular exercise, I was always too busy and engrossed in making money to even think about serious dieting and exercising, however, around a year ago I finally made the decision to change my eating habits and to start exercising regularly.

You see, although I have been successful in business and I have been able to keep my mind fit and very positive, I had really neglected my body and looking back on it, I now realise that keeping fit and watching your weight is an important part of success and it is something that we should all take notice of.

Why being fit contributes to your success

The first thing I've noticed is that carrying around less weight gives you more energy, it makes you more confident, more assertive and generally makes you feel more cheerful, which are many of the qualities that help us to feel good and become successful, you must have heard the slogan "Look good, feel great."

I've also found that working out on a regular basis has helped me to reduce fatigue, contrary to popular belief exercise builds up your energy level, it doesn't take it away.

Do you suffer from fatigue or do you tend to feel lethargic?

Well the problem could be your diet, lack of exercise, cigarette smoke, either as a smoker or by passive smoking and the general air quality. Let me briefly discuss these subjects:

Your diet

I will discuss over-eating in greater depth in a moment, but what I actually mean here is not over-eating or under-eating, but the actual foods we eat. Certain foods give us more energy and help our minds to think better, others can cause us to slow down and feel sleepy. A big lunch in most cases kills your productivity for the rest of the day.

Cigarette smoke

I am not here to pass judgement on smokers, however, medical research has shown that smoking can kill your energy level. Nicotine is a vasoconstrictor, causing the blood vessels to narrow, which means less blood reaches the brain. The blood that reaches your brain has more carbon monoxide, so the affect is low energy and some drowsiness. The next time someone says that a cigarette helps them to concentrate, I suggest you tell them to do some research. Don't forget that you don't have to be a smoker to be affected, passive smoking is just as bad, if not worse. A smoke free work-place is more productive.

Lack of exercise

Many people who work in office or desk based jobs, just don't get enough exercise. Humans were not designed to sit in front of a computer for 8 hours a day. By simply standing up for a few minutes, stretching or moving around, you will find that fatigue can be reduced. Try standing up when you are on the phone, instead of sitting slouched in a chair. If you get a lunch break try and walk around or go out and get some fresh air.

Air quality

Most offices have very poor air quality, even the ones with air conditioning. I have found that an ioniser can help to improve the air quality. An ioniser has a cleaning and calming effect which gives the air the same feeling as after a thunderstorm. Some ionisers can be used with essential oils that give out fragrances which can stimulate and invigorate you. If your company doesn't have an ioniser you could buy a small personal ioniser. If you suffer from allergies or have breathing problems, then you will notice a big difference by using one.

My big health tip

Here is my big health tip which is fairly painless, any women who want better looking skin should definitely read this.

> It is a fact that most men and women DO NOT DRINK ENOUGH WATER. By water I don't mean tea, coffee, soft drinks or beer, I mean straight mineral water or filtered water, preferably still and not sparkling.

Water seems to be a neglected cure for many problems, including fatigue, dark and puffy eyes, kidney problems, bad skin and much more.

Experts vary in their recommendations on daily water intake, but my view is to drink as much as you possibly can, as I have never heard of anyone overdosing on water. I always push myself to drink at least 6 to 8 glasses of water a day.

I am not going to turn this book into a health and fitness guide, there are many good books on exercise and healthy eating, however, all I can say is do think about what you eat and about starting a regular exercise routine. From my experience it is better to exercise for a shorter period every day or every other day, rather than exercising for 4 hours all at once.

You are what you eat

Let's start off with the fact that most diets don't work, in fact most people will regain all the weight they lose, normally within 1 to 2 years. Many people will also gain extra weight on top of this, so they would have been far better off if they had just maintained their heavier weight!

My personal mind diet

If you are lucky enough to be in good shape and you are at a comfortable weight, then you don't need to read this section, however, if you are looking to lose weight and most importantly keep it off, then read on.

The first point to realise about overeating is that in nearly all cases it is in the mind. Yes, your body needs food, but it doesn't need to be over fed. The main cause of overeating is not that you need or in most cases like eating lots of food, it is the fact that you have some other problem, where you console yourself with food. People overeat because they are depressed, they are lonely, bored or experiencing other negative feelings. If you are excited, busy, happy and generally feeling good about yourself, you will be less inclined to snack and overeat.

If your brain is very busy, it hasn't got time to focus or think about food. If you follow the plan outlined in this book and start setting goals and feeling happier about yourself, you will find that losing weight will be easier. Now don't get me wrong you still need to eat, I still enjoy eating, and going out for a meal with my friends and family is an enjoyable experience.

The media and advertising has a great deal to do with overeating, walk down any high street and you will see many fast food outlets and adverts for food. Do you know that fast food outlets circulate food smells outside the restaurant to get you in? Well it's true, it is a subtle marketing technique. Supermarkets use the smell of freshly baked bread to get you to shop more, because it is a fact that hungry shoppers buy more.

Impulse eating, if your brain sees an advert, poster or smells chips, it sends a signal that says, "I'm hungry and there's a fast food outlet where I can buy some chips from."

The key to losing and keeping weight off is to avoid in-between meal snacking. If you really need to snack then try low calorie and nutritious alternatives. Many supermarkets and chemists/health-food stores now sell a low fat range of foods, these include low fat chocolate bars, milk-shakes, sandwiches and even crisps. You'll be surprised how good they taste in view that they are low in calories.

A point I want to mention here is diet drinks that contain a sweetener which I won't name, but you probably know the one I mean. This sweetener is Aspartame based and a cause for great concern. I was a heavy consumer of diet drinks, in fact I would buy them by the case load, however, now I don't buy any drinks that are diet. I stick to drinking water, fruit juices and occasionally full fat drinks. I have found that since cutting out drinks with Aspartame in, the many headaches that I used to suffer from have miraculously disappeared.

If you have access to the Internet, go to a search engine like Yahoo or Infoseek and type in "Aspartame" and read the various articles that come up. I doubt that you will ever buy another diet drink again!

My 90% good, 10% bad rule

I don't believe that 100% of anything is good for you. I think that the "carrot in front of the donkey" trick works, so if you've been sensible for 6 days of the week and you feel like a treat, then by all means have one. Looking forward to a treat can be used to motivate you, but make sure that your treat doesn't cancel out all of your good efforts, also remember to get the order right, eat the sensible foods first and then have the treat at the end of the week.

> **JOKE:** An overweight man went to the doctors because he needed to lose weight. The doctor drew up a diet and said that as long as he ate 1,500 calories a day he would lose weight. 1 month later the man went back, he hadn't lost any weight and in fact he had put more on! The doctor was baffled and the man said that he has taking his 1,500 calories a day allowance, however, he forgot to tell the doctor that he had taken an advance on his future allowances and he was up to the year 2010!!!

A diet is for life

This is the hardest fact to face, if you diet for 1 month, 6 months or even 12 months and then STOP, and go back to your pre-diet habits, what's going to happen? You'll start putting it all back on again.

The key is to re-educate your eating habits and to make healthy food fun and taste good. With the introduction of lower fat alternatives and the great range of chocolate bars, crisps, low calorie meals and sandwiches, you can still think that you're eating "nice" foods, even when they are low in calories.

Summary

A healthy diet does not have to be boring, I've managed to prove that and with a combination of exercise and a better diet at the time of writing this book, I have lost over 4 stone (56 lbs/26 kilos) in weight. I was around 18 stone (252 lbs/

114 kilos) when I started, so that is a loss of around 20% of my total body weight. The diet has given me more energy, helped to reduce fatigue and with all the weight loss and exercise I have managed to reduce my back pains, I walk better and I can sit straighter.

Even if you don't need to lose weight, you can still increase your energy levels by watching what foods you eat and by taking up regular exercise.

Here's a final word on a good diet and exercise, it is a sad fact that many people die every year from diseases that are caused by being overweight, smoking, lack of exercise, bad diets and alcohol.

If you don't care about living a long and healthy life then that is fine, but if you achieve success which I am sure you will by following this book, you will want to live a long and healthy life.

Once you get your life into shape and you start to actually achieve wealth, you don't want to worry about bad health, disease or death, you'll want to enjoy your new found success, what could be worse than dropping dead with millions in the bank? I don't think they take credit cards when you cross over to the other side!

Here's something that you may want to add to your lifetime goals list:

> **"I want to be fit and active so that I can live to over 100 years old, I want to be able to drive my Ferrari, sail my yacht and travel around the world for as long as I can and by investing in a good diet and exercise now, I can help to make this a reality."**

Dealing with poor health

Many illnesses today have come from modern day living and the way we conduct our lives such as, eating, drinking, smoking, drugs, stress and so on. There are also illnesses that start in the mind. It has been proven that Hypochondriacs, people who are convinced they are sick, even though there is nothing wrong with them, experience the same symptoms of the actual illness. It is possible to make yourself ill by generally feeling down about life and through constant worry or by over-reacting to situations, you've probably done this yourself, I know I have.

A sick and negative mind is the worst illness that anyone can have, because without the power and belief that you will get well, your body will never be able to recover.

It is a fact that people who feel that they have no purpose in life or are unhappy with their job and surroundings, tend to have more sick days than those who are happy at work and are positive about their life.

Let me tell you that since owning my own business, which has been for over 10 years, I have never had one day off due to illness. Sure I've had a few coughs and colds, which I have worked through, but that's about it.

A great deal of time and money is spent on quick cures for illnesses, however, very rarely does anyone ever stop and think about prevention and about the link between the mind and the body.

☺

Change your image

A businessman called Ron, was going through a serious mid-life crisis. To fix things, he decided to have a face-lift, a tummy tuck and a hair transplant. He cut down on fatty foods, stopped smoking and started going to the gym every day. Ron felt and looked like a new man, so what went wrong?

Well one day Ron was crossing the road and was hit by a truck and died. When arriving at the pearly gates, Ron cried out in anguish "Why me, God, things were going great?" God looked at Ron and with a perplexed look said "Oops, I'm sorry I didn't recognise you, I thought you were someone else!"

CHAPTER 13

Smart education and investing in yourself

It's funny that when I was at school, I wouldn't be seen dead in a library or bookshop, now it's an outing for me and an enjoyable pastime. I buy many books, training videos, magazines, attend seminars and now surf the Internet for information.

I have found that information and knowledge is power and is priceless. Knowledge is a commodity that we all need and as much as we may already know about a subject, you can always learn more. Knowledge and education can never be taken away from you, once it is in your head it's yours forever. If you were to lose every possession you own in an earthquake tomorrow, you would still have all of your knowledge wouldn't you?

Successful people study

It is a fact that the super successful are perpetual students, you've heard the saying, "the rich get richer" well it's true. I have sold various "How to" information including, newsletters, training videos etc. and it never ceases to amaze me that many of the buyers are already very rich and successful.

I have hundreds of doctors, dentists, lawyers and businessmen/women as clients, all of whom are already very successful and yet they still want to know more and they are willing to seek and pay for new knowledge.

Join and use your local library

Most large towns and cities in the U.K., Europe and the USA have excellent libraries and the best thing about these is that they are free.

I am very fortunate that my local library is a large one and as well as books they have:

> Magazines (including difficult to find trade magazines), newspapers (including overseas), training video tapes, audio tapes, reference directories, access to the Internet and much more.

A good point about the library is the librarians, if you approach them and ask them nicely, they will do anything to help you. It's like having a free researcher.

Why a book is excellent value

Just think about it, for a relatively small amount of money a book can inform, entertain and even change your life.

Most people could not afford for me or a successful motivation speaker to be their personal tutor for 1 week, I would need thousands of pounds to make it worth my while, yet for a fraction of that amount you have me in a book format forever!

I love to read biographies of successful people, without ever meeting these people in real life, I feel that I already know them and I can learn the techniques that they have used to get to the top.

Buy books, videos and attend seminars

The fact that you have invested your time and money into this book, shows that you are already a smart learner and you are on the way to being richer, however, you need to understand that this is a beginning and learning is an endless journey.

I strongly advise you to invest in education, buying books, videos, audio tapes and attending seminars, you are never wasting money when you invest in any of these.

There are 3 ways that you can obtain real business and life changing information:

1. The school of hard knocks, trial and error method.

2. Find someone who has experienced and overcome the same problem that you are facing and quiz them.

3. Books, tapes and seminars offered by those who are "practising what they preach."

Practising what they preach

There are many books in print which are books of theory, especially in business. I've read many of them and they are terrible. They are written by professors who you can tell have never, ever, done anything except lecture.

Let me give you an example, I've read many books about marketing and advertising, a subject which I am very knowledgeable on, now I know that many of those books contain theories that just don't work in real life.

A good way to tell if you are reading a "theory" book is to read how the author is introduced.

Which of the following books would you read?

A) If the introduction is "Professor Smith is a recognised expert and lecturer on direct marketing at Oxford University for over 30 years."

B) If the introduction is "Mr Smith built up a successful direct mail business, starting from only a few hundred pounds in savings, to a multi-million pound business and his book contains many of his top secrets."

I'd go for B, because he's done it, he has been in the trenches and not in a classroom.

Another way to tell if a book is written by someone who actually does things is if they refer to their own experiences for example, "When I was selling" or "I found that advertising agencies would always..." You see Professor Smith can't say that because he's never sold anything in his life!

Losers don't invest in education

I have met many men and women in business who really need help and if they would only spend some time and money on learning, they would be in a far better position than they are now. Instead of investing in themselves, they waste money on their cars, clothes and other gadgets and then they say that they don't have any spare money for books or seminars, these people are LOSERS!!!!

I would like to point out that the saying "Knowledge is power" is very true, but unless you put that knowledge into practice, then you're no better off than if you didn't have the knowledge at all.

I know it all and I've done it all

As you start to gain some success, confidence and money, you may start to suffer from complacency, take your eye off the ball and start to get the "I know it all" disease. Be very careful and get ready for a BIG FALL if you think you know everything.

Life is a constant learning process and it's amazing how quickly things can change, for the better or worse. Here is a good example of the know it all syndrome:

Someone sets up a business and they do very well, they continue to do well, in fact they can't do anything wrong. Everything is going their way and then they decide that because they are so great they will start up another business and then another one and what normally ends up happening is that they start taking their eye off the ball. They spread themselves too thinly and before you know it trouble starts and they lose everything. Now this may sound far fetched, but believe me I've seen it happen so many times in real life.

Now I'm not saying that you shouldn't be ambitious and confident, of course you should, unless you are ambitious and confident you will never get anywhere, however, don't become too big for your own boots, understand that you are not 100% bullet proof and definitely understand that you can never know enough about anything.

Here is another example, if you have ever been to a casino in Las Vegas or Monte Carlo and you start playing a slot machine, the chances are that you'll win some money, but do you walk out with any money? I doubt it, what happens to most people is that they put it all back in, along with some more.

Go the extra mile in everything you do

If you would like to know one of my key secrets for success, it is that I always ensure I give a little bit extra in all areas of my life. I've already touched on this subject, however, it is so important that it's worth going into in depth.

The attitude that is taken by many today is, "I want to get by," or "I want to do just enough," well unless you can get into the habit of giving extra service and providing more than you have to, then I don't think that you are ready for success.

If you are in the service industry, for example, a supermarket and a customer comes up to you and says, "Please can you tell me where the tinned tomatoes are?" now you could get by with saying, "Four aisles that way and they're at the bottom, on the right," or you could say, "I will show you, please follow me." And that's the extra mile service, it doesn't take that much effort, but believe me the customer will appreciate a personal escort, rather than directions, wouldn't you? Also going the extra mile should make you feel better, I know I feel better when I've done a good deed.

The service industry is growing rapidly, whether it be in retail, restaurants, mail-order or telephone selling. and unless you learn to like helping customers and enjoy going the extra mile, then I strongly suggest that you stay out or get out of these type of businesses.

Shining by going the extra mile

As most people are negatively programmed and go about their lives on a minimum effort basis, it is very easy for you to shine if you start going the extra mile. By doing simple extras such as, working 10 minutes extra a day, going in 10 minutes earlier in the morning or ensuring that the job is completed a little earlier than expected, are all excellent ways of demonstrating the extra mile process. Also make sure that you say, "Thank You" and "Sorry" to customers and I don't mean on autopilot, I mean truthfully and in a sincere manner. It is also nice to address the person by "Sir" or "Madam," again sincerely.

I recently heard about a man who went to a large American store and as he went through the check-out the cashier handed him his change and receipt, but he was shocked when the cashier didn't say thank you and he said, "You've forgotten to say thank you" and the cashier replied, "It's printed on your receipt!" Let's ensure that this doesn't become the norm.

People and businesses who provide that bit "extra" will always rise to the top, even if the benefits to you may not be apparent in the short-term, they will always come through in the long-term.

Whatever your next task is, whether you are a road-sweeper, a bank clerk, a doctor or a waiter, try putting a bit "extra" into your work and before you know it, you'll benefit both financial and personally.

On the same subject, whatever profession you are in and however menial you may think your job is, act as though it is the most important job in the world and do it to the best of your abilities. Here is a quote I recently read:

> If a man is called to be a street sweeper, he should sweep streets as Michelangelo painted, or Beethoven composed music, or Shakespeare wrote poetry.

> He should sweep streets so well that all the hosts of heaven and earth will pause to say, here lived a great street sweeper who did his job well.

> Martin Luther King Jr.

I remember one of my very first jobs at the bank in which I worked, I would key data into a computer, which most people treated as a menial and boring job, however, I would key the data in with enthusiasm, accuracy and skill, it was almost as if one wrong digit would set off World War 3.

Believing is seeing

You may be thinking, isn't it "seeing is believing," after all, if I don't see it with my own eyes it can't be true? Well I have to tell you that in life there are many times when it is far better to adopt the "believing is seeing" philosophy.

For myself and millions of others, FAITH and BELIEF are stronger than the actual seeing, let me be totally honest with you about this book:

> The book was finished before the first word was even typed into my computer!

> The book sold 1 million copies before the first one had even come back from the printers!

> The book was translated into various languages before it had even been finished in English!

So what does this mean? Well that faith and belief came first for me, the actual reality and seeing came after and for some of my projects, very much after. You must also adopt the "believing leads to seeing" philosophy in all aspects of your life.

We need people in the world who are willing to believe without any hard evidence. Just think, there are thousands of people employed in the pharmaceuticals industry around the world, who are all working hard in the belief that they will discover a cure to Aids, Cancer and other life threatening problems, these people have faith and belief in their work, they have little hard evidence in many cases, but they still keep going. Do you want these people to give up just because they are not "seeing" instant results or do you want them to keep "believing?" I think you'll now agree why the world needs believers. Today's trial drugs and vaccinations, become tomorrow's reality cures and saviours to millions.

We reap what we sow

I believe that deep down regardless of what we do for a living, we are all farmers and our lives are based on the "reaping and sowing" principle, in fact the Bible actually states that we reap what we sow.

Whether it is in business, health, love, friendship or whatever, if you sow hard-work, diligence, care, precision, perseverance, faith and belief into your life then you will reap a bumper harvest and crop, you won't necessarily reap this reward instantly, but in time it will come. You will have to preserve, take care and water your crop.

Now if you sow half-heartedly, with fear, doubt, in haste and carelessly, then you will be lucky to harvest anything, either in the short or long-term.

Remember this in everything that you do and you will become a winning farmer and your harvest will be everything that you truly want out of life.

CHAPTER **14**

Achieving non-monetary goals

As we are now coming to the end of this section I would like to reveal how to achieve your non-monetary goals. In the next section you will discover how to achieve the monetary goals.

The reason I left this section towards the end was because I wanted to get you set in the right frame of mind and help you overcome as many obstacles as possible, which I believe I have now done.

Now remember the importance of believing in yourself, visualising, believing before seeing and all the other techniques that we have mentioned, however, without any ACTION your goals will not be fulfilled.

Before we go any further, I will presume that you do have non-monetary goals. If your life is that shallow that you have only put down monetary goals like a big house, yacht or car etc. then I can safely say that you will never achieve true happiness or success.

In this section I will concentrate on the aspects of your life that you want to improve such as, losing weight, getting into shape, improving your confidence, finding a partner, to be more assertive, to speak well, or any other personal achievement that you wish to have. I know I have said this before, but if you want to make and save money, you do need these personal skills.

Goal assessment sheet

This sheet should be copied out and one copy should be made for each asset that you wish to improve, for example, public speaking. I suggest you put them in a ring binder and treat them as a diary, keep updating them until your goal has been achieved.

☺

Tom: I wish I had enough money to buy an elephant.

Frank: What do you want an elephant for?

Tom: I don't. I just wish I had that much money.

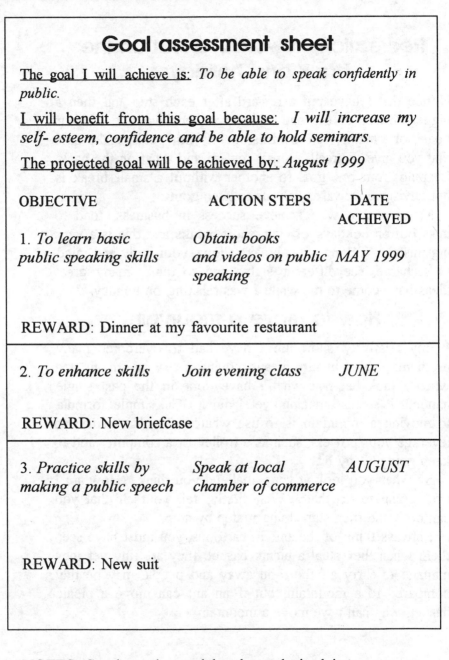

Goal assessment sheet

<u>The goal I will achieve is:</u> *To be able to speak confidently in public.*

<u>I will benefit from this goal because:</u> *I will increase my self- esteem, confidence and be able to hold seminars.*

<u>The projected goal will be achieved by:</u> *August 1999*

OBJECTIVE	ACTION STEPS	DATE ACHIEVED
1. *To learn basic public speaking skills*	*Obtain books and videos on public speaking*	*MAY 1999*

REWARD: Dinner at my favourite restaurant

2. *To enhance skills*	*Join evening class*	*JUNE*

REWARD: New briefcase

3. *Practice skills by making a public speech*	*Speak at local chamber of commerce*	*AUGUST*

REWARD: New suit

NOTES: See how the goal has been devised into steps, as mentioned in the getting things done section, it is easier to break big tasks into smaller tasks.

Recreation, rewards, a pat on the back and holidays

Notice that I have put a reward after each step and then a bigger reward at the end. When you achieve one of your goals, or a major step towards one of your goals, make sure that you give yourself a small reward and a pat on the back. Leaping from one goal to another without a small break is not advisable, rewards help us to keep going.

Many people who achieve success in business, tend to miss out on holidays or even short breaks and this is a very big mistake. Taking short breaks allows your body and mind to recharge, see different sights and to think, many great ideas have come to me while I was relaxing on holiday.

How to move a mountain

In my relatively short life I have had to overcome many problems, which in turn meant moving a few mountains and when I look back at what I have done in the past single handed, it seems amazing, yet I did it. The simple formula to moving a mountain is to use whatever tools you can to leverage your powers, such as a trolley or a computer and to keep going bit by bit.

So when you look at your goal and you think, "How am I ever going to do that?" Well firstly, tell yourself that you can do it and then start doing it step by step.

I always think of the ants in cartoons, you must have seen them when they steal a picnic basket, they are tiny yet they manage to carry all the food away and people may be tiny compared to a mountain, but if an ant can move a picnic basket, why can't we move a mountain?

CHAPTER 15

Summary to section 1 of this book

We have now come to the end of this section and I'm sure you will agree with me that this section is the foundation for a successful life. Take the time to study and put the principles discussed into action every day, for the rest of your life and you will build strong and broad foundations which will allow you to build the highest skyscraper of success, wealth and happiness.

Skimp on the foundations and whatever you try to build will always be shaky and in the majority of cases, it will topple over. Too many people rush into business or try to make money without understanding the basic principles of putting your life in order first, without your health, both physical and mental and a good balanced life-style, money will not come your way and even if it does, it will not fulfil you.

I have disclosed some life changing tools in this section and if used correctly you too can start to achieve your dreams, however, remember that this is a journey and you will need commitment, perseverance and vision to overcome obstacles including, the many sceptics and doubtful people that you will meet along the way.

It is easier to give up than carry on, especially when things don't appear to be going your way, but by giving up and admitting defeat, you join the ranks of the other millions of life's losers and no-hopers who are living shallow, empty and worthless lives, hoping that Lady Luck will help them to win the lottery!

Now although success does take some effort, it really is worth it and I speak from first hand experience.

Remember that you have a long way to go yet and reading the first part of this book is only a tiny step up a long ladder that you will need to climb, however, now that you've started, keep going.

The next section is the making money section which will allow you to fulfil your financial goals, combine the new skills that you have learnt in this section, together with the money making secrets that I will reveal to you and you will become seriously wealthy.

So let's carry on with our incredible journey...

CHAPTER 16

Section 2

Making Money

In the last section we explained the importance of setting goals, increasing your self-confidence and the importance of positive thinking. As previously stated, it is very important to continue with your daily declarations and it is very important that you believe in yourself.

Positive thinking and believing in yourself are very important qualities which are the beginning to your new successful life, however, positive thinking is not enough on its own. The next two qualities that you require are the ability to make money and save money.

You could say that the first section of this book was the preparation, we are now into the ACTION section and then the saving money section will be the final icing on the cake.

I will repeat this a few times during this book, but it's so important that it's worth it. Knowledge without any action is worthless, you could read this book 1000 times, in fact you could learn every word off by heart and you'd know the book better than me and I'm the author, but what would you prove and achieve? You will have the knowledge and you'll be a textbook expert, but unless you AIM, FIRE AND

TAKE ACTION nothing will ever happen. So remember, if you want things to improve then JUST DO IT! Talk is certainly cheap and worthless, it is the action that speaks louder than words.

Now before we go on to making money, don't think that you won't have to read the first section of this book again, because you will. You MUST still practice the various techniques that we have discussed. I will occasionally remind you of this during this section. Without a focused and Positive Mental Attitude it will be very difficult to make money. To stay positive and charged up you must keep up with the techniques outlined in the first section, it's the same as keeping your physical shape, if you stop exercising or practising cautious eating, before you know it you'll be back to square one. Keeping positive is the same, start skipping your daily declarations, start thinking a few negative thoughts and before you know it your mind will be out of shape. It is a lifelong commitment, but it's one that I have found is worth making.

Can you juggle?

Well you need to learn quickly and I don't mean with balls or oranges. Making money is like juggling, you need to juggle various qualities and areas of your life all at once. You need to juggle your mental health, physical health, your personal relationships, the actual making money and learning how to save money.

Being your own boss

I am not going to mince my words and mess about, instead I am going to tell you straight and as it is "You'll never get rich working for someone else" and these famous words came from John Paul Getty, one of the world's richest men.

The only way that you will ever make real money is to own your own business. I've worked for companies on salaries and commission, and without a doubt running my own business has been much more profitable and enjoyable.

Yes, there are some drawbacks to being self-employed and we will go into these later, however, on balance I guarantee that you will be better off working for yourself.

You are already self-employed

This is where people will say "No I'm not, I work for an oil company, a newspaper, a hospital or the government etc." Well I can tell you that you ARE self-employed, you work for YOURSELF and you are really Joe Smith Plc or Mary Robbins Inc. Your employer is just a vehicle at the end of the day, you work for yourself and the benefits that it brings to YOU and your family.

Why owning your own business is the only option today

If you do some research and go back say 100 years ago, or maybe even less, you will find that nearly everyone was self-employed, go back to your grandfather or your great-grandfather and the chances are that they worked for themselves, many people worked from home and we had the cottage industry businesses, then it all changed with the big factories etc. fewer people were in charge of their lives and they started to rely on the big companies to look after them.

Well, we all know what's happening today, most of those big companies are becoming smaller companies, they are breaking up into smaller divisions and the staff are being laid off. The buzz word for this is "downsizing" or "corporate restructuring." People who have provided 20 to 30 years plus of loyal service are being laid off.

If you are still employed for a large company you will know that your employer demands more and more from you, you are expected to come in early, work late, be responsible for your actions and yet in good times the company rarely increases your pay or benefits, but in bad times they are quick to cut your pay, the hours you work and even lay you off. Anyone who's in the airline business will know exactly what I mean!

So back to my point about "Are you self-employed?" I think you must agree with me that you are, and it seems that you are getting all of the negatives yet you are receiving none of the benefits.

I have recently been looking at recruitment advertisements and it amazes me what employers expect. They write long descriptions of what you must have, experience, leadership, qualifications etc. and then when you look at the benefits to you they are minimal. I see jobs advertised for directors and other senior positions that pay in 1 year what I would earn in 2 to 3 weeks, I am not saying this to gloat or to say how great I am, I wouldn't be offered one of those advertised jobs even if I wanted one. I am trying to demonstrate the injustice and the rewards gap between working for a real company and being your own boss. Now throw into the equation that many employers whatever they tell you, still have very old fashioned ideas about who goes to the top and promotion prospects are even less. If you are a woman, black, Asian, have any foreign blood in you (like me) or suffer from a disability etc. then YOU MUST set up your own business and be your own boss.

There are a few fair employers who treat everyone truly equal, but these are very rare.

Why working for yourself is the key

Why are you working for someone else?

The main reason I worked for someone else is that I left school at 16 with a few qualifications and very little experience and getting a job was really my only option. Even at this age I knew that working for a big company was just a stop gap. After 3 years in the London financial markets I managed to move to a company that paid a salary and commission, which was better than just a salary as I would start to be paid for my efforts, regrettably that was in 1987 which as many of you know was the big stockmarket crash.

Now although I was a good salesman, even I couldn't sell shares to someone after the crash. Many clients had lost thousands of pounds, some hundreds of thousands and it was then that I learned my first important lesson in business which is:

You can't sell something to someone if they don't have any money!

It is so simple but I see companies and shops making this mistake every day. I will explain later how to make sure your potential customer has money.

Anyway, although there was some hope that the financial markets and confidence would recover, I knew that it would take years and it was time for me to leave. After looking at other jobs I came to the conclusion that I had to make my own job and hence starting a business. This was difficult as I had little or no business experience and only a few hundred pounds in start-up capital. So my starting position was probably much worse than your current position.

One thing I can say for sure is that once you have worked for yourself there is no going back, sure you may change directions, sell different products etc. but you will always want to be a business owner. As a business owner you do have to take some calculated risks and stick your neck out a bit more than if you worked for someone else, but the rewards are worth it.

Let me tell you about my sister who with a bit of help from me, set up her own business doing exactly what she used to do working for someone else. Now she was doing OK when she worked for a company, she had a good salary+commission+car, but we both knew that if she set up on her own she would earn far more.

My sister was earning around £25,000 p.a. plus benefits which was not too bad, in her first 12 months running her own business she earned over £150,000. Now that is a true example of why you should be the boss, sure she had to stick her neck out and take some risks, but look at the benefits.

Now back to you.

Why are you working at the company you're with?

Are you truly happy with your job?

Are you happy with the income?

Are you being treated as you should?

Is getting to and from work a job in itself?

What would you do if your employer went broke or sacked you tomorrow?

I suggest that you write the answers to these questions down and answer each one, truthfully.

How did you get into the line of work you're in?

I have asked this question to hundreds of people and most people can't answer it. It seems to me that people spend very little time on choosing their careers and employers, it is almost a case of they'll take whatever comes. I think that most people spend more time choosing a car or house than they do selecting employment. The other reason people get into a profession is because of pressure from parents, teachers or other family members for example, your mother or sister was a teacher so you became a teacher.

I think that there are very few people on this earth who can truly say that they are happy with their work.

When I worked for my first employer which was a large bank, I came across many unhappy workers. They would moan about their pay, conditions and anything else they could think of, but if it was that bad why were they there? Simply because they were lazy and were too scared to either challenge their employer for a better wage or to look for a new job.

I am sure that many of those people are still in the same job and they are probably still moaning to themselves.

Are you working in the wrong job or business?

Most people are in the wrong profession for the reasons already mentioned. The easy way to know if you are in the right job or business is to answer a few simple questions truthfully:

1. Do you jump out of bed in the morning to go to work, or do you hate going?

2. Do you clock watch and can't wait for breaks or for the end of the day?

3. Are you enthusiastic, motivated and proud about your work or do you do it because you have too?

4. Do your superiors motivate you and set good examples or do you find that they couldn't care less?

5. If you didn't earn any money for what you did, would you still do it?

If you are totally satisfied with your profession then congratulations and the best possible avenue for you is to become a consultant, set up your own business doing the same thing or find any other angle, such as writing a book, newsletter or course on your profession. If you are happy with your profession, by branching out on your own you can still enjoy your profession and increase your income from it.

If you are not happy with your profession, then it is time to get out and this is where people will say, "What at my age?" Yes, change now because every day is another day wasted, the chances are that you were never meant to be in that profession in the first place.

If you are unhappy in your job or profession you could be doing yourself serious damage, many unhappy people over-eat, under-eat, smoke excessively, make themselves ill through stress and poor working conditions and generally cause themselves unnecessary pain and suffering.

Analyse your skills, what makes you happy and your desires

Let's go back to the drawing-board and take stock of yourself.

What skills do you have?

What skills would you like to obtain or improve?

What job or profession would make you jump out of bed in the morning?

Deep down, what was the job or profession that you always wanted to do, before others put doubts into your mind.

I believe that it is never too late to acquire new skills and to move into another profession or business which truly stimulates and excites you. Obtaining new skills is going to take some time and perseverance and you may have to attend evening classes or night school after a hard days work, but if it means improving your life, then surely it's worth it! You may also have to take another job on a lower pay so that you can gain experience in your new profession, which will of course cause you financial hardship in the short-term, however, the long-term benefits are worth it.

Don't go through life working in the wrong profession, you are wasting your life and all the talent which is locked up inside you, you will never be happy or excel in a profession if your heart is not 110% in it.

CHAPTER 17

Improve your current position now

As I have already stated, having your own business is the only way for you to make real money and to obtain total freedom, but this won't come overnight. Now considering you are in current employment I suggest that you carry on with this, as it would be foolish to stop your income, however, I would at least try to increase the income from your current employment.

Asking for a pay rise

> "The quality and quantity of the service you render, plus the attitude with which you render it, determine the amount of pay you get and the sort of job you hold."
>
> Dr Napoleon Hill

The first thing to do is to be honest with yourself. How much money do you deserve?

Look at your own work, your attendance and your contributions. Are you putting 65 minutes into an hour or are you just coasting by? Imagine that you were the Managing Director of the company, would you be happy and delighted with the performance and the service that you provide to the company? If you cannot truthfully say that you are giving your job 110% attention, then you cannot ask for a pay rise until you do.

Those who do no more than they are paid for have no real basis for requesting more pay, because they are already getting all they deserve to earn. You see, you need to deliver the extra benefits to your employer before you can ask for extra pay, some people might say that if they had a pay rise they would work harder, but it doesn't work like that.

If you are totally truthful and you strongly believe that you have an excellent case for a pay rise, then you should challenge your employer for a higher wage.

If you are just coasting by then you should be happy with what you're getting and start putting your efforts into your new business.

Preparing a case for a pay rise

It is very important to write down the reasons that you feel you are entitled to a pay rise or better job position. Write a letter stating the facts. Ask for a meeting with the relevant person in your organisation and before the meeting preferably the night before, use the declaration technique and say, "I have increased my wage by..." and use a specific amount. Visualise yourself in the meeting, you are smiling, calm and you are in control of the situation. Visualise yourself being given the pay rise.

On the day of the meeting, stay calm, speak slowly and clearly, sit up straight and demand what you deserve. Hand over a copy of the letter you have prepared and read it out. (Use the techniques in section 1 of the book.)

IMPORTANT:

Keep your mouth shut and never tell anyone in your organisation even your closest work-mate, what you are doing, whether you get a pay rise or not is between you and your employer. Many employers will be worried that they will now have to give everyone a pay rise, but by keeping quiet about it both before and after, you will be able to eliminate that problem.

The outcome

A yes answer

If the answer is yes, then well done, you have increased your salary, however, don't let your guard down and remember that having your own business is your ultimate goal. It is good that you have increased your salary, but this is still not acceptable and remember to continue with your good work.

A neutral answer

Your employer may agree with you that you are worth more, but they are not able to pay you any extra salary this time. Now this is where you need to start bargaining and you should have made a list of things that you will accept other than money such as:

A better job title, attending a training course, extra paid holidays, better company car and any other benefits that you can think of, even if it's an extra £10 a week in Luncheon Vouchers then at least you've walked away with something!

A no answer

It is regrettable that your employer does not see the value of your talents. You haven't lost anything by asking and you are not the loser, your employer is. It is very important to stay calm and either go back to your employer or write a letter stating that you are very disappointed, however, you will continue to work at your best level and you hope that a review could be made in the future. Now you know where you really stand and just as if the answer had been positive, your ultimate goal is still to aim for your own business.

Summary to raising your salary

If you don't ask you don't get. Most companies will not come up to you and say, "Here's an extra £1000 a month." You need to make the first move. Yes it takes courage, but with good preparation and using the techniques outlined in this book you can do it. Whichever way it goes you are a winner for asking. If you get a pay rise, you win and if you don't, you now know where you stand, at least you have tried and that makes you a winner in my eyes.

NOTE: Don't make threats which you are not willing to carry out and even if you are willing to carry them out, soften the threat. For example, don't say, "I am walking out today" say, "This leaves me in a very difficult position and I will have to consider my options."

I do know that sometimes our emotions overcome common sense, but please THINK before you say something that you may regret, pause for thought. Wherever possible leave your employer on good terms, it really is a small world and there may come a time when you need to do business with them or ask for a favour in the future.

A point about your current employment

Although I said earlier that it was wise to keep your current employment while you're getting started in business, don't make the mistake of feeling too comfortable for example, "It doesn't matter if I fail, I've still got my daytime job."

Many people work far better under pressure, when I started my business I was under serious pressure, I had to make it work almost immediately and I did. Now if I had the comfort of another income I may not have achieved this success. If you are reading this and you do not have any current employment you may discover that this is a real blessing. Not having any money coming in scared me into success. I'll talk more about why having too much start-up capital can be a DISADVANTAGE, yes, I did say disadvantage! Many people think that throwing money at a problem is the easy solution, however, I know from my own business experience that this is not the case and you can outsmart the larger "Fat cat companies" who have massive budgets.

☺

What has two hands but can't feed itself?
A clock!

What part of a clock is never new?
The second hand!

CHAPTER 18

Starting your own business

As we have already outlined, you don't want to give up your daytime job just yet, so you will need a business which is flexible, can be run out of hours, can be run from home and started on a small budget. At the same time you want a business which can grow and expand with your needs and aspirations.

Now I know of various ways to make money and I could have listed them all here, but most of these businesses have a ceiling, however, I know of one business that is better than all the others and is the only business that I will suggest you go in to. Now this business does divide into 2, but the principals are the same for both businesses and I will explain as we go on.

The best business in the world

I owe everything to this business, I came into it without even understanding what I was doing. I started from my bedroom with a few hundred pounds and built up various businesses worth hundreds of thousands of pounds in a fairly short space of time.

This business has been around for many years and will continue to thrive. It is truly the last business where the "little man or woman" can compete with the large multi-nationals and beat them.

The business is called DIRECT MAIL/MAIL-ORDER/ DIRECT MARKETING and there is probably no other business in the world where so many men and women including me, have started from scratch and become millionaires and even billionaires. I could list thousands of names and companies who owe everything to mail-order they include, Richard Branson of The Virgin Group, who started selling records via mail-order with adverts in student magazines and working from a bedsit. Another person who owes everything to mail-order is Anita Roddick of the now world-wide cosmetics and toiletries group the Body Shop. She started by selling a few beauty products and advertising them in teenage magazines.

My list can go on and on...

What is so great about mail-order?

The life-style and riches that mail-order/direct marketing can bring are beyond your wildest dreams. With mail-order you can choose the hours you work, you can work for 3 months of the year and then take the rest of the year off. You can work from the comfort of your own home and you can operate in your pyjamas if you want! You can live anywhere in the country and it can be in the middle of nowhere. Now, there maybe days when you will be working for 15 hours a day, fulfilling orders, sending out mail etc. but this should not bother you because firstly, it's your business and secondly, you're making money.

The key to this business is choice, freedom and the fact that there is no ceiling or limit. You can start the business from your kitchen and it can grow like Virgin and the Body Shop into a world-wide business.

What mail-order is not

Mail-order is not a get rich quick scheme, however, if you get the right product you can make it big very quickly. It is not an opportunity to deceive people and sell shoddy goods. As already mentioned there will be days when you will work so hard that you'll be wreaked, however, the up-side far outweighs the down-side. Please don't confuse mail-order with multilevel marketing, chain letters or any other type of home business scam that you may have read about. Mail-order is a legitimate and well established business that I am proud to be associated with.

What you need to succeed in mail-order

What you need is some get up and go, a certain amount of self-discipline, determination, a desire to succeed and the wish to start developing all the abilities you know you have inside you, but have never had the opportunity to tap into. In mail-order you need the ability to adapt and think quickly. You need to learn new techniques and copy successful formulas.

You need to be able to do a bit of everything, one minute you'll be working on your computer, then you'll be answering the phone, then you could be packing goods or sending out a mailshot and then a few hours later you might be researching products and designing adverts.

You need to be flexible and willing to do whatever it takes, if you're the only employee and the bin needs emptying or a sack of post needs to be taken to the post office, you can't say, "It's not my job" or "It's not my department," EVERYTHING is your department, especially in the early days.

Hold on, this sounds a bit difficult!

Listen, I never promised you money for nothing. I promised you a legitimate business where you can earn as much money as you want and I promised you a business that will give you freedom and a great life-style.

This business will however take some time, effort and hard work. Large amounts of money may come to you very quickly, however, I hope it doesn't come too quickly, because when you earn money over a period of time it will TASTE much better than if you inherited it or won the lottery.

To succeed in this and any other business you need to really want to be successful. Sure people will say that they believe they can make money from direct mail, but deep down inside they know that money doesn't really come that way, they truly believe that they will win their fortune, or they will inherit millions from an unknown, long lost relative.

Well I didn't inherit or win my money and everyone else I know didn't win or inherit their money, we all made it ourselves through our own businesses.

One thing I have noticed is that people who succeed in business have a plan just like personal goals, they have a plan for their business and they plan for success. Not everybody who has a plan for success achieves success right away, but those who stick to it, adapt and change their plan to meet the changing conditions in the market-place, usually succeed.

So before you read any further I must ask you to go back to your goals sheet and read them through. (If you haven't made a goals sheet, then please don't read any further and go back to the section and make them.) I'm sure that you have some materialistic items on your list, maybe a nice car or house etc. but how badly do you really want these items? How badly do you really want to increase your standard of living? If you are totally truthful and you are genuinely willing to do whatever it takes, then the business plan that I will disclose to you will work, if however you are not sure, you doubt yourself and you are not willing to make the short-term sacrifices for the long-term rewards, then now is the time to GIVE UP.

It is pointless going into business if you think you're not

going to make it or that you'll be happy to earn just an extra £200 or £300 a week, it's not worth it, you need to go into business knowing that you will succeed and that you will earn all the money that you deserve.

So if you are 100% with me then read on, if you're not, then don't bother starting, you'll end up losing what little you have.

Just do it

During this section I will disclose a great deal of information on how to get your business up and running. I have worked very hard to give you as many secrets as I can, however, there is one element that you must do and that's PUT IT INTO PRACTICE, as quickly as possible. I don't expect you to be able to put all of the information into practice at once and I don't expect you to be perfect, however, I do expect you to start! You see, many people will say, "I can't start yet, I don't know everything" and while I believe in good research and planning, I also believe in just going for it.

In the first section of this book under "Doing it now" you will recall that I listed many excuses people make to not do something and many of those same excuses are used everyday by people who drop out or never start their own business, please don't be one of them.

Contrary to popular belief, I believe in starting something badly or in a small way, rather than doing nothing. If you keep putting off starting your business until you know everything about everything, then you will never start.

Here is a classic quote which sums up my argument:

> **"Better to do something imperfectly than to do nothing flawlessly."**
>
> R.H. Schuller

And that is a fact, I started my business with far less knowledge than you will have after reading this book. My circumstances forced me to start my business even though I wasn't ready, but I don't regret it. Looking back I cringe at some of the mistakes I made in the early days, but at least I started, I was a player, not a spectator and that's the difference between me and everyone else. I was always crazy enough to believe in what I was doing and I was mad enough to dream. I kept going even through all the low points and set backs, I knew that I was doing the right thing and that I would be rewarded one day.

I am not a textbook businessman

You may have already gathered but in case you haven't, I am proud to say that I am not stiff, pompous, theory based, or any other word that sums up a regular businessman or woman.

If you want the theory on how business works, then go to the library or a business bookshop and you'll find hundreds of guides on starting your own business. I can truthfully tell you that these books on the whole are terrible and the easiest way for your business to fail is to follow these theory books. They are normally written by people who have never made any money in business, they are spectators and they have never played the game.

The information I will disclose to you is "as it is today" it is not what the book says should happen, it is what really does happen. If you were going to war would you want to read a book on "how you should fight the war" written by a researcher, or would you want to read a book by someone who's just won a war and has had first hand experience of war, not textbook theories?

Come to war with me and I'll show you the real secret weapons and facts that you need to know, not the theory.

Now back to business...

What is mail-order

Mail-order is supplying goods and sometimes services to clients who you have never seen and they have never seen you or the product. The initial contact comes through an advert or a salesletter, inviting the customer to buy your product. The customer either phones the order through or returns an order form, you then process the order and send the goods either by mail or in most cases today, by courier.

Today you can purchase almost anything through the mail, this includes books, video tapes, computers, compact disks, clothes, toys, furniture, vitamins, loans, adult orientated goods, keep-fit equipment, food, flowers and just about anything else you can think of.

The most important factor that is leading to the explosion in growth of mail-order is the convenience and ease of direct mail shopping. Another big factor is the customer's attitude towards direct mail. Today's shoppers are different and they will buy goods from strangers hundreds of miles away. Nearly everyone has a phone and most people now have a credit card.

Imagine 100 years ago, nobody would buy anything via mail-order. You would have to go to a local store and buy the product face to face from someone you knew. In many cases you would barter. No one had a phone or credit card and there wasn't a reliable postal service.

The agency/consultancy side of this business

Now here is the second part of this business. The basics and principles are the same and you will need the same qualities and the same equipment, the only difference in an agency/consultancy business is that there are no direct products, you are more of a middleman. Examples of agency/consultancy businesses are Recruitment Agencies, Advertising Agencies, Finance Agencies and Computer Consultants etc.

Let's take the example of a recruitment agency, the agency is a middleman between the prospective employee or candidate and the employer. The agency earns a fee from the employer, so unlike a traditional mail-order company where you sell a product or book, this time you are selling a service, but the principals are the same.

A consultancy is where you offer your expert advice to companies on your chosen subject, it could be marketing, motivation, advertising or computers etc. The product in this case is therefore YOU.

Getting started in mail-order

The first item that is worth either buying, borrowing or renting is a computer and a laser printer. The computer does not have to be state of the art, as long as it is an IBM compatible 486 or better. The laser printer should be a Hewlett Packard LaserJet type. If at all possible buy a modem, as this will give you a link to the Internet, more about this later. You will also need a phone and a postal address, again I will show you how to get a real postal address.

Now if you have a computer and a basic word processor/desk top publisher then that is excellent, however, if you don't, it is crucial to your success that you get one and learn how to use it.

You see, I want to show you the EASY way to make money in business. I want to steer you away from all the mistakes that amateurs make. When I started in 1988 I had an electric typewriter which was quite advanced at the time, but not today. About 6 months later I bought a computer and laser printer with my first profits and this was the best money that I ever spent. Back then a computer and laser printer cost thousands of pounds, most big companies didn't even have a Hewlett Packard printer in those days and here's me, a guy in a bedroom producing state of the art documents, with images and different fonts.

If you want to be successful you have to look successful and this starts with the letters and correspondence that you send. I am afraid that people do judge a book by its cover and in direct mail, your salesletter is your cover.

A good friend of mine is a mail-order millionaire in America. When he started out in business his home had just been destroyed by a tornado and he was living in a mobile home. He did not have any indoor plumbing and his phone was fifty yards from the door, attached to a temporary poll. He was living in poverty conditions and yet he had a computer and a laser printer.

Why?

Even though he was down and out, his letters and correspondence were perfect and gave the impression that he was a massive corporation working from a big office. His direct mail offers were convincing and had credibility, after all no one could see him!

You need to be able to do the same. If I wrote you a salesletter on a scrap piece of paper with stains all over it and using an old typewriter, would you take much notice and would you send me any money?

Now if I wrote to you on a professional piece of letterheaded paper with a beautifully formatted letter in a nice font, you would take me seriously.

First impressions count and in direct mail you need to make a good impression.

Learning how to use your computer

It is pointless having the best equipment if you don't know how to use it. Take the time to learn the basics of writing a letter and producing documents using a desk top publisher. Luckily software is very user friendly these days and come with very good manuals. A point about software, you don't need the most expensive software on the market, in most cases you can buy cheaper versions that do 90% of what the expensive packages do.

Computer training

Most schools and colleges offer evening classes and short courses on computing and if you need help then I suggest that you enrol on a course. It is not important to know everything about computers, you just need to learn the basics so you can produce the results that you need. For example, you probably don't know how a calculator works, but you know how to use one and get a result from it and that is the same with a computer.

Buying computers, software and peripherals

The best way to buy computers today at the lowest prices, is through mail-order. I have bought all my computers this way and I suggest you get hold of a copy of a magazine called Computer Shopper.

Incorporating a company in the U.K. and USA

If you plan to be successful in business, which you do, then I strongly recommend that you set up a Limited Company. The process can be handled by a company registration agent and the whole service should cost no more than £150. A U.K. Limited Company requires 1 Director and 1 Company Secretary. In most cases you would be the director and your partner, sister or brother etc. could be the company secretary. You will also need a registered office which is the legal address that any documents will be served to, many companies use the address of their solicitor or accountant, you can of course use your trading address.

Deciding on a company name

Think very hard about a company name as you need to give a good impression, however, make sure that the company name is credible and not too long. I have seen names like "European International Overseas Import And Export Limited," and that is just too long.

Now you will probably want to think of 3 or 4 company names, as your choices may already be registered at Companies House. I would also be careful about registering a name that is too similar to another company. Let me explain, it is possible to fool Companies House into registering a name that has already been registered, by adding words such as U.K., COMPANY or DIRECT etc. let me give you an example:

If you discover that "First United Direct Limited" is already registered, you could register "First United Direct (U.K.) Limited" and Companies House will normally allow it, and I know because a company did it to me! Now although Companies House will register it, the company that was already registered could easily sue you for passing off, especially if you are in the same or similar business, so tread carefully when registering your company name.

Another point to mention is, try not to make your company name sound too specialised, as the chances are you may do more than one type of business.

Why should I set up as a Limited Company when I haven't even started yet?

Well, when you start your business you will need to print stationery, get a telephone line, open a bank account etc. and by registering a company, you will be ready to give the details that they require.

Now the reasons why I have always traded as a Limited Company are as follows:

a) It gives the impression that you are not a one man band, people assume that a Limited Company is a real business.

b) A Limited Company provides just that, limited liability and although legislation has reduced the amount of protection a Limited Company gives you, you are still able to keep your personal assets safe, should your company be sued for something or hits trouble.

c) It's easier to sell the business. You are setting this business up to succeed and when you become successful you may decide to sell your business, you could be taken over or you may decide to list on the Stock Exchange. A Limited Company is far easier to sell and value than an un-incorporated company, such as a sole trader or partnership.

d) It is easier to raise money without using your personal assets, money can be raised on the strength of the company's accounts and assets.

e) You can sell shares in your company to equity investors and friends etc.

Disadvantages:

a) You have to file an annual return, which is public information for a U.K. company and your company accounts are also available for inspection by anyone who wants to see them at Companies House.

b) Accounting costs are normally higher for a Limited Company, although there are provisions for simplified accounts for smaller companies, which reduce the costs.

c) National Insurance and Taxation is more complex for a Limited Company.

Now I am not a solicitor or an accountant and at the end of the day the choice is yours as to whether you incorporate, you may also choose to incorporate your company overseas, to take advantage of possible tax benefits. I have listed 2 U.K. companies and one American company who are reputable which I have used and they will be able to send you more details on incorporating a company. I also recommend that you go to your library and take out some books on limited companies and company law.

NOTE FOR USA: It still seems that Delaware has a great deal to offer and I believe that it is still the best state to incorporate in. One of the best US company agents is The Company Corporation, Wilmington, Delaware. I have also read and heard a lot about the different tax advantages of different US companies and I strongly believe that the "S" corporation is still the best way to incorporate and to protect your personal assets. The Company Corporation publish various books and leaflets on this subject.

Take some time to think about the legal status of your company, i.e. sole trader, partnership or limited company. You may wish to ask people you know why they trade as a Sole Trader or Limited Company.

Let me summarise by saying that if you are going to incorporate a Limited Company, make sure that you use a good registration agent and even if you have to pay them a bit more, let them help you with all the various legal forms, shareholder certificates, minutes and company seal etc.

Note: When you form a Limited Company make sure that they incorporate the company from scratch, some agents use ready made companies and then they file a name change to the company that you wanted, I don't like this practice.

My recommended Company Agents are:

For U.K. (Ltd, Plc) Channel Islands and tax havens:
Overseas Company Registration Agents Ltd. (OCRA)
Companies House
Tower Street
Ramsey, Isle Of Man
IM8 1JA
Telephone: 01624 815544
Fax: 01624 815548
Internet: WWW.OCRA.Com
or
Spencer Company Formations
Scorpio House
102 Sydney Street
Chelsea, London
SW3 6NJ
Tel: 0171 352 2274
Fax: 0171 352 2260

USA companies
The Company Corporation
725 North Market Street
Wilmington, Delaware
19901
USA
Tel: 1 800 542 2677
Outside the US call: 00 1 302 575 0440
Internet: WWW.Incorporate.Com

Let me add that I am not being paid by any of these companies to recommend them. I found that they provided me with a good service and at reasonable rates in the past, hence I am recommending them. Feel free to do your own research, you may find others that you would prefer to deal with.

Setting up a bank account

You will need a bank account to pay money in and to pay company expenses. A business bank account is totally separate to your personal account. If you are trading as a Limited Company, you are the Director of the company and technically an employee, so don't pay any business expenses out of your own account and don't pay your personal bills out of the business account.

Opening a business account is fairly simple and all the banks are desperate for your business, so you will get FREE banking for the 1st year at least.

Depending on your position with your current bank, you can either open a business account with them, or if you're not on best terms with them, then start a fresh with a new bank. I will talk more about banks, accepting credit cards and borrowing money etc. at a later stage.

If you are trading as a Limited Company the bank will require:
  a) Sight of the original certificate of incorporation
  b) Copy of the Memorandum and Articles of Association

These documents will be given to you by the company registration agent.

Please remember: The bank works for you, they are your servant and not vice versa! As with anyone, treat the people who work there with a friendly and courteous manner, whether it's the junior cashier or the senior manager, but expect and demand the highest level of service and respect from them. You should be addressed as Sir or Madam and nothing should be a problem, just because you are small fry today, doesn't mean that you won't be a big fish tomorrow. Over time a bank can make a lot of money from you and they should start treating you well from day one.

I will talk later about why you should treat the "little guy" with respect and my own personal experiences, but here is a true story that I will always remember:

The late Sir Gordon White who was the other half of the successful 80's conglomerate, Hanson Trust Plc, went to his bank many years ago, this was when the company was in its early days, as he needed to do some business, I won't mention the bank but they were an American bank.

Gordon White was left waiting in a draughty corridor for over 30 minutes, he wasn't offered any tea or coffee and when he finally saw someone, it was a junior manager who clearly wasn't qualified to deal with his query. Frustrated with the service he demanded to see the senior manager and after a further delay he finally saw a manager, he then asked the manager to confirm what his company's balance was with the bank (the balance was in the millions) and Mr White then replied, "No, that's the balance I did have with your bank" and closed the account there and then, and transferred his money elsewhere.

For over 30 years that bank has tried to get Hanson's business back and they have never succeeded. Just think of the millions that the bank lost in future fees just because of simple courtesy!

On the subject of banks, I don't know why, but most people think that they're in business to provide a service to the community or that they are some sort of government body, this is not the case. Banks exist for one reason only and that is to make as much money as they can, they have no morals, feelings or any loyalty to anyone other than the directors and shareholders.

Letterheaded paper

To be taken as a serious business and that's what you must be seen as, you need a professional letterhead. A letterhead may not seem important to you, but it is the first contact that most of your clients, contacts and customers will have with your company. And if your letterhead doesn't build confidence in your ability to get the job done, it will cost you business.

Creating a letterhead

I normally design the letterhead myself using my computer and then take the artwork to my printer. If you don't want to design the letterhead yourself, then your local print shop will be able to do this for you and it is normally FREE, as long as you print the paper with them. If you have a friend who is good at art then they could design a logo for you.

Letterhead Rules:

1. The letterhead should have a clean and uncluttered look.

2. The font (typeface) should be easy to read, especially the company name, address, telephone number, fax number and e-mail address/web address. Never use these type of fonts in a letterhead as they are too hard to read and look very bad.

SAMPLE BAD FONTS

This is a bad font for business

This is a bad font for business

This is a bad font for business

3. Don't make your letterhead look like a rainbow, too many colours do not look good and they end up costing you more money. Use 2 colours such as, blue and red, or black and green. You can also use tints if you wish.

4. Try and formulate some company colours and a logo, or typeface style that you can carry throughout your business. Look at what other big companies are using. A one man/woman business can still have a corporate image.

5. Use white paper (it makes black text stand out better) normally 100gms or 110gms. You will want the paper to be thicker than normal photocopier paper, but it doesn't have to be so thick that you need a crow bar to fold it with! That is a total waste of money and is what most solicitors use who charge huge fees.

6. Don't have a raised letterhead, you will find that laser printers do not like it and the heat from the printer can make it crack. (I know because I had raised paper once.)

7. Don't forget that if you are a Limited Company you will need to put the company registration number and registered address etc. at the bottom of the paper.

A good letterhead won't be as expensive as you think. Print a small quantity to start with, normally 500 and then take it from there. Shop around for printing prices as there can be big variations, check your Yellow Pages for printers. Now although a cheap quote is vital, don't sacrifice quality for the sake of a few pounds, some back street printers use old machinery that produce awful results.

At this point I must stress that it is very important to build up a good relationship with a printing firm. Depending on how big your business gets and your requirements, you will need a printer who is very flexible, has the latest technology, is able to print in colour and produce brochures etc. Over the last few years I have spent over £500,000 on printing and I have learnt a lot about the printing trade.

Business cards

A business card is an essential item to carry in your wallet or purse. It should have your details on just like a letterhead and your name in a clear font, with your title underneath, i.e. Managing Director.

A trend at the moment is to print on the back of the card with a brief description of what your company does, for example:

Computer Consultancy
Software Programming
Computer Training
Computer Installations

Phone/fax

You need a dedicated business line and it's easy to get a phone put in, just make sure that you set the phone up in the name of your company and that the bills are made out to the company.

Normally you will start with one line and one number, try and get an easy number to dial and remember. As well as taking the line I would also recommend that you get caller divert, which will allow you to divert the number to another number and caller display, this will allow you to see the number of the person who is calling you. This is very good for direct mail when taking orders, in case you get cut off. As well as your phone you will probably want a simple answering machine.

Fax machines

I've had a fax machine for many years and would be lost without one. You can either rent or buy a fax machine. If money is tight, there's nothing wrong with buying a second hand fax machine, my machine is 8 years old and still going strong.

Now here's a big mistake that small companies make, to save the extra line rental they put the phone and fax machine on the same line, BIG MISTAKE, don't do it, it proves that you are a little guy, get a separate line installed for the fax. If you are installing 2 lines at once, the phone company will normally give you a discount on the second line anyway.

Mailing address

This is a big stumbling block for most home businesses, as they don't want to advertise their home address and even if they do, a residential address doesn't look good on a company letterhead. The simple solution is to use a Business Centre, sometimes known as a serviced office.

Business centres

A business centre gives you a permanent office address that you can use, but you don't have to have physical space at the office. All your post and messages are held for you and can either be posted on to your home address or preferably you can drop in and collect them.

Business centres offer an excellent service and are ideal for the home business user. Most business centres offer many other services such as, secretarial services, outgoing post handling, faxing and photocopying etc. You can also hire an office or boardroom by the day or in some cases for just 1/2 a day, which is excellent if you have meetings etc. and you don't want to hold them at home.

I have listed some U.K. business centres here and you can also consult your local Yellow Pages. For those that may require an overseas office, then H.Q. have a network of business centres all over the world.

U.K. Business centres

Premier House offer good facilities throughout the U.K. including, Birmingham, Brighton, Bournemouth, Bristol, Hull, Leicester, Manchester, Nottingham, Sheffield, Southampton, Walsall, Wolverhampton and various locations in locations in the London area.

For details of your nearest office check your Yellow Pages or contact Tel: 0181 951 5656.

World-wide business centres

HQ Business Centres offer business centre facilities in Germany, Canada, Mexico, France, Belgium and a massive network throughout the USA including, New York, Chicago, Florida and Los Angeles to name a few.

For a current H.Q. directory call 1-800-227-3004 if you are in the USA.

If you are in England call HQ in London on 0171 917 6000.

NOTE: If you have caller divert, you can divert your calls to the business centre when you're out, it is better to have a live person answer your phone rather than an answering machine, especially during office hours.

Accepting credit cards

Today most people have a credit card or at least a debit card. I strongly recommend that you set up merchant facilities to accept Visa, Mastercard, American Express and in the U.K. the debit cards Switch/Delta.

Credit/debit cards make payment very convenient, you must make it as easy as possible for the client to be able to pay you and it is far easier for a client to give you a credit card number, than it is to pay by a cheque or postal order.

Now there are a few disadvantages in accepting credit cards firstly, there is a fee which you have to pay and is about 4% on credit cards and 70p per transaction on debit cards, regardless of the sale amount and secondly, you are liable for "Charge Backs" which means that if there is a problem with the credit card you can be forced to give the credit card company the money back.

Now I have accepted credit cards for many years and although you may experience a few fraudulent transactions, on the whole the benefits far outweigh the disadvantages. In mail-order you have to be more vigilant than most, as you will be accepting credit cards over the phone and through the post (you will not normally see the actual card) which leaves you open to fraud, however, there are steps that you can take to reduce credit card losses and here are my rules:

1. Authorise every single transaction, whether it is £5 or £5,000. If you have an online terminal then it is easy.

2. When taking an order over the phone, make sure that you take the full address and telephone number. Ask if this is the address that the card is registered to. If you are at all suspicious then phone the number back and see who answers the phone, it is possible to tell if it's a phonebox because you will normally hear a beeping noise in the background. You can also check with Directory Enquiries to see what number comes up under that name and address.

3. Only ship goods to the address that the card is registered to, never allow the client to send a taxi or their own courier to collect the goods. If the client wants to pick the goods up from you, then make sure that you treat the transaction as a retail transaction i.e. ask for the credit card, swipe the card and get the client to sign the slip in front of you.

4. Depending on the value of the goods, I suggest that you send them by courier or by Recorded Delivery post, so you will have the signature of the recipient, this way if someone phones up claiming they haven't received the goods, you will have proof of the dispatch and who signed for them.

5. Be alert, watch for very large orders and watch out for repeat orders very close to each other. Look out for such things as someone ordering 5 of the same item, especially if it is unlikely that it's a gift item. If in doubt phone your credit card clearing company and ask for their advice and explain to them what has made you suspicious.

Why you may not be able to get credit card merchant facilities:

Firstly, I want to make this very clear, it is a PRIVILEGE to be able to accept credit cards, not a RIGHT. Remember this throughout your negotiations with the bank and you'll get on fine.

The credit card company will be wary of you, especially in the early days because many banks have suffered huge losses through fraudulent credit card transactions. For example, you get a merchant account, charge up thousands of pounds in orders, you get paid, you don't deliver the goods, you skip town and the credit card company is left with the loss and they have to refund all the cardholders.

Now I hope and expect that everyone reading this is honest and is in business for the long-term benefits, however, there are people out there who will set up in business to do this and unfortunately due to these idiots (most of whom end up getting caught) the rest of us have to suffer.

Proving that you are legitimate

You need to prove that you are legitimate and you are an honest person and have things such as:

1. A good credit rating. If you have defaulted on any loans or credit cards then it won't look good, however, if you can show that you pay your debts, keep your credit card payments up to date and you are genuinely trustworthy, then this will help your case.

2. Trade references/personal references. Any evidence which backs up that you are trustworthy. If you know someone in business who accepts credit cards then maybe they could give you a reference.

3. Show that you are serious about business, a good letterhead, a business phone line, a fax line, a

brochure or catalogue etc. shows that you are not a fly-by-night operation. Also have some stock to show the bank/credit card representative. Even if you are working from home you can still show that you are serious.

4. Explain to the bank/credit card representative that you offer a full money back guarantee and that any queries that arise will be dealt with by you promptly. The credit card company wants an easy life, it doesn't want hundreds of customers complaining that they haven't received their goods or that they're not happy with your company. Also offer to indemnify the bank against any credit card problems and explain that you will never take payment from the credit card until you are ready to ship the goods.

You may think that the above seems a little excessive, but believe me it's worth it. I've never seen any other book explain the importance of accepting credit cards, but just ask anyone in the mail-order or retail business how crucial credit/debit cards really are.

Borrowing money

I will start by saying that I hate borrowing money and I believe that if you have to borrow money to start a business, then it is a bad business. Fortunately the businesses that I am going to show you require little start-up capital, therefore you can avoid borrowing money. Every business that I have started has been with my own savings and money earned from another business.

The only time I have ever borrowed any money was in my early days, which was a mortgage on a flat which I used as my office and home. Today I am fortunate enough not to have a mortgage and that is a goal that you should all aim for. To own your house outright is a great sense of security, if everything goes wrong you still have somewhere to sleep at night.

Back to borrowing money, I suggest that you use your own savings and try to avoid raising any money from your friends or family, unless you really have to.

Stand-by credit/credit cards/overdrafts

As I mentioned in the first section, I have always been a good worrier and therefore I have always had and still have many credit cards and access to large amounts of credit, should I ever need it. In the saving money section I will tell you who the best credit card companies are.

I suggest that you do the same and have some credit to fall back on, just in case things don't go as planned or your timing is slightly out. Now only you will know if using credit will make matters worse or will in fact help you out of a temporary problem, for example:

Scenario 1

If things are going badly and your business is genuinely not going as planned, then it would be foolish to start using up credit and running up debts. Throwing money at a problem doesn't cure it.

Scenario 2

Business is genuinely going well, however, due to a few factors that you didn't calculate, you have a temporary shortfall. Now you will know whether it is temporary or not, don't fool yourself. Another scenario would be that a genuine opportunity has come up to buy some stock or equipment at a reduced price, for example at an auction, where payment is required immediately.

In this scenario I would suggest that you use temporary credit, however, my number one goal would now be to pay that debt off as quickly as possible because long-term debts, just like a mortgage or a long-term loan end up costing you a fortune, but a short-term debt, even if the interest rate looks high, always works out cheaper when you pay it off within a few months.

Don't forget that if you can buy something on a credit

card you can get up to 50 days interest free credit, which may just be long enough to get you out of your shortfall. This doesn't work on a cash advance, as most credit cards charge interest from day one.

Another advantage of borrowing on a credit card is that you can pay back variable amounts. For example, you take an advance of £2,000 and the first month you pay back the minimum amount, which is say £100 and the next month you can pay back the whole amount without any penalty.

Now if you were to take out a loan you would be fixed to a payment schedule i.e. £200 over 60 months and although you can pay the loan off early, most banks charge early redemption penalties that can be very high.

Overdrafts

Never, ever, take out a bank overdraft, either authorised or unauthorised, it's not worth the hassle. This goes for personal and business accounts and I know that a few banks now offer interest free overdrafts for small amounts, but don't even use this. If you are going to be short of money in a personal or business bank account, then you should raise the money elsewhere to cover the shortfall (a credit card cash advance) and pay the money into the bank.

Always stay in credit with your bank, even if it's only a small amount. I want you to have a good credit rating and standing with your bank.

As you can gather I am not a big fan of borrowing money, especially from banks, but I do believe in using credit cards wisely, both for business and personal use. The nice thing about a credit card/cash advance is that it's instant because you already have the credit line, the last thing you want is a meeting with a bank manager or lots of forms to fill in.

The only point you have to watch is when you invest any money into your business, make sure that you account for this as "cash introduced" or "a loan to the company" and show the money going back out again when the company repays the loan. Your accountant will be able to advise you more on this matter.

My final word on credit cards is that you must be disciplined enough to get the balance back down to zero as soon as possible, paying off the minimum amount month after month is the road to disaster, however, paying off the minimum amount for a month or two and then paying off large chucks or the whole sum thereafter, is a very sensible way to borrow.

NOTE: Never sign a personal guarantee or offer any bank, finance company or supplier any security in the shape of your family home, it's just not worth it.

Summary

If someone had told me everything that I have just disclosed to you when I first started out, I would have paid them at least £5,000 because that's how valuable this information is. Simple things can make a big difference!

CHAPTER **19**

Finding products to sell

Now that you have a computer and the ability to produce quality correspondence, your next step is to look at products that you can sell.

Research

This is one of the most important factors that will either make or break your direct mail business. The biggest mistake that most people make in mail-order and retail businesses is that they do little or no research into the product they are selling and the market they are selling to.

Look at any high street and you will see that new businesses come and go very quickly, the story normally goes like this, Joe Public is made redundant and has a few thousand pounds, he opens a shop, gets advice on sorting out tax and business bank accounts etc. but forgets the biggest factor, MAKING MONEY BY MAKING SALES. You see, Joe Public hasn't done any research, he doesn't know what the market wants, he sells at the wrong price and when he goes broke he puts it down to bad luck! My advice is to forget about tax and accountants etc. because if you don't sell anything, you won't have any tax to pay! Make some money by concentrating on your marketing, sell the right product at the right profit margin and you can then higher the best accountants and solicitors etc. later to look after the paperwork.

The market will make or break you

Unless we identify our market first we will end up like Joe Public. We need to put the market first and the product second. We need to know how people think, what they want and feel. What people buy today is not the same as ten or even two years ago. What they buy depends on current news, politics and many other things, even the movies. The film Jurassic Park has trebled the sales of wooden dinosaur kits at the Natural History Museum, visitors are up and all of a sudden everyone is interested in dinosaurs. You may not be in the dinosaur business, but you should take my point that you need to know what is going on around you. Watching the right programmes on TV is very important.

Gary Halbert, a top marketing guru, was addressing a seminar in the USA. He gave an example of a business which was a hamburger stand. He told the audience that they had a hamburger stand and he had a stand in competition with them. He would allow them any advantages they cared to name, and he only wanted one advantage.

The audience came up with such advantages as, the best meat, the best position and the biggest stand etc. Gary said that they could have all those things. All he wanted was one advantage which they hadn't mentioned and he would beat them easily. "What can it be?" they asked, "Easy" said Gary, "The only advantage I need is a HUNGRY CROWD!"

You see, the whole point of this story is the word "HUNGRY." Vast fortunes have been lost and many companies have gone broke, because the products they sold were not wanted. No one was hungry for them. Of course, with enough time and money you can use the media, press and television to convince people that they need something. Take the example of deodorant, it took nearly twenty years and literally millions to convince people that they must have it. You and I simply don't have the time and budget to convince people that they want something.

Picking the easy targets

Unlike most people, I am not in the business of reinventing the wheel, I don't care if I am the first to think of a business. In most cases I would prefer to be second or third. What I do want and what you should be looking for are easy targets, markets that are desperate for what you are selling and they must be "HUNGRY."

The biggest mistake that nearly all companies make, is that they spend too much time and money developing a product and then they say, "Who shall I sell this too?" Sounds obvious, so why do most companies do it?

Instead of going to your market and saying, "This is what I have for sale, do you want to buy it?" You should be able to go to your market and say, "Here's your chance to get the product you've desperately been looking for!"

Having exactly what the market wants is a sure way to achieve success in business. If you want to buy a car and I try to sell you a boat, it's going to be very difficult for me to sell you a boat.

People buy what they want and not always what they need

Before I go on, I want you to remember that people buy what they WANT and not what they need, let me give you an example, my sister who is a successful business woman recently purchased a new Mercedes SL sports car with all the extras, her previous car was nice enough and got her from A to B in comfort etc. so she didn't really NEED a Mercedes, she just **WANTED** one.

Let me give you another example, most people NEED

life insurance and health care insurance, but they don't have it. Why not? Because they don't want it, people don't want to think about death or illnesses and that is why life insurance is so hard to sell.

In the next few pages I will give you products and specific markets that you can sell to. I have sold these products myself, so I speak from experience.

Before I give you these opportunities on a plate, I want to teach you how to fish.

How to fish

If you were starving and I gave you a few fish, you would eat for a few days, but if you were starving and I gave you a fishing rod and taught you how to fish, you would eat forever!

So although I will give you specific opportunities that are available, I will also show you how to look for new ones.

How to find out what people are buying and what they want

Where to start your research

A large newsagents is a good place to start. Look at the magazine racks and see what topics have the biggest display space. If you go to a large newsagents at the moment, you will see that the following sections are the biggest:

1. Women's magazines and related interests
2. Magazines relating to cars
3. Computers
4. Money/investments
5. Adult titles

A new trend is men's fashion and life-style magazines.

From our investigations these 5 topics were taking up more shelf space than any other topic. I have also spotted a big trend in new men's magazines, such as GQ.

So what does this mean?

That there is a market and interest for these subjects. People want to know more about them and are willing to spend money on buying these magazines. If they didn't, then the magazines wouldn't be there.

Another way to find out what people are interested in is to go to a bookshop or look at the weekly book charts that show which books are selling the best.

Looking through the non-fiction book chart will give you a very good idea of what people are desperate to know more about.

A bookshop will also reveal what the most popular selling titles are, by the amount of space given to a subject. From my recent investigations at an average bookshop, I saw a large amount of book space being given to travel and computers.

Tip: Don't go to a specialist bookshop, i.e. a business bookshop, as this will give you a false impression.

Another good way to find out what people are buying is to watch QVC, the shopping channel, also look out for the infomercials on Sell-A-Vision and tune into late night satellite TV channels.

If you're watching QVC and you see that 8 hours of their programming schedule is designated to jewellery, then you know that this is selling well. Now I know for a fact that jewellery ranging from £20 to £200 is a very big seller. I also know that the profit margins are huge in jewellery.

How to find millions of mail-order buyers

Today names, addresses, purchasing behaviour and other general information is bought and sold quite freely. If for example you purchase something from a catalogue, sub-scribe to a magazine, fill in a competition entry or return a guarantee form and so on, then this will be registered on a mailing list.

In the U.K. there is a book called BRAD Direct Marketing, in the USA it is called SRDS. This book contains about every mailing list there is in the U.K. A sample page of the book follows. You should be able to get a copy from larger reference libraries. A copy of BRAD currently costs £85 and is worth buying.

BRAD which stands for British Rate And Data, can be contacted at:

BRAD
Emap Media
33-39 Bowling Green Lane
London
EC1R 0DA
Tel: 0171 505 8246
Fax: 0171 505 8264

NOTE: It is BRAD Direct Marketing that you need for mailing lists because there is also another publication, which is the BRAD that lists all the newspapers and magazines.

Just by looking at these lists I can get an instant idea of the size of a market and their profiles. Let me give you an example, there are 2 lists, one list contains women's dress sizes 12-14 and the other list, women's dress sizes 8-10. From the list entries I can see that there are around 500,000 size 8-10 names and addresses and over 2 million size 12-14. So if I am going to sell dresses I would make sure that I cover the 12-14 size, as that is where the main market is.

Renting names

As you can see from the sample BRAD entry page the details of the list broker/owner are listed. You would contact them and they would supply you with the names and addresses on a disk or on sticky labels.

List brokers will also provide you with more detailed information about the list, including how many new names are being added monthly.

Sample entry from Brad Direct Marketing

reproduced with permission from BRAD.

The newest way to research and find information for FREE

I have used the internet and newsgroups for some time now and I am starting to realise that it's a very powerful research and information tool. The best point about the internet is that I can access it at any time from the comfort of my own home.

In the next few pages I want to explain why you should have access to the internet. I will keep it brief and as non-technical as possible.

What is the internet?

It's basically lots of computers all over the world that you can access from your computer with a small box called a modem, which plugs into the telephone socket and your computer. When using the internet the box dials out, normally on a local number and connects you to the internet.

1. Research, information and market testing

Whether you are looking for new business ideas or if you want to find information on your current business, then the internet is a cheap place to start. For the price of a phone call, which is now as low as 1p per minute at weekends, you can research almost any subject.

Imagine that you are writing a newsletter or booklet on tropical plants and you need some more information for this month's issue. With a few searches on the internet you will find pages of information and photos. The scope in which to convert information found on the internet into manuals and "how to" guides is massive.

2. E-mail

E-mail is far cheaper than sending a fax, letter or using a courier. Once you have an internet account you can send letters, photos, video clips and sound clips to anyone world-wide for just pennies.

Example:

You can send a 10 page text document to Los Angeles, USA for the following:

    First Class Post (5-7 working days) = £1.56

    Fax (5 minutes X 40p per minute) = £2.00

    Courier (2 working days) = £29.27

    E-mail (a telephone call at BT local rate 4.94 per minute) = 15p

E-mail is almost instant and would cost about 15p. If you send your E-mail at weekends it would only cost 3p!

3. Lead generation, promotional material and direct sales

The internet is one of the most cost effective ways to distribute sales information and generate leads.

Direct sales are still a new concept on the internet, however, the trend is growing and the fears of using credit cards are being overcome.

4. Newsgroups and chat areas

Contrary to what the media makes out, all chat areas are not sex related, there are chat areas on law, sports, computers, business, stocks and shares etc.

A chat area allows you to ask questions, send replies to other members, or just read other people's questions and replies. An interesting chat area which I use is in the stocks and shares area. Here you can ask a question and normally within 20 minutes someone will give you the answer. For example, XYZ company's shares have fallen sharply today for no apparent reason. I can post the question "Anyone know why XYZ shares are falling today?" and I would receive an answer shortly.

Getting on-line

At the end of this book in the reference section, I have given the name of a good internet access provider which I use and they will send you free internet trial software and information. It is also now possible to obtain free internet access through providers such as Dixons Freeserve and many others. A full list of free internet service providers can be found in magazines such as Internet Magazine.

Costs

Your costs are the telephone bill, as the modem is talking on your phone line and a monthly subscription fee to your internet service provider if you are not using a free one. My internet provider charges £12.00 a month and that's it. It's a flat fee and you can stay on for 1 hour a month or you can stay on for 200 hours a month. I still use a paid for provider as I get a few extra facilities that free providers do not give.

Tips to help keep your phone bill down

Whether you are on-line now or you are going to be, here are a few tips:

1. Make sure that your modem/internet provider is using a local phone number i.e. 0345.

2. Use off-line readers. This is software which allows you to read E-mail and web pages after you have disconnected.

3. Learn how to use your internet software. Most browsers, such as Netscape, will allow you to view pages without the graphics. This allows the page to load much quicker. If you find the page of interest, then you can request the graphics.

4. Watch out for the slow times on the World Wide Web. The transfer speed is affected by the traffic on-line and the location of the page that you have requested. Good times to work at top speeds are early in the morning.

5. Join "Friends and Family" with B.T. and register your local internet access number.

Summary

In this chapter I have explained the importance of research and I have explained the way that I find new markets.

CHAPTER 20

The ideal mail-order product

The ideal mail-order product should be fairly small, lightweight (posting an elephant is expensive), not too fragile and the product should normally not be available in local stores and most importantly the product must have a high perceived value and offer at least a 200% mark-up and in most cases a typical 500% mark-up.

Now let's look at that pricing.

A lesson that I learned very quickly in mail-order is that selling your product too cheaply is always worse than selling it for too much. It is the mistake that most new businesses make, they think that because they are new in business they should work on small margins. This is not the case.

Let me give you an example: If you needed a heart operation and there were two doctors, one quotes you £250 all in, and the other one quotes you £3,000. Which one would you trust?

I know I would go for the most expensive one, you see, price and quality have a psychological connection, it's cheap so it must be rubbish!

Now I'm not saying that you should sell a paper-clip for
£500 and don't think that you'll get away with it either, you
still need to make sure that your customer is happy and that
they believe they have received more than good value for
money.

You can always go down in price, but it is very hard to
increase a price. For example, let's say that I am selling a
new home-study course. You enquire and I send you my
salesletter, my selling price is £97.77. Now let's say that
you haven't responded to the offer after a few weeks. I can
then write back to you again with a new salesletter and I
could offer you a special LAST CHANCE offer of £67.77.

Selling products that you like

I feel it is important to enjoy and understand the product
that you are selling. It is very hard to be enthusiastic about a
product which you don't like for instance, I personally
wouldn't like to sell clothing or cosmetics.

Remember that you could be spending 12 to 14 hours a
day working, so make sure that you like what you are doing.

Now at the same time I must warn you about selling
products just because you like them, that don't have good
profit margins or a big market. Your hobbies do not always
make good businesses.

Specific products

Some of the best mail-order products are:

Information products

This includes books, "how to" manuals, correspondence
courses, self-improvement courses, newsletters, video
cassettes (training/seminars), spoken word cassettes (self-
improvement/spoken books) and computer software/
peripherals.

Information booklets, "how to" guides and manuals

People pay good money for information. Awhile ago I sold

a 4 page document for £50. Now the ink and paper cost me less than £1, but the value was of course the information on the paper.

Information that currently sells well includes topics on, how to make money, diets/fitness, how to attract the opposite sex, money saving tips, how to win at gambling, computers, self-defence and cosmetics etc.

Producing a "how to" manual

You have 3 choices:

> **1.** You can write and research the manual yourself. For example, let's say the topic you have chosen is "How to pick winning racehorses." You can research the manual by collating information from the internet, newspapers, other books and by interviewing people etc. and format it yourself using your computer.

> **2.** You can pay a researcher to find out the information and produce you a script.

> **3.** You can find a manual on the subject and purchase the reprint and resale rights, or you can enter into a wholesale agreement to buy the manuals.

Audio information

Anything written on paper can be put on to an audio tape. Today's time starved consumers are willing to pay for information on tapes and the success of books on tape proves this. Audio information can also be put together very cheaply. An audio cassette costs around 50p and the original master, including using a professional voice-over artist, will cost no more than £300 to £400.

Videos

The videos that I am talking about here are very low-tech information videos, not big budget feature films. There are some things that are easier to explain by showing people in real life, rather than in writing.

Let me give you an example:

A friend of mine in America runs a company that cleans computers and offers other maintenance services to companies. The market for this service is very large and so he decided to make a low budget video, showing people what he did and how they could start their own business doing the same thing. All he did was set up a desk in his own house with a computer on and demonstrated how he cleaned computers. He also goes on to explain how he markets his business and what he charges etc. His video was made with the help of a friend as the cameraman and a home video camera.

To go with the video he produced a short "how to" manual and workbook. The manual and the video cost him only US$10 to produce and ship, which is around £7.00 and he sells the course for US$127 (£90). The last time I spoke to him he had sold over 15,000 copies of this video, via mail-order. Now in case you're not too good at maths, that's over 1.9 million dollars!

Simple ideas like this work. Notice the high profit margin and how by only selling 15,000 he managed to make so much money, now if he was working on a smaller profit margin i.e. he sold the package for $39, he would have had to sell over 45,000 videos to make the same amount.

Another way to make money with videos is by recording trade shows and seminars/conferences. You see, for every one person that attends a seminar/trade show, there are probably 10 others that couldn't make it, or didn't want to spend a large amount of money attending the seminar.

Example:

Let's say that there is a national seminar for Doctors and it costs £300 to attend. Now you could arrange to video that seminar and sell it to the list of doctors who didn't attend for £40 to £60. You can even sell it to those who did attend!

Getting video tapes produced

Videos do cost more than audio tapes, however, they also sell for more. For a very simple video, you could produce it yourself at home using a video camera. For seminars you'll probably need 2 video cameras, extra lighting and a professional microphone.

Editing

Once you have your footage you will want to edit it, add some titles, fades and music etc. A studio will normally charge around £70 an hour, which includes an operator. After the various chopping you will end up with a master tape, this is what you make the copies from. Before you go into a studio be prepared because studio time goes past very quickly and before you know it you've spent a lot of money.

Have a plan ready of what you want to do, have titles ready on paper, or produce them yourself on your computer and bring them in on a disk.

A video tape costs around £2.00 for 30 minutes and around £2.50 for 60 minutes. This includes the blank tape and the actual copying. Prices vary and can be reduced significantly depending on volume. Again just like printing, price is important, but so is the quality, badly copied videos look very bad.

You can also print inlay sleeves for your video and put the video in a professional video case, which cost around 40p each.

More about producing videos

There are various books on producing videos and there is also quite a bit of information on the internet about this subject. There are even videos on how to produce videos!

If you are serious about this, I would recommend going on a short course, various companies advertise these in the back of video magazines.

Buying the rights to a video

I own the rights to 26 videos at the last count. Most of these videos were purchased from the USA and I edited them, converted them over, repackaged them and sold them in the U.K. and Europe.

Anyone reading this could buy the rights to a video and do the same. Most of the videos I own are "How to" videos, which I package together with books or paperwork etc.

How to buy the rights to a video

The first step is to get hold of a copy of the video and the salesletter. Identify the market that you think would be interested in the video. Look at ways in which you can improve the video, what you could add to the video, i.e. a workbook, help-sheets or computer disk etc. What do you think of the title? Could you improve the title name and make it more marketable?

Once you have decided that you can sell the video, then you need to write or phone up the copyright holder and explain what you want to do and how it will benefit him.

You could either make a one off offer for the U.K. rights, such as US$1,000 or you could offer a small advance of say US$250 and a percentage of the sales, say 5% of the sale price on each video etc.

You see, the chances are that Joe Smith, the copyright holder, has never even thought about selling the video outside his home country, and by you selling the video in the U.K. then he's got nothing to lose, it's BONUS money to him.

If the copyright holder is in the same country as you, you can still buy the rights, I know that there are many saleable videos that are just sitting on shelves collecting dust, including some of mine. Contact the copyright holder and make them a reasonable offer, you'll be surprised how many will agree to your offer.

Newsletters

A newsletter or small magazine is a very good way to get into the media business, with little or no up front costs. I have written a workbook specifically on this subject, which comes with 2 videos that show step by step, how anyone with a little common sense can earn around £100,000 pa. from a newsletter.

Most people are totally unaware of the vast profits and multi-billion pound empires that have been built up through the publishing of books, newspapers, magazines and newsletters. Some of the richest people in the world have made their fortunes through owning media companies including, television and radio. Unfortunately unless you have millions to invest in buying a television/radio station or a newspaper, there are no opportunities for the small businessman/woman to get into the profitable publishing and media industry, except by publishing a newsletter or small magazine.

What is a newsletter and why do people pay for them?

Information is now one of society's biggest needs and most valuable commodity. People will pay large sums of money to find out more about a particular subject. Whereas newspapers and to a certain extent a magazine, provide a broad overview of a subject, a newsletter would provide very specific information on a particular subject.

Unlike most other forms of media, newsletters can be set up on a very low budget and produce staggering results. Let's say that you have 2,000 subscribers to a newsletter, each paying £40 a year, that's £80,000 a year! The costs of running a newsletter are very low, in fact an 8 page newsletter can be produced, printed and posted for less than £1 per month.

The big advantages of a newsletter are:

　　1. It can be started and run from home.

　　2. A computer and a laser printer are the only tools

you need.

3. You get paid up front. For example, I sell you a 12 month subscription and you pay me now, but I don't have to deliver the newsletter all at once, so technically I am getting an interest free loan from the subscribers.

4. You have a residual value. Depending on how good your newsletter is you will get renewals, so after 12 months your income doesn't stop, it keeps going! A good newsletter should get around 80% renewals.

5. You can sell your newsletter business when you've had enough, for a substantial amount.

6. There are numerous extra ways to make money on top of subscriptions, including renting out your mailing list, carrying loose inserts and reader's offers etc.

Let me give you some examples of successful newsletters:

Competitors Companion

This newsletter has over 150,000 subscribers all paying on average £45 a year. 150,000 X £45 is 6.75 million pounds! Now even after running costs such as, printing and stamps etc. the newsletter still makes over 6 million pounds a year pre-tax.

So what is this newsletter all about?

It's very simple, every month they publish all the competitions that are open in the U.K.

The sort of information they give includes:

Where to get entry forms from.

What are the competition restrictions and if any proof of product purchases are required, i.e. 3 tokens from the side of a packet.

What the prizes are.

The closing dates.

Help with answers.

Sample competition slogans and tie-breakers.

And any other news the competitors need.

What a simple idea!

The information is always changing and the information is free. (They just have a few researchers who track down all the competitions.) With the public's massive appetite for winning competitions, this newsletter will continue to grow.

Government Auction News

This is basically a monthly newsletter on where all the various auctions are to be held, what type of goods are available and general buying advice.

Other successful newsletters are:

Discount travel newsletters
Health and medical newsletters*
Finance and investments newsletters*
Food and wine newsletters
Computer newsletters
Accountancy and taxation newsletters*
Classic car newsletters
Model railway newsletters
Gardening newsletters
DIY newsletters

* Note

Any newsletter that relates to medical advice must be written by a suitably qualified person. Take legal advice before proceeding.

Investment newsletters must be regulated in the U.K. by the P.I.A. and again must be written by a suitably qualified person.

Why everyone in business should publish their own newsletter

I strongly believe that everyone reading this should publish a newsletter, whatever business you are in and even if you give the newsletter away FREE, then you will benefit greatly from it.

Now I know you are thinking, this guy's mad, why would I give my customers a FREE newsletter? How do I make any money?

How to make money with a FREE newsletter

Making money by giving something away FREE!

There are many regional newspapers in the U.K. that are distributed free. The advertising revenue of course pays for the printing, distribution and staff's wages. Many of these newspapers are of good quality and make very good profits.

In England the ITV, Channel 4 and Channel 5 television channels are free. Their massive overheads are paid for by the commercials.

Can a free newsletter work?

On advertising alone it can be difficult to make your newsletter profitable, but with a combination of reader's offers and selling your own goods, it can be very profitable. Unlike a paid for newsletter, you can sell more advertisements and try to sell a bit harder to the subscriber, as they haven't paid for the newsletter.

Giving a newsletter away free to existing customers

Let's say that we own a computer software company and Joe Smith buys our latest program, instead of forgetting about him as we have now had his money, wouldn't it be a nice touch to offer him 12 month's free subscription to our computer newsletter?

In this newsletter we would have:

General computer news.

Updates about the software that he has just bought.

Hints and tips.

And details of our other products that we have to sell, including upgrades.

You will sell more software to Joe Smith by sending him a free newsletter every month, rather than sending him a salesletter.

So that is how you make money with a free newsletter, remember that a newsletter doesn't cost that much to produce and send out. If it's a free newsletter you don't have to send one out every month, it could be quarterly. Your newsletter can also be literally 1 or 2 A4 sheets.

Keeping in regular contact with your customers is very important. Most companies take your money and forget about you, yet if they only sent you a newsletter or a catalogue on a regular basis, the chances are they would get more sales from you and they would be able to create goodwill and a good impression.

NOTE: The firm of Accountants that I use now have their own newsletter, which contains all the latest tax news etc. and is sent out to clients free of charge, on a regular basis. This creates goodwill, keeps their customers informed and keeps their name to the forefront.

How do you make a newsletter a winner?

There is one thing that will make or break a newsletter and that is the topic. Pick the right topic and everything else will fall into place. Remember what we said earlier about "the hungry crowd," well that's what you need for a newsletter, it doesn't have to be a massive crowd, but there needs to be one!

The other thing that you need to concentrate on is marketing your newsletter, in fact 90% of your efforts will go into marketing the newsletter and the other 10% will go into writing the newsletter.

Summary

A newsletter is a very profitable home business, which can be started with little up front money. A newsletter is also an ideal product that can be sold alongside your existing profession/job.

If you want to get into this business, then drop me a line and I will tell you how to get my videos and workbook on starting a newsletter, at a special reader's reduced price.

Computer software/peripherals

There is no disputing that the computer age is with us. The first thing that I recommended to you was to get hold of a computer and some software. As I write, the richest man in the world is Bill Gates, the founder of Microsoft. This company went from nothing in 1980 to the biggest software company in the world.

Computer software is a fast changing market and sells very well as a direct mail product. If you decide to sell software, then you have the same 3 options as if you were selling a book or "how to" manual:

1. You could write the software yourself, if you have the skills and are that way inclined, however, this could take you a lifetime!

2. Find someone else to write the program, or find a program that someone has already written and offer to buy it or license it.

Let me tell you a little bit more about the software industry, as I have been involved in it for some years. There are many talented programmers and some excellent pieces of software, however, 99% of programmers haven't got a clue about business or marketing, therefore in most cases these programmers are totally broke. They have great products, but they don't know how to sell them, and that's where you can come in. Bill Gates is not a billionaire because he's a good software programmer, it's because he is a good marketer. I read that for every 1 programmer that

Microsoft employs, they have about 10 people in sales and marketing.

As already mentioned, Bill Gates is the richest man in the world and the program that started his career was MS-DOS, but the amazing fact that most people don't know is that Microsoft never wrote DOS, it was bought from someone else for a few thousand dollars! Microsoft then licensed the program to IBM and the rest is history. So Bill Gates, the richest man in the world, did exactly what I am talking about, find a good programmer and get them to write the program.

3. Purchase the software from wholesalers/publishers. You can buy software wholesale or direct from the publisher. Software carries a good profit margin, normally a program that retails for £40 can be purchased for around £15 or less, depending on quantities.

You can also import software from overseas, normally America. I distributed a very good CD-ROM compilation in the U.K. which I imported from America. The software cost me around US$5 (£3) a piece, including shipping and taxes and I sold it for around £20 retail and £10 wholesale, which is a very good mark up. The best point about this deal was that I only had to order a small amount from the publisher, so I didn't have to carry a large amount of stock. Thanks to couriers like DHL I could have more stock within days.

Peripherals (extras)

These are the extra add on pieces to a computer such as, computer speakers, sound cards, video capture boards, extra memory, scanners, modems and memory back-up drivers etc.

I know the owner of a successful company which sells peripherals in the U.K. He regularly goes to the large computer trade shows in America such as COMDEX and CES, looks for the latest add-ons and imports them over to the U.K.

Don't get involved in selling computer hardware

I strongly advise you against selling mail-order computers, it is a very competitive market and is best left to the big companies. The margins are far better on software and peripherals, and you don't need much start-up capital to start selling software and peripherals, in most cases you only need to order a small amount of stock, then you can place orders only as and when you receive your orders.

Novelty items, kitchen gadgets, health & fitness, jewellery and personalised items

One of the best salesman/direct marketers in recent years has to be Ron Popeil, better known as RONCO. His products include many kitchen gadgets and time saving devices. His top tip in direct marketing is to make sure that the product can be sold as a gift. Without Christmas, Mother's day, Father's day, birthdays, weddings and so on, most retail stores would go broke!

I recommend getting hold of his book "The Salesman Of The Century," in this book Ron Popeil explains how he went from selling kitchen products on a market stall, to being one of the biggest direct advertisers in America. Details are listed at the back of this book and anyone who is interested in promoting their products through infomercials or on home shopping channels should definitely read this book.

Products and information that solve people's problems

It seems that most people today have so many problems. As a direct marketer, any products, guides or services that can help to solve problems are very big sellers. You see, if you have a product which solves a common problem, the customer will not even think about the price.

Let me give you a few examples of problem solving products:

The problem: Chopping food and preparing vegetables is difficult and time consuming.

The solution: The Chop-O-Matic. It cuts and slices food thinly in just seconds with no mess.

The problem: A diamond necklace is very expensive and is impractical in view of crime and fear of losing it.

The solution: Fake diamonds, such as Diamonique. Affordable jewellery that looks good and costs very little.

The problem: Back pains.

The solution: A massager which straps to your chair and vibrates. The ideal gift for someone you know who suffers from back pains.

Packaging products together

This is a very simple way to make a new mail-order product out of existing items. Let me give you a true example that went from being a wacky idea to a very big Christmas seller.

The product is Christmas stockings for cats and dogs. For years confectionery manufacturers realised that you could take a few bars of confectionery, put them together in a pretty box or stocking and stick an extra 50% on to the price. The idea came from the USA and now animal lovers in England and Europe are buying them by the millions.

All you need is a cheap Christmas stocking and some small dog or cat treats, toys and balls etc. Many of the goods in the stockings are samples/trial sizes, which can be obtained from the manufacturers for nothing!

Put a nice printed card at the top of the stocking with a picture of a cat/dog and a name tag, so that you can write TO: Tiddles, and you then have a finished product.

So by taking existing products and putting them together, you have made a new product.

Another very successful packaging concept was the introduction of compilation records, tapes and now compact disks. This was pioneered by a Canadian company, called K-Tel in 1970 and later Ronco. Now you have Telstar, Soundsdirect and numerous others. These companies would approach the record companies and pay them a set price and a royalty, based on the hit status of the song. The songs were then put on to a tape or CD and sold on, in the old days mainly direct through TV and radio.

This concept can be copied for many other products, the computer software CD-ROM that I mentioned was a compilation.

Importing products and ideas

What do the following products and services have in common, jeans, T-shirts, pizzas, pasta, popcorn, shell-suits, home delivery of fast food, tool hire, karaoke and dancing coke cans/flowers?

They were all ideas and products that came to the U.K. from America or other countries.

The opportunity to import ideas and products from overseas is enormous. Whenever I go away I'm always looking at possible new products to bring back.

It can also work the other way. The Americans love things connected to the British Royal family, they like fine English teas and Scottish shortbread biscuits etc.

Summary

To summarise, you need to find products and services that people want. You need products that can easily be shipped. You need products which have big profit margins and a high perceived value. If you follow the guidelines that I have given you, I don't think you'll have any problems in finding successful mail-order products.

A NOTE ON STOCK: Go easy, especially in the early days on buying stock, you will probably have to hold a small amount of stock before some newspapers will let you advertise, but you don't want to be left with thousands of books or videos etc.

The key is to have some stock and a good supplier, so that if you receive thousands of orders you can obtain more stock within 7 to 14 days.

Adding value

A large box gives the impression of more value. As previously mentioned, never get into price wars in business, the only winner is normally the consumer and not you, pricing higher is better than pricing lower, however, a good trick is to add value to your product.

Let's say that you are selling a set of kitchen knives, now to add value you could add a cookbook or a guide on how to use the different knives to their best effect, you could also throw in a few other small kitchen gadgets. So even though your price may be slightly higher, you are giving more value.

I deal with a company in America and when you order something they always throw a few extra bits in the box like newsletters, brochures, a mug and even a baseball cap!

How to source products

Most people will not want to invent and manufacture their own products, especially if you are new to mail-order. The best way is to source a product through a wholesaler, direct from the manufacturer or if it's a book or video, from the publisher/author.

The best starting point is to obtain a copy of the book, video or product that you are interested in selling and this way you can get the name and address of the publisher or manufacturer.

The second step is to write them a good letter on your official letterheaded paper, explain what your company does and that you would be interested in selling the XYZ product. In the letter you need to demonstrate that you are serious, but at the same time be truthful.

Now we both know that you are just starting out and this could possibly be the first product that you've ever tried to sell, however, there is nothing wrong with writing in your letter "We are a dynamic, young company which specialises in marketing products such as... and from our initial research, we believe that we will be able to sell a substantial amount of units."

I would also state in your letter that you are happy to place an initial test order of 50 or 100 units, depending on the price and that you are happy to pay for these immediately.

You see, if I received a letter like this from you I would take note, sure you're not a big retail chain, but you have already offered to make a small order and you've offered to pay for the goods on delivery.

This format will work in nearly all cases. The above scenario takes into account that you will be dispatching the product, now in some cases it could be possible for the manufacturer or their dispatch agent to handle your orders, the only down side to this is that you lose some control and you are then disclosing the names and addresses of your customers to the manufacturer.

An easy way to find good ideas for products

An easy way is to "follow my leader," watch what other successful mail-order companies are doing. An important tip is to get on as many mailing lists as you can, you need to get all those little mail-order catalogues and see what they are selling. Watch for the mail-order products that are being repeated over and over again.

At the time of writing this book there is one product that is everywhere, it's a fitness product which gives you a flatter stomach by toning your abdominal muscles. There are many variations, but the principals are the same and their names are all very similar, AB FLEX, AB CRUNCH, AB ROLLER etc. all of which I better add are registered trademarks. By the time you read this you will have no doubt purchased one, I have!

My favourite mail-order catalogue is:

Innovations
Euroway Business Park, Swindon, SN5 8SN, U.K.
Tel: 0990 83 83 00 Fax: 01793 48 70 02
Internet: WWW.Innovations.co.uk

This catalogue will give you some great ideas for mail-order products and will also show you how a good catalogue should be laid out. The best point about this and other catalogues is that they are FREE, it's unbelievable that you are getting ideas for products and examples of advertising copy and it costs you nothing.

A note on copyright and copying others

There is a very thin line between getting ideas and learning from other people and STEALING their ideas. If you take a book and copy it word for word, or if you illegally duplicate a video that you don't have the rights to, then that is STEALING, there is no other word for it. Don't do it because it's not worth it, you may get sued or even have a nasty visit from someone! Believe me it's been done, especially in the music and video business.

Be a smart copycat

A smart copycat reads a book or an advert etc., gets ideas and formulates a plan from other people's work. They then write their own book or produce their own video along similar lines. Nobody can copyright ideas or generic words like "AT LAST" or "HOW TO." Take for instance the supermarket's own brands, their products are so similar to the brand leaders, sometimes the packaging even looks similar, however, as long as the own brands do not purport to be the actual brand, then there is nothing that the brand leaders can do.

Don't forget that you can be a legal copycat if you buy the rights to a product or buy it wholesale.

Improving other people's ideas with a superior product, advertising campaign or creating a more appealing package, can be a very quick route to success and it is completely moral and ethical.

A very important lesson

I mentioned earlier about the bank that lost the Hanson Trust account, well you need to remember this. If you make it big one day, which I'm sure you will, and a little guy writes to you asking to buy 50 or 100 units of your product, ALWAYS do business with them and treat them fairly and with respect. Treat them as if they are the biggest chain store in the world and they are placing an order for 10 million units. Why this great treatment? Because firstly, you don't know who that little guy is, he could in fact be a very big guy, but is just testing the market and secondly, one day that company working from a studio flat, could become the biggest corporation in the world and they will remember you and it will be to your benefit.

Let me tell you a true story, some years ago when I first started producing and selling videos, I needed to make 10 copies of a video, I was new to the business and phoned a few companies from the Yellow Pages, most weren't very polite to me or that bothered, and others tried to rip me off on the pricing because I was only ordering a few copies and I was "a little guy" in the video business. What they didn't know was that I was already a big guy in publishing and I was regularly ordering 10,000 audio tapes at a time.

Anyway, one company was polite enough and they offered to copy the 10 videos at a fair price and turn them around as quickly as they could find a gap in their duplication schedule.

The company is still the company that I use today for duplication and copying, that "little guy" who started with a 10 video order, went on to duplicate over 300,000 videos plus, possibly more by the time you read this. Now just think if all those idiots who wouldn't deal with me for an order of 10 had done business with me, they would have had a very big customer.

Let me add something else about people in business, especially those who have built up a business from scratch and have climbed up the ladder, THEY HAVE LONG MEMORIES AND THEY ARE VERY LOYAL.

If anyone reading this ever wants to buy 50 or 100 videos or books etc. from my company and they write to me on a professional letterhead and with a laser printed letter, I guarantee that I will do business with you and deal with you on fair terms. All I ask is that you have the same attitude towards other new entrepreneurs.

☺

Policeman: I'm afraid I shall have to lock you up for the night, Sir!

Prisoner: What's the charge?

Policeman: There's no charge, Sir. It's all part of the service!

CHAPTER 21

Advertising and marketing

What we have talked about up till now is nothing without advertising and marketing. You can have the best product, the best piece of letterheaded paper and a good address etc. but if you don't know how to advertise and market your product or service cost effectively, then you will fail and you will go broke.

I just cannot stress how important this subject is, if you can imagine that a successful business is a cake, then this is 90% of the cake.

Let me tell you the facts of life, THE BEST PRODUCT does not always win, it's the best marketed product that wins, it's the product that the market likes the most that wins.

Let me give you some examples:

Some years ago you had the video wars, the 2 standards were VHS and BETAMAX, now anyone who is technically minded will know that BETAMAX was the better product and in fact is still used in the TV business, but VHS won the consumer market, they gained the support, they won the marketing race and now everyone has a VHS.

Another example is the IBM compatible PC and the Apple PC standard, the apple PC is technically the better machine and is probably easier to use, yet IBM PC's outsell Apple PC's at more than 10 to 1. Why? Apple just never got the marketing quite right and they never managed to get the public and the software developers behind them. Notice which computer I advised you to get and what computer I use, it's the IBM compatible.

So never think that it's the best product that wins, it's not.

Promoting your product

Let's say that we have done our research and we have negotiated the rights to a product (the cleaning a computer video). We now need to write a winning advert and response pack to sell our product.

Trying to sell a product without advertising is like smiling in the dark, you know you're doing it, but no one else does! Good advertising will normally sell an inferior product, but bad advertising will always make even a good product fail.

There are two ways to advertise and I have shown them both:

> **1.** To offer the product for sale from the initial advert. This is normally called "off the page" advertising and means taking out a larger advert.

> **2.** Inviting the public to write/phone in for free information concerning the product (two stage selling) and these are smaller adverts. For most things I prefer this method and over the years I have probably written over 2,000 small adverts.

Sample two stage advertisements

Sample off the page advertisement

Now you also have 5 major media outlets for your advertising which are, newspapers, both regional and national, magazines, the internet (World Wide Web), TV and radio. As well as the media, you have the power of press releases and competitions that you can use. You also have direct mail.

As a beginner I would stay out of TV and radio for the moment. I would definitely use newspapers, magazines, press releases, competitions and direct mail.

Newspapers

Although it is true that newspapers are losing some market share, there are still many larger regional and national newspapers that are worth using. Newspapers are ideal testing grounds for products, since the advertisements can be relatively cheap and your advert can appear within days of it being placed. Newspapers also offer instant response. If one of my adverts appeared in a newspaper on a Monday, I would start receiving calls from 7.00am that day.

The down side with a newspaper is its short life, if the advert is in Monday's paper, it would pull in the most response on a Monday with some follow through to Tuesday, but after that the advert will be finished because newspapers get thrown away very quickly.

The other point to remember about a newspaper is that it is very general and although you can target your market by having your advert placed in a certain section i.e. the business section, your product needs to be fairly general to work in a newspaper.

How the paper is divided

Most newspapers have special days and sections. For example, Wednesday's is money and Thursday's is travel etc. and you may find that if your product relates to one of these days, then you should advertise on this day. For example, if your product is a "How to cut your tax bill" book, you could advertise on the money day, or on or around the financial pages.

There are two types of adverts, "CLASSIFIED ADS" and "DISPLAY ADS." Classified adverts are composed of words only, in ordinary type and listed under the heading supplied by the publication itself. Classified adverts are charged either by the word or by the line.

Display adverts are where you only buy the space that you use i.e. 1/2 a page, 1/8 of a page or 1/16 of a page etc. I mainly buy the exact space, such as a 5cm X 2 column advert.

Newspapers normally sell by the column for the width. The column width can vary from paper to paper and can also depend on whether the newspaper is a tabloid (i.e. the SUN) or broadsheet (i.e. Daily Telegraph). In a tabloid the typical column width is 3.1 cm, so my 5cm x 2 column advert would be 5cm X 6.2cm.

In a display advert you can have pictures, diagrams, boxes and use different type faces, which allows you to produce a higher impact advert.

Reference publications

British Rate And Data (BRAD) will provide all the information you need concerning rates, printing specifications and circulations etc. on almost all the newspapers and periodicals in the U.K. BRAD is generally kept in the reference section of a public library.

Profile

When selecting a newspaper you need to know about the type of person who is going to read it. The person who reads the Financial Times will not be the same as the person who reads the Daily Mirror. The Audit Bureau of Circulation (ABC) provides information on circulation and readership.

Readers are graded into classes, according to the reader's occupation and other characteristics. For example, A = managerial, B = professional, C1 = administrators, C2 = skilled/semiskilled labourers and D = unskilled labourers.

These classes give some indication about the reader's life-style, level of education, attitude and purchasing power, which are all very important factors when deciding whether the profile matches your product.

Media packs and sample copies

If you contact the advertising department of your chosen newspaper or magazine, they will send you a free sample copy of the publication and a media pack, which contains their advertising rates and profile details.

Tip: When you advertise in a publication it is very common to receive calls from sales people who work for other newspapers/magazines, wanting you to advertise in their publication. Some of them will be from publications that you may have heard of, but many will be unknown, therefore ALWAYS make sure that you get a voucher copy and media pack first, before you advertise. I've had so many sales people call me, telling me that they have a special deal and I must place the advert right now! I would never do that unless I saw a real copy of the publication and a media pack.

Before placing an advert in a newspaper, I would buy at least one week's worth of the newspaper if it's a daily, or a few editions if it's a monthly. Taking the example of a daily newspaper, if you look at every day's paper, you will then be able to see all the different sections/different daily features and you can then decide which day suits you best.

Magazines

Magazines are a very good media for mail-order. While it takes longer for your advert to appear, magazines have a longer life than newspapers. I have hundreds of magazines which I keep for months and even years, but I never keep a newspaper for longer than a few days. Magazines are also left in doctors/dentist's waiting rooms and offices etc.

The big advantage with magazines is that they are targeted. If you are looking to attract fashion conscious women, then you can advertise in women's fashion magazines.

I believe that newspaper circulations are dropping and magazine circulations are rising, because people are becoming more focused and interested in their selected interests. If I am a woman, why should I buy a daily newspaper which has sport, financial news and motor news etc. in it, when all I am interested in is fashion and cosmetics? In the U.K. at the time of writing this, there hasn't been a launch of a new daily national newspaper for years, whereas there seems to be a new magazine launch every week!

Your research into different magazines will give you a solid foundation and "feel" for the types of products advertised in the various publications. Hobby or sport's magazines lend themselves to mail-order, since the readers are always on the look-out for an article that could assist or benefit them in some way. Trade journals provide a perfect vehicle for specialised products which appeal to only one particular segment of society, such as lawyers, architects, accountants or hoteliers etc.

Choosing the right magazine or newspaper

Q. If you pick up a magazine and find that there isn't one single mail-order type of advert in it, do you think that this is a good sign or a bad sign?

A. It's a bad sign. Let me explain why, it is better to "follow my leader" than to be a pioneer. You see, if a magazine carries mail-order adverts, month in month out, you can safely say that the magazine is working or the advertiser wouldn't be in there. So if the advert is working for other mail-order advertisers, it is likely that the magazine will work for you as well.

I have noticed that Saturday's national newspapers carry many mail-order adverts (buy a copy and see for yourself), so you can safely say that Saturdays must be a good day for mail-order advertising. The Sunday colour magazine supplements are also very popular with mail-order adverts, possibly because people are more relaxed on a Sunday and buy more.

Summary

Matching the right publication to your product is very important and you must spend some time researching the various publications carefully. Good research will avoid you making costly mistakes. For example, choosing the right section of the newspaper and choosing the right day makes a big difference. Watching other advertisers is the key.

I quickly learnt that I could have the best advert position, with the best copy and a brilliant headline, but if the publication was the wrong publication for my offer, then I would get little or no response.

Magic words

If you remember in the first section we mentioned how important words are, how they can make you laugh, cry, be sad and most importantly SELL PRODUCTS.

Choose the right words to use in an advert or salesletter and you win, choose the wrong ones and you lose.

Over the next few pages I will give you as much information as possible, which will increase your chances of selling your product. At the back of the book I have listed some excellent books which go into advertising and marketing in further depth and I suggest you invest in a few of them.

What makes someone respond or look at an advert?

In nearly all cases it is the headline. The words at the top of the advert in large print are read first, then if the reader is interested he will continue and if not, he's on to the next page. The headline is the appetiser or the hook, it should appeal to the reader in some way and provide a striking statement, or promise of some benefit. I will go into this in depth in a moment as this is very important, but in a nutshell people are basically very self-centred and respond to appeals that promise gratification of some personal or intimate aspect of their life, improvement in their status, increasing their income, admiration, love and success etc.

I have spent a great deal of time researching and looking into what people want out of a product or service, and listed below are my findings. A headline either in an advert or salesletter etc. that can appeal to one of these categories is a winner. These categories are in no particular order and they are all winners:

1. Earning money. I don't know anyone who isn't interested in this!

2. Improving health. There are very few people who can say that they are 100% happy with their health.

3. Saving time, everyone wants to do this.

4. Being appreciated by others. People like to feel special and wanted. They also like to receive compliments.

5. Improving appearance and being fashionable.

6. Avoiding criticism and pain.

7. Avoiding losing money or possessions. Everybody likes to think that they are smart with money and they haven't been taken for a ride. Ask anyone who has achieved something, for example a nice house, what their biggest fear is, and it will probably be losing their assets.

8. Leisure.

9. Improving social status and getting promoted.

10. Attracting the opposite sex.

11. Avoiding work and/or effort.

12. Security and comfort in old age. This concern starts later on in life, no one wants to end up in a state-run nursing home.

You will no doubt be interested in some or all of these twelve categories.

Anyway back on to adverts and headlines.

"On average, five times as many people read the headlines as read the body copy. It follows that, unless your headline sells your product, you have wasted 90 percent of your money."

David Ogilvy

Words that work in an advert

Some of the words that I will list here have been used for many years and although they may sound like a cliché and they are used over and over again, it's because they work, believe me.

Words to use:

NEW, AMAZING, STARTLING, REVOLUTIONARY, MIRACLE, THE TRUTH, ANNOUNCING, NOW, SUDDENLY, AT LAST, LAST CHANCE, HOW TO, WANTED, EASY, FREE, COMPARE, DISCOVER, BE A, DO YOU.

The two most effective words that you can use in an advert are FREE and NEW.

Look at any successful direct mail adverts or salesletters and I guarantee you that you'll see these words used. Watch the infomercials on satellite TV and you will see and hear words like, "AMAZING DISCOVERIES" and "ANNOUNCING THE NEW REVOLUTIONARY...," these people know what they are doing.

Spend time on your headline, and never ever run an advert without one. In larger adverts you will tend to have a headline and a sub-headline. <u>I cannot stress enough how important the headline is.</u>

Here are a few tried and tested ways that you can start your headline with:

How to... (one of my favourites)

Seven steps to...

The secret to...

Are you...

An absolutely sure-fire way to...

Should you...

Your guide to...

TIP: Anyone who is thinking of writing a book, manual or marketing a video, do remember that the title is very important. I treat the title of my books and videos just like headlines and I use many of the same words. A good opening title for any book or video is "How to."

WARNING: Don't try and be clever in a headline, that's what advertising agencies do and they normally end up killing the response. Your headline should be direct and easy to understand.

HOW TO CUT YOUR HEATING BILLS NOW!

This is a very direct headline with short words and is not too long. I like to keep my headlines down to 10 or 15 words maximum.

An advertising agency style headline is, "If every wife knew what every widow knows, no husband would be without life insurance."

This is a clever headline, but it will not grab the reader's attention and most people will not understand it, do you understand what the story is?

Here is the key to writing a good advert, salesletter, press release or sales speech:

A = Attention, grab the reader with a powerful headline or opening.

I = Interest, keep them interested, make the copy persuasive yet informative and make the copy believable, back up any claims with research and testimonials.

D = Desire, make them want to know more, make them desire your product or service, you want the reader to feel that "this is what I have always been looking for," or "this is the answer to my dreams."

A = Action, ask for an action, phone now or return the coupon and close the sale.

The first paragraph

The next step to a good advert is the first paragraph. We've got the reader past the headline, but we now need to keep them reading, we need to get them excited, worried, curious or whatever it takes. For example:

"Did you know that thousands of men and women are making £500 a week plus, working from home in their spare time?"

or

"It's hard to believe but it's true, you are currently wasting thousands of pounds in tax benefits because you simply don't now how to claim what is legally yours!"

Body copy

This is where the main copy goes and depending on the size of your advert and the type of offer, this is where you list all the benefits and facts to the reader. The body copy needs to be easy to read, believable and sell the idea to the reader. It needs to explain how your product, book or service etc.

will benefit the reader. It is pointless saying in your copy, "My company is the best, we've been in business for years and we're the biggest..." This is rubbish and the reader will say, "So what!"

The reader is selfish, self-centred and is reading your advert or salesletter for his pleasure and to see "What's in it for him." Remember these letters WII FM, no it's not a new radio station! It's "What's in it for me," which is the question that everyone really wants to know the answer to, people want the BENEFITS such as:

> The stainless steel chopping blade, which means it's easy to clean, chops quickly and easily with no effort and will stay sharp forever, saving you time and money.

> Superwax polish, gives your car a long lasting, showroom shine. Easy to apply within 20 minutes, goes on and comes off with the minimum amount of effort and leaves you more time to drive your car instead of polishing it.

See how these examples give the benefits to the customer, they tell the customer what they want to know and what the benefits are to them. If your advert is full of "WE ARE," then scrap it and start again, you should have "YOU WILL" and "YOU" and also make sure that there are not too many "I," "We," "My" or "Our" words in your advert or salesletter.

A point about the length of the copy

You can never have too much copy, but you can have boring copy. I often see full page adverts with sometimes no more than 10 words in them, what a waste! It has been proven time and time again that it is the copy combined with a picture that sells, not just a picture. Long text copy can also be made to look interesting by using a good layout, using appropriate paragraphs and using bullet points ● . A quick point on using photos in adverts or salesletters, make sure that you write a small caption underneath it or beside it, some people will see a photo and not understand what it is trying to represent, the caption will also reinforce the photo's message. (See sample advert on page 213.)

In salesletters you can have longer copy, but obviously with an advert because you are paying by the centimetre, space is a premium. Don't make the mistake of trying to cram a full off the page advert into a small space, it normally doesn't work. If you cannot afford to go for a bigger advert, then you need to go for a 2 step advert.

> TIP: Editorial is read and believed far more than adverts, that is why many of my adverts are set to look like newspaper articles.

A good way to tell if your copy is too cramped and hard to read, is to look at it at the end of the day when your eyes are quite tired, now if you find it hard to read, then so will your potential customers.

Closing copy

This is the action space, it's amazing how many adverts don't ask for any action or don't try and close the sale. Even if you are not asking for any money or commitment at this stage, you still need to make the reader act. For example:

> "Phone now for your FREE 24 page report, which will reveal the tax secrets you should know."

or

> "Take action today, for the special introductory offer of only £19.95 you too can be enjoying the benefits of ..."

Don't be afraid to tell the reader what they should do next.

Summary on advertising

There is no way that I can tell you everything about advertising in such a short space, however, if you stick to the guidelines that I have given here, you will have a far better advert than most and you'll certainly have a better advert than any advertising agency could produce for you.

I have listed some of my favourite books on advertising at the back of this book, that are worth investing in. You can never know too much about advertising and marketing.

What's grey, and has four legs and a trunk?
A mouse going on holiday!

What's brown, has four legs and a trunk?
A mouse coming back from holiday!

SAMPLE advert written in an editorial style. Research shows that this type of layout works very well.

CHAPTER 22

Salesletters and direct mail

I want to start by saying, "There is no such thing as junk mail," if someone calls your mailing piece "junk mail," then you've made either one of these mistakes or possibly both:

Mistake 1

You've made your sales piece look like all the other stupid banks, insurance companies and book clubs etc. who haven't got a clue about direct mail and take their advice from advertising agencies, who are worse than their clients, talk about the blind leading the blind!

Mistake 2

You're mailing the letter to the wrong person.

Bad direct mail

Let's deal with mistake 1. No doubt you've received mail from life insurance companies, banks or book clubs etc. In most cases you put them in the bin without even opening them! You know what they are trying to sell you before you even open the envelope, because they have stupid teaser copy on the envelope or they have the company's name and logo on the envelope, and as if that isn't bad enough, they send you the letter by MAILSORT or BULK MAIL, as they call it in the USA, which means that you and another 10 million others have received this "special message!"

Why do these big sensible companies do it?

Well firstly, they have more money than sense and they are so big that no one normally knows what's going on and secondly, they do get some results because if you mail 10 million letters out, even with a bad mail piece and teaser copy all over the envelope, there will always be a few fools who will respond! These companies use the "shot gun" approach, they guess that if they fire enough bullets they are bound to hit something!

Now, I'd like to think that we are a little bit smarter than these big companies and I know a few things about successful direct mail, in view that I have made a lot of money from it! Over the next few pages I will tell you the right way to use direct mail.

Mistake 2

A good piece of direct mail should be addressed to someone who is interested in what the letter is selling, simple isn't it? If I receive a letter trying to get me to subscribe to Knitting Weekly, I class that as JUNK MAIL. I am not interested in knitting and I don't plan to take it up either! Now if I receive a salesletter about investing money or the latest computer software, then I am interested in that and as long as the mailing piece is good, it will certainly not go in the bin.

Making money with good direct mail

Direct mail works, get it right and you will be making money so quickly, you won't know what's hit you! You'll be going to the bank every day with huge piles of cheques and if you accept credit cards, your terminal will be doing overtime!

It's hard to describe in words the excitement and feelings that a successful direct mail project will provide, hopefully in the near future you'll experience it first hand. At the end of this section I will show you how a winning salesletter can turn a few hundred pounds into over 1 million!

So why does my direct mail work?

Well first of all my direct mail is targeted, I don't just write to any old fool, I qualify the person who I am writing to before I start. By using the RIGHT MAILING LIST, I have secret information about the recipient. Now there is nothing underhand about the way I get my information, it's from the lists that are in BRAD, which I have already mentioned and by getting more information from the list broker or list owner.

As well as good research I use recent lists and I use lists of buyers, not enquirers. I don't mind paying extra money for fresh, good quality names and addresses, it's worth it. I also use buyers because they have parted with money before, which means that they are more qualified.

Unlike the big insurance companies, I want the recipient to enjoy reading my salesletter and I want them to respond and buy from me.

So the first key is to match the right person to the right offer. If I am selling a subscription to Knitting Weekly, I will look through BRAD and find a list of people who are interested in knitting and crafts.

The mailing piece

In this section I will tell you how to put together a good mailing piece.

The envelope

First of all never, ever, use teaser copy on the envelope. The envelope should not have anything on it, other than possibly a return address (no company name) and possibly PRIVATE & CONFIDENTIAL, TO BE OPENED BY ADDRESSEE

ONLY or URGENT FIRST CLASS MAIL.

> **TIP:** If you are using 2 step advertising and you're sending out information to an enquirer, it is a good idea to make up a stamp that says, "Here is the important information that you have requested," it will normally get your letter read before everyone else's.

And that's it. The name and address can either be hand written if it's a small mailing, directly printed on to the envelope or you can use a window envelope. Stick to a white envelope for most mailings.

It all depends on the volume of mail that you are sending out. I've used hand addressed envelopes, directly printed envelopes and window envelopes and all 3 methods have worked fine. I would never use STICKY LABELS on a piece of mail as it looks like "JUNK MAIL."

Now I have read books which say that you should print on your envelope because it is your "shop front," and maybe 20 years ago printing on an envelope may have worked, but today people are smarter, they probably get lots of direct mail and they are time starved.

Stamps

A real postage stamp with a postmark on it is the best option to make your letter look personal. If you are a real perfectionist you can use a colourful stamp that has some sort of appeal to your reader, such as sports or flowers.

A few direct mail companies have also started to mail out from abroad, so that the envelope has a foreign stamp and postmark on it, I know a time-share company who did this very successfully.

Let's summarise the envelope before we go any further. If you can't get the recipient to even open your letter, then everything else is pointless. See how I am making the envelope a mystery, you can't tell anything from the envelope, no company name, logo or teaser copy. There is no way that anyone throws mail away when they don't know what's inside it, it could be money for all they know. I always use a thicker envelope so that you can't tell what's inside the envelope by holding it up.

The letter

Using the discreet envelope method you will get past the bin, but you're not home and dry yet, far from it, you now need to get the recipient to read your letter. The basics here are the same as a newspaper or magazine advert, we need a headline, hook, statement etc. that will appeal to the reader.

Imagine that the reader is the judge and jury, before I set the stage, this is a unique concept and way of thinking and if any other book tells you this, then they copied it from me!

Anyway, imagine that you have been charged with murder and you are defending yourself, your salesletter is your defence and the customer is the JUDGE and JURY. If you convince him/her, then you've got their order, if you don't convince them, then your salesletter goes to jail, well in the bin, but it's the same thing really!

So what do we need to defend ourselves? We need to make a very strong argument, we need to appeal to the judge, we need to make our story believable, we need to back up our claims and finally, we need to pull a few rabbits out of a hat as a finale and close our case.

Wow! Sounds dramatic, but writing winning salesletters is dramatic, it's the difference between eating bread and water for dinner or Champagne and lobster!

Back to salesletters...

Now remember that we have targeted this person, so we should know a little bit about them and we know what they've purchased in the past etc.

A great example of headline writing was a letter sent to recent investors of certain companies. The letter was selling investment books and an investment newsletter, the headline was:

Your shares in British Telecom, should you buy more, sell or hold them?

Now imagine receiving this letter and you are a shareholder in British Telecom, would you read it? Of course you would. Now for those of you saying, "How did they know he had shares in British Telecom?" It's simple, you can buy shareholder's names and addresses, if you look in BRAD you'll see millions of them.

Another great headline was:

Those valuable coins you've recently bought, are they real?

Again we know that the reader has just bought valuable coins, because his name is on a list of valuable coin collectors. This headline was used for a product called the "Gold Tester," it's a sort of electronic pen and when you run it over metal, a light indicates whether it is gold, how pure the gold is, or if it isn't not gold at all (fake).

The sub-headline

This is where you can expand a bit on the headline for instance, a sub-headline for the gold tester offer could be:

"Introducing a new and amazing way to test gold coins within seconds."

> **TIP:** It seems that people remember and believe
> headlines that are in quotation marks, for example,
> "Discover how to prevent cancer."

The salutation

The best salutation and one that I nearly always use, is the person's name, Dear Mr Smith or Dear Mrs Davidson. It takes some time and effort to get your computer to mail-merge the address, but it's worth it. It makes the letter look personal and official. If you can't manage mail-merge, then you could get a bureau to do it for you.

> PLEASE DO NOT USE Dear Friend, especially in the U.K. I suggest that if you can't use a personal salutation, you should skip it altogether and just go straight into your letter.

Opening paragraph

This is the same as newspaper or magazine advertising, we've got the reader past the headline, but we need to keep them reading and we need to get them excited, worried, curious or whatever.

The body copy

This is the main part of the letter which needs to tell all, remember what I said earlier about WII FM "What's in it for me," keep answering that regularly during the letter.

Also keep the letter personal, as if it's to someone you already know. A technique that I use in letter writing is to ask questions and then answer them myself. I try to answer any questions that I think the reader would ask, as if I were talking face to face with them, for example:

Can you really make money from the goldfish business?

Yes, there are thousands of men and women all over the country who are earning excellent first and second incomes from goldfish breeding.

A good layout, fonts, bullets, bold text, underlining and italics

It is important to make the letter easy to read and you need to leave some white space or the eye will drown in a sea of words! Don't let the sentence go from edge to edge, leave a margin at both ends because the reader's eye can only go so far across the page. Make sure the space between each word is enough and the space between each line is adequate. These parameters can easily be changed on your word processor or desk top publisher, so you can experiment with different settings.

Make sure that you keep your paragraphs fairly short and use bullet points to make the benefits stand out, such as:

- Learn how to get FREE advertising!

- Discover the secrets that advertising agencies won't tell you!

- Why starting on a limited budget is an advantage!

I also use sub-headlines to break up any large blocks of text, which I normally centre, for example, "Free bonus report," "Why you must take action today," or "Full Money-Back Guarantee if you are not 100% satisfied."

Fonts

The only 2 fonts that I use for the body copy are Courier, which looks like this `AaBbCcDdEeFf` and gives a typewriter look and Times New Roman, which is the font this book has been written in and is fairly easy to read, for big headlines I like **Switzerland Black.**

A good graphic designer will tell you never to use more than 2 fonts in an advert and I think that is very good advice for a salesletter.

Bold text, underlining and italics

These features should be used in a good salesletter, but you must not over do it. Treat them as if they are special effects and less is more. If you underline every other line it will look terrible and I once saw a company's salesletter who did this in red!

Bold text is good for sub-headlines and the occasional line. Italics can be very hard to read and I don't often use them.

Back to the salesletter...

Testimonials, quotes and research

These are all good ways to break up your salesletter and most importantly, they add credibility and back up your claims. Salesletters need to be believable and backing up your claims reinforces your message.

NOTE: I want to tell you about making your offer sound too good, unfortunately many people are negatively programmed and if your offer sounds too far-fetched, even though it's true, you can lose a lot of sales.

Let me give you an example: Someone I knew ran the headline, "Earn £25,000 a year running your own successful part-time publishing business." Now I knew that this was a realistic figure and in fact many people would make far more than that, yet when he changed the headline to "Earn £1,000 a month running your own successful part-time publishing business," he had a far better response, it seems that people BELIEVED that they could make an extra £1,000 a month, but they didn't believe they could make £25,000 a year!

So remember this story, sometimes you have to actually scale down the offer.

Testimonials

Hopefully you will receive letters from satisfied customers and I suggest that you write back to them thanking them for their kind remarks and request permission from them to use extracts of their letter in your marketing material.

Another way to obtain feedback and comments which can be used, is to mail out a questionnaire to people who have recently purchased your product. Ask them a few simple questions and ask them for a brief comment on what they liked about XYZ.

On the questionnaire you need to state that some quotes may be used by the company in their promotional material, however, assure the customer that you will not give out their address and that their confidentiality will be respected. Also state that you reserve the right to edit their testimonial.

You MUST always give the customer something back if you expect them to help you. I would suggest a headline on your letter along the lines of "Help us with our marketing and you can claim a FREE gift."

The gift could be a pen, book, report, video or a discount voucher off future orders etc.

By the way, if anyone wants to write to me with some nice, honest comments about this book then please do, there's a form at the back of this book and YES, you will get a FREE gift for your time and effort. You can never have enough feedback.

You won't normally print the whole testimonial letter, you would just choose a few lines.

For example:

Here's what a few of our customers had to say:

> "I really enjoy reading your marketing newsletter. It is the best resource available. Keep up the good work." - J.Y. Hampton VA

> "Here's my cheque for the renewal of my subscription to the Video Marketing Letter. I value your tips highly." - D.S. Hope, London

> "Superb! Literally hundreds of ideas which will make or save me more than 10 times the cost of the seminar!" - G. Thomas Atlanta GA

Quotes and research

Statements such as "Dr Brown, professor at the London University, recently tested XYZ and his tests concluded that the XYZ was one of the best ways to..."

or

"A recent article in the Wall Street Journal claimed that over 54% of people are terrified of speaking in public."

Obviously research and quotes have to be true and do

need to originate from the source you say they do.

Free gifts, bonuses and discounts for prompt action

People like to get something for nothing, remember in my magic advertising words, FREE was one of the best words. Offering an extra bonus such as a video tape or report etc. can clinch the deal. If you remember the investment newsletter that we mentioned earlier with the headline "Your shares in British Telecom, should you buy more, sell or hold them?" Well the free bonus with that was a special report on British Telecom shares, which was a very powerful premium and I'm sure that many people bought the newsletter just to get the report!

The aim of the premium (bonus) is to give something that the reader thinks is very expensive, yet costs you very little. One of my concepts was the FREE cellular phone which became a very powerful premium, yet only cost a few pounds.

A discount or extra premium for prompt action

The aim of our salesletter is to make the reader act immediately, we need to create some urgency and we want the reader's order now, not in 12 month's time, therefore we need to politely ask the reader to send his money now. It's amazing how many companies don't offer any incentives to the reader to act immediately. I use words to the effect of:

> Act today and you will qualify for an extra free gift.
> If you act promptly and submit your order to us
> before 1st August XXXX, we will also include an
> extra bonus as a special thank you for acting
> promptly.

Price

A lot of people ask me when they should spill the beans and

reveal the price, in most cases leave it until the end, by then you will have stated your case to the reader, who really is the JUDGE and they will have read everything you've had to say and if you've made your case strong enough, the price will be insignificant. I have occasionally used the price in the headline, for example, "Now for only £5 a week you can own..."

P.S.

A few people have asked me if I use a P.S. because I have forgotten something, I don't think so! The P.S. that I and many other successful direct mailers use is very deliberate, in fact now I never send any salesletters without a P.S. and in many cases I have a P.P.S.

I don't know why, but people always take note of a P.S. and that's all you should know. Use a P.S. to summarise your offer and state the strongest benefits, a P.S. is really like a headline, but at the end of the letter. For example:

> **P.S.** Don't forget that if you order today you will receive the full "How to breed goldfish course," the free ????, and the special bonus ???, not for the normal price of £50.00 but for the special price of only £17.77.

or

> **P.S.** Act today because you really can't afford to waste another day without the XYZ. Don't forget with our FULL MONEY BACK GUARANTEE, you have nothing to lose and everything to gain.

Signature

Never send a letter without a signature, I have signed mailings up to 5,000 by hand, it's a pain but it's worth it. Use blue ink and if you can use an ink pen to give a thicker look to your signature, this is very impressive and gives the ultimate personal look.

For larger mailings your printer will have to print your

signature and although it won't look as good as the real thing, as long as they use a good blue ink, the match will be acceptable. You can now get your signature made into a rubber stamp.

Brochures

For many products and services a good salesletter alone will not be enough and you will need a sales brochure. Before I go any further, never mail out just a sales brochure on its own, without a letter it doesn't work. I've found the best combination is a good salesletter and a fairly brief brochure.

A brochure should be designed to look interesting and be informative, but at the same time you must remember that its purpose is to sell the product or service.

A good brochure should be a joy to read, look good and ultimately help to finish your sale. Remember to think of the customer first in the brochure, list all the benefits to the reader and keep technical terms down to a minimum, if you must have a technical specification page, then put it at the back somewhere.

A good brochure should be well planned and needs to hold the reader's attention. Start the brochure with an introduction, then go on to the main benefits and then close the brochure with a strong summary.

> **Tip:** It's a good idea to have a quote or an important statement towards the bottom of the page such as, "I've never used an easier car polish," Bill Green, Texas or "A lifetime guarantee comes as standard when you buy an ABC."

Another tip is to have a phone number and fax number at the bottom of each page.

The order form

The order form, tends to be the most underrated part of the direct mail package, yet it is crucial to your success, if no one fills in the order form then you are finished!

Whenever I design an order form I try to make it as easy as possible for the customer to complete. I leave lots of space and I try to use tick boxes rather than make the client have to write something. If an order form is difficult to fill in, then the prospective client may give up or put the form to one side.

On many of my mailings I already fill in as much as I can on the order form such as, their name, address and account number, I would then add "If the details shown are incorrect, then please amend accordingly." (See sample order form.)

The other thing I always do is to summarise the offer again on the order form. I also try to make the client feel good about making the order, for example:

> Yes, I am ready to make money with the ABC course. Please rush me the course at the special reduced introductory price of £29.77. I understand that if I am not 100% satisfied with the course I can return it for a refund. Please also send me my FREE BONUS.

> I enclose my Cheque, Postal Order, Draft made payable to "ABC" for £29.77, alternatively please debit my credit card as below.

You should also state the expiry date of the offer, which can be stamped on the order form, for example: This order must be received at our office no later than Friday 26th July 1999.

A catalogue type order form

If you are selling more than one product then you will not know the total price, but you can still state your offer and your guarantee. On an order form I always like the first item to be listed as FREE. For example, say the free gift is a Rolex watch, then the order form would look like:

1 Gold Rolex Watch = FREE

Sample order form/coupon

This form is the type used when you have a fixed price and product.

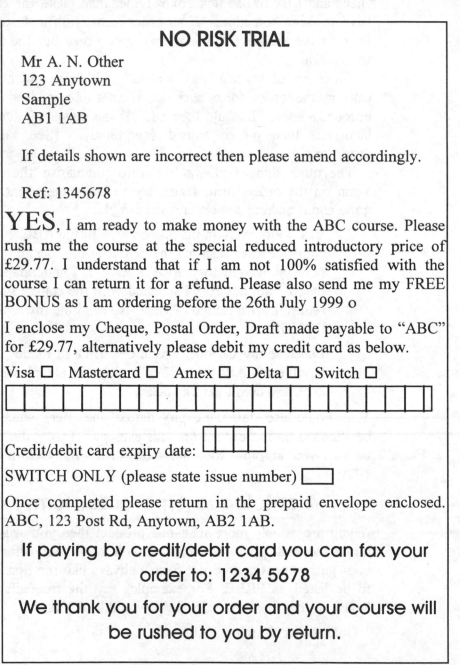

NO RISK TRIAL

Mr A. N. Other
123 Anytown
Sample
AB1 1AB

If details shown are incorrect then please amend accordingly.

Ref: 1345678

YES, I am ready to make money with the ABC course. Please rush me the course at the special reduced introductory price of £29.77. I understand that if I am not 100% satisfied with the course I can return it for a refund. Please also send me my FREE BONUS as I am ordering before the 26th July 1999 o

I enclose my Cheque, Postal Order, Draft made payable to "ABC" for £29.77, alternatively please debit my credit card as below.

Visa ☐   Mastercard ☐   Amex ☐   Delta ☐   Switch ☐

Credit/debit card expiry date:

SWITCH ONLY (please state issue number) ☐

Once completed please return in the prepaid envelope enclosed. ABC, 123 Post Rd, Anytown, AB2 1AB.

If paying by credit/debit card you can fax your order to: 1234 5678

We thank you for your order and your course will be rushed to you by return.

Sample order form/coupon

This form is the type used when you have more than one product such as a catalogue, where you do not know what the total order will be.

The MOTHER of ALL OFFERS?????

We put together a package of everything you'll need to get your video production business off the ground. We call it the 'Mother of all Offers' because it includes everything but the kitchen sink . . . This is what you get:

- ☐ Desktop Video for Profit video tape – *(see description on page 3)*
- ☐ Desktop Video & the Amiga video tape – *(see description on page 4)*
- ☐ Setting Up a Low Budget Video Studio video tape – *(see description on page 4)*
- ☐ Advanced Guide to Guerilla Video video tape
- ☐ Three years of The Video Marketing Letter Back Issues *(over 300 pages on how to make money as an independent video producer)*
- ☐ Plus, a one year subscription to The Video Marketing Letter

This is over $400 worth of goodies, but in our 'Mother' offer, you get it all for $189!!! And it doesn't stop there either. With the 'Mother' offer you also get Free use of our Video Technical Hotline, and opportunities to discuss your video needs with our studio professionals. What a deal!

#GM119 The MOTHER of ALL OFFERS..............................$189

ORDER FORM

Name: _____

Street: _____

City: _____

State: _____ Zip _____

Daytime Phone#: _____

For Even Quicker Service Call in Your Order!

1-501-321-1845
1-800-247-5188 (24 Hrs)

Item #	Qty	Item Description	Price	Total
GM900	1	Guerilla Video Hour	FREE!	

My check or MO is enclosed for $_____
Make checks payable to Group M Inc.
(COD orders must be placed by phone)

Subtotal	
S&H	$4.00
TOTAL	

Card No. ☐☐☐☐☐☐☐☐☐☐☐☐☐☐☐☐   Exp.Date ☐☐☐☐

Please Sign _____

Group M Productions 321 Ouachita Ave. Hot Springs, AR 71901

TIP: More and more people have access to fax machines these days, so make sure that you encourage orders to be faxed to you if payment is made by Credit/Debit cards.

Thank the customer

Make sure you have something like "Thank you for your order," or "We appreciate your business and we will dispatch your order as soon as possible." Customers like to think that they are smart and they are doing the right thing by dealing with you and thanking them is a good way to reassure them.

How to judge if your order form is any good

Once you have produced your order form, print one out and take a good look at it and imagine that you are the customer, does it look easy to fill in and does it inspire confidence?

Another way is to test the form yourself, give yourself a maximum of 2 minutes to fill in the order form, if you find it difficult, then the chances are that your customers will as well.

Money back guarantee

To be taken seriously in direct mail today, you must offer a money back guarantee, you could hold back the postage and packaging charge, but most companies give a full money back guarantee. Most people work on a 30 day money back guarantee, some companies offer up to 12 months, it all depends on your product.

A money back guarantee inspires confidence in your company and helps to take the risk out of buying. As long as your product is good and you ship it correctly and on time, you shouldn't get more than 1 to 2% back, which you can live with. In most cases you can sell the returns on again.

Note: Take care on packing your goods, use padded

envelopes, packing material etc. and although it costs a bit extra and takes a little time, it's worth it, there is nothing worse than customers screaming on the phone that the goods have arrived in a damaged state. If you are shipping goods overseas, then make sure that you pack with even more care.

Prepaid envelopes

Never expect a customer to find an envelope, a stamp and then write your address out, it's too hard. Always enclose a reply paid envelope, which is printed with your address on and no stamp is required. The extra cost is worth it.

Note: Occasionally a prepaid envelope may be missed out or lost by the potential client, so make sure that you have your address printed on the order form as a back up.

Your questions answered sheet

This is probably one of the best things that you can add to a direct mail package. In my various direct mail businesses I would listen to what people were asking and from these questions, together with other questions I imagined the customers would want to know, I would produce a question and answer sheet, for example:

Q. Can I work from Home?

A. Yes, many people started or still work from home.

Q. What happens if I need help?

A. Once you join you will be given a special telephone number which is manned from 8.30am - 6.30pm weekdays and 8.30am - 1.00pm Saturdays. We will answer your questions immediately or come back to you within a few minutes.

Many of the questions would have already been previously answered in your brochure, however, stating them again in this format helps.

Note: The aim of your salesletter and brochure is to sell to the customer from start to finish. I have sold to thousands of people without them ever even calling my office, and that is your aim, the last thing you want is thousands of people on the phone with long lists of questions, if you're getting that then you're brochure/salesletter is letting you down.

Pulling rabbits out of a hat

Here I will explain some extra tricks which can be used to increase your hit rate and your profits.

Attach a post-it note to the letter

Now if you're mailing out thousands of letters you will not want to hand write each note, but there are now companies that will print on a post-it note for you. I would suggest that you hand write the note and then get it printed in a good blue ink, so that it looks hand written.

What to say on the note:

"Take action today, you won't regret it!"

"You will be delighted with the results from XYZ, I guarantee it!"

"This is the best offer that I have ever made, don't let it pass you by!"

Use a lift-letter

This is where you include a short letter in addition to your primary letter in a direct mailing. The aim of the lift letter is to give a second opinion or a different opinion. It should be written in a different style to the main letter and preferably signed or endorsed by someone else, other than the main letter writer.

The lift letter should have a handwritten look to it or as if it's been written on an old typewriter. The letter should also be put in a separate small envelope with words printed on the front such as:

"Looking for another professional's opinion?"

"Still not convinced? Then open this envelope!"

"Are you sceptical? Open this envelope for more proof!

The letter should go along the lines of a testimonial or endorsement such as:

"I've been using XYZ for 10 years now and I can remember being wary about the claims that were made, but I can truly say that it has been the best..."

How to make the customer buy more than they planned

This technique is ideal if you are mailing out a catalogue of products which are all related. Let's say that we are mailing out a catalogue of "how to videos," the prospective client has gone through the catalogue and maybe seen a few videos that he likes and one or two others that he definitely likes, now right at the end try a "Mother of all offers," this is where you state that the client can have one of everything in the catalogue for a special price. Believe me, even if you have to cut your margins a little, it's worth having an offer like this.

Buy 2 get 1 free

This is very successful in retail stores at the moment and can work very well in mail-order as well. Another good idea is to have on your order form something like "Buy a second XYZ for a friend or a member of your family for only £??" and offer them a good price.

Response rates and testing

Let's talk about the bottom line, which is money. If you follow everything I have told you up till now, you will have a winning salesletter and as long as you are mailing out to a good list, then you are going to make money. Now it's impossible for me to tell you how much, you will only find this out once you have sent out your initial test mailing, which should be around 2,000 pieces. Now many people like to talk about what percentage response they get i.e. 1%, 3% or 10%, I never really look at percentages, all I care about is CASH!

It's the cash that counts, response rates are for vanity, cash is for sanity!

I've had projects that have only brought in 0.5% response, yet they made thousands of pounds because the profit margin was very high. My minimum aim is to double my money in direct mail and in almost all my projects I have done this, if not more.

For example: Let's say that I am mailing out 1,000 letters, the cost to print and stamps etc. is £400. I am selling a product for £60 which makes me £40 clear profit each time, all I need is a 2.5% response and I've brought in over £800, which is double my investment. I don't count the 0.5% as this covers the costs and shipping the product etc.

Costing out a project

I use a simple spreadsheet program for costing out my direct mail, this way I can see within minutes if a project is viable, what my break even point is and so on. The printout shows what to include in your costs, basically your printing, stamps and envelopes etc.

If anyone wants a copy of the program that I use, then drop me a line and I'll send you a copy, you just pay for the handling and postage which is £7. The program is really simple and runs on any IBM computer with MS-DOS, the program is about 10 years old, but it's so simple why use anything else? I've sent thousands of these disks out and everyone agrees that it's so simple to use.

Notice how hard it is to make money by selling products at £20, yet when you make £60 or £100 per sale, your break even point is much lower.

Sample Direct Mail Marketing Evaluation

CREATIVE COSTS

Copywriting Fee	0.00
Other Creative Costs	0.00
TOTAL CREATIVE COSTS	**0.00**

VARIABLE COSTS

Names (per 1000)	85.00
Postage (per 1000)	198.00
Printing (per 1000)	152.64
Envelopes (per 1000)	24.00
Labour (per 1000)	0.00
Other Costs	0.00
TOTAL VARIABLE COSTS	**459.64**

FULFILMENT COSTS

Product Cost	15.00
Packaging Cost	1.00
Shipping Cost	4.00
Order Taking Costs	0.00
Cost Of Premium	0.55
Other Fulfilment Costs	0.00
TOTAL FULFILLMENT COSTS	**20.55**

PRODUCT PRICE   **89.95**

(Note: Test several product prices to determine optimum proft.)

Continued......

PERFORMANCE ANALYSIS

Cost per piece to mail	0.45
Total Number of letters mailed	1,000
Sales needed to break even	**6.62 0.66%**
Profit on 3% Response	1622.36
Profit on 5% Response	3010.36

Notes:

a) Ideally, it is better to test a minimum of 3,000 names.

b) The selection of the right mailing list is crucial for a valid test result.

c) Notice the low break even figure, this is what you should always be aiming for.

You can cost out your direct mail projects with pen and paper, but it's much easier to use a computer and spreadsheet program. If you would like a copy of this spreadsheet on 3.5" disk which works on any IBM compatible PC with DOS, then drop me a line.

How using a salesletter and a winning direct mail offer can turn a few hundred pounds into over 1 million!

First of all, the technique that I will explain here has nothing to do with multilevel marketing, chain letters or any other scams. The method I will disclose to you is totally legal and is just simple mathematics. This is the first time that I have put this in writing, but I and many others have done it in reality. I was reluctant to give out this secret in this book, but in the end I thought what the heck, I always try to give people much more value than what they paid for or expected.

So here we go, using the techniques that we have discussed in this section we can safely say that you can produce a good salesletter and offer, which brings in £100 profit for every £250 you invest, remember that many products will bring in far more, but let's stay with this figure as it makes the maths simple, watch how by investing the profits what happens:

Table assuming only a 40% profit

Time	Starting Capital	Net Profit
1st time	£250	100 (+350)
2nd	£ 350	140(+490)
3rd	£490	196(+686)
4th	£686	274 (+960)
5th	£960	384 (+1,344)
6th	£1,344	538 (+1,882)
7th	£1,882	753 (+2,635)
8th	£2,635	1,054 (+3,689)
9th	£3,689	1,476 (+5,165)
10th	£5,165	2,066 (+7,231)
11th	£7,231	2,892 (+10,123)
12th	£10,123	4,049 (+14,172)
13th	£14,172	5,669(+19,841)

14th	£19,841	7,936 (+27,777)
15th	£27,777	11,111(+38,888)
16th	£38,888	15,555(+54,443)
17th	£54,443	21,777(+76,220)
18th	£76,220	30,488(+106,708)
19th	£106,708	42,683(+149,391)
20th	£149,391	59,756 (+209,147)
21st	£209,147	83,659 (+292,806)
22nd	£292,806	117,122(+409,928)
23rd	£409,928	163,971 (+573,899)
24th	£573,899	229,560 (+803,459)
25th	£803,459	321,384
=	**1,124,843**	

And that's how simple it is, the power of direct mail can turn small profit margins into big results. Now let's answer some possible questions that you may have about this multiplying system:

Firstly, I've used a small starting figure of £250, if you start with £500 then of course you will achieve 1 million much quicker. Secondly, I've been realistic and I have used a figure of 1 million, this is because if you carried on forever there will come a time when you're mailings are so large that you would be mailing the whole world! What I suggest you do if you need to earn more is to find another product that makes the same return and start again. Thirdly, in the real world the maths will not be as precise as the table, but the end results will be the same or very similar, so on one mailing you'll get a bit more and on another you'll get less. This technique also works very well in the stock market and trading. Buy one company, sell it, plough profits in to another and so on.

How the same principles work in advertising

On a recent trip to America I saw someone who claims that he went from nothing to a millionaire, by using the same concept of multiplying, but he did it with classified adverts.

His system was to book a small advert, selling products that would net him around US$40 from one advert, which is very realistic. He would then repeat the same advert in over 200 newspapers throughout the USA, working on US$40 X 200 that's US$8,000 a week. He would run 2 or 3 different adverts selling different products, normally information type products. You can now see how lots of small adverts, which don't make that much money on their own, can make a big profit when added together.

I will shortly be testing something in the U.K. along these lines, mainly in magazines and anyone else could do the same.

Why you should go back for a 2nd, 3rd or even 4th try

Let's say that you've sent out a mailing of 1,000 letters, and 50 people buy, which is a very realistic figure of 5% response. Now it makes sense to re-mail the 950 people that didn't buy, as the chances are that a second letter will normally result in at least another 25 to 30 buyers out of the 950.

You see, even with the best letter you will have people that are undecided or need a reminder to make them act. I also found that a follow up letter was essential because some potential customers would say that they had never received the first letter.

How to re-mail

1st Reminder

The best thing is to use the same letter as the first letter and add on "SECOND NOTICE" or "URGENT REMINDER," you could also print "COPY" on the letter in the background.

You should also send a new covering letter, I would start with "Perhaps you misplaced my last letter as I have not heard from you, therefore I am enclosing another copy."

2nd Reminder

Depending on your product you could go straight to this stage, which is the "Last Chance/Reduced Offer" letter. Here you should explain that you have not heard from them and you would like to give them a last chance to order and as an incentive, you reduce the price slightly or you could offer them an extra special bonus. If you are selling an expensive item, you could allow the potential customer to spread the payment over 2 or 3 instalments.

A note on re-mailing rented lists

If you have rented a list of say business opportunity seekers, the chances are that they were for one time use only, therefore you must go back to the list broker/owner and negotiate a deal with them to re-mail the names. Most lists can be rented out at normally half the price you paid for the first time mailing. Of course, if it's your own list i.e. people that have phoned you in reply to your advert or names that you have compiled, then of course you can re-mail them as many times as you like.

How many times should you re-mail?

The simple answer to this is, until it is no longer profitable, some companies mail out 4 or 5 times and can still make it pay.

Getting ideas from other direct mail users

I suggest that you start keeping every single piece of direct mail that you receive, try and get on as many mailing lists as you can, I would also suggest that you ask your friends and family to keep their unwanted direct mail and pass it on to you.

It is always good to see how other companies put together a direct mail piece, look at what you think they have done wrong and make sure that you're not doing the same. You can also pick up on any good points and incorporate them into your salesletter. Try to get on the mailing lists of registered charities, Reader's Digest, Linguaphone language courses, companies selling magazine/newsletter subscriptions and any other company that is an effective user of direct mail. Take notice of how they write to you on the 1st, 2nd and 3rd time.

Summary

Everyone reading this should use direct mail in some shape or form. Even if you are not selling a direct product, you should still use direct mail. For example, if you are an advertising agency, recruitment agency or a fashion consultant etc., then direct mail should be used to get appointments and build up your relationship with new clients. If done correctly as previously outlined, then it will be a very cost effective way for you to sell your product or service.

> NOTE: Don't mistake direct mail with leaflets or door to door distribution, I've found that leaflets are not a particularly cost effective form of marketing and they are too much like "shot gun" marketing for my liking.

Testing is the key

I've already mentioned that you need to test your mailing piece first, normally to around 2,000 people. Testing allows you to get a feel for the offer, you will find out what people are phoning you to ask, why they are buying and what they don't like etc. It is through testing that you can develop things like the question and answer sheet previously mentioned. If your mailing piece works on 2,000, then you can start mailing out to larger numbers.

What you need to know about the Post Office

If you are going to be in the direct mail/mail-order business, then the post office is going to be an important part of your business, even if you are using a private courier to ship your goods, you will still be using the post office to send out your mailings and responses to enquiries etc.

The first thing to remember is that the post office needs people like us, it's the businesses that keep them going, not granny buying 2 second class stamps! I suggest you make contact with your local sales manager and tell them that you're going into the mail-order business and you would like to build up a good business relationship.

The Post Office can help you in the following ways:

1. Freepost and Business Reply. The Royal Mail have a free pack on this, which will answer all your questions.

2. Postal collections. If you are mailing out 2,000 letters you don't want to have to take them to the post office, let the post office come to you! The post office will send a van round to pick up your mail, this is a free service if you are mailing large amounts, you can either have a daily collection or you can have a collection as and when you call them.

3. Special promotions. The post office want you to succeed and have special promotions from time to time. I while back there was a promotion where you could mail 1,000 letters for the price of 800.

4. Packet Post and other special pricing arrangements. If you are a big mailer of letters or small packets over 60 grams, you could apply for Packet Post, this is where you pay per gram and not by price bands as consumers do.

As your company grows your needs will change and different post office services will apply.

Using a courier

Depending on the weight of your product, you will probably want to use a reliable national and international courier. A good courier is an extension to your business and gives a great image, imagine your parcel being delivered in a shiny great image, imagine your parcel being delivered in a shiny van by a uniformed courier, it gives a great impression to your customer.

It is also important to use a reliable courier who will deliver your goods in good condition and on time. Remember, if you make a promise of 48hrs delivery and the parcel doesn't arrive, it's YOU the customer screams at, not the courier.

When should you post your direct mail out?

I have always tried to aim for my direct mail to arrive on the potential customer's doorstep on a Saturday. This means mailing out late on a Thursday/Friday for First Class mail and Wednesday for Second Class.

For mailings that are mainly business addresses, then aim for the mail to arrive midweek, as most businesses are not there on a Saturday and that means your mail will be opened on a Monday, which is the worst day.

For households, mail that arrives on a Saturday stands more of a chance of being read, as most people still have Saturdays off and they have more time to relax and read their post. If your salesletter arrives on a Monday morning the chances are that the potential customer is harassed and the mail could end up in the bin or put to one side.

Note: If someone has requested your information from an advert, then send the information out and reply as soon as possible, regardless of the day, it is very impressive when you phone up for information and it's on your doorstep the next morning. Many people have commented on how efficient my company is and how impressed they are when they receive the information by return.

How to address your letter properly

If you are advertising and people are phoning in or writing in for information, it can sometimes be hard to take down the right address, however, there is a computer program which can really help with this called QuickAddress. This program has all of the addresses in the U.K. stored in it, and all you do is simply type in the post-code.

For example, John Smith phones up for some information, you type in his name and the next thing you ask him for is his post-code, you then type this in and up pops the full address, all you need is the house number or house name.

You've no doubt experienced this when dealing with large organisations and until recently this type of software was very expensive, however, now you can get this facility from as little as £99.

If you would like a free demo disk and further details, write to QAS Systems Ltd, 7 Old Town, London, SW4 0JT.

☺

Teacher: If you found a five-pound note in one pocket and a pound coin in another pocket, what would you have?

Child: I would have someone else's coat!

CHAPTER 23

Press releases

Press releases are a very effective form of marketing which most businesses totally ignore. Writing a good press release/article and sending it to the right people is usually the quickest and least expensive way for any business to generate a lot of new customers and orders. Yet the majority of businesses don't write or make available to newspapers, magazines or newspaper editors a single press release.

What many people don't realise is that many magazines and newsletters depend on press releases to fill their pages.

What is a press release?

A press release is an announcement or story that you write about your company, or a product that you believe is news worthy. Your aim is to get the editor to either print the press release word for word, which does happen in many cases, or for the editor to write a piece based on your press release.

The key is to provide some informative information for the reader and at the same time to plug your product and give out a contact number and/or address.

Another way to get free publicity is to write an article about a subject which you know about and that there is an interest for. The topic should be related to the product you are selling for instance, I have written articles relating to topics in this book and at the end of the article you would plug yourself, for example: Vince Stanzione is the author of "How to stop existing and start living," published by First Success Publishing, to find out more about his book Telephone or write to...

> **TIP:** When you write a press release it should be written as though a journalist has written it from their point of view. For example, you would not say, "I am the Director of ABC Computers and I would like to announce that I have invented a new laser printer," you would say, "Fred Smith, the Director of ABC Computers has invented a new laser printer."

If you need help writing a press release you could consult a P.R. consultant/agency, or you could contact a journalist from a local newspaper who could write the press release for you. Most journalists are underpaid and are always looking for some free-lance work.

A good format for a press release should answer:

> **Who** - Fred Bloggs, ABC PLC, the B&B Partnership
>
> **Where** - London, New York, Bristol
>
> **What** - New Car, Computer, Travel Service
>
> **Why** - To help small businesses, to save energy
>
> **When** - Now, open on 1st January 2000
>
> **How** - Details on how to get more information, the stores selling the product

A guide to getting a press release/ article printed

1. Identify magazines, newsletters and newspapers whose readers are specifically interested in your product or service.

You can look through BRAD for the names and addresses of magazines and newspapers.

2. Once you've identified a particular magazine or newsletter that reaches your audience, call and get a sample copy of the publication.

3. Write your press release/article in a similar style to the articles that are currently running. For instance, you could copy their typesetting style, the size of their headlines and columns etc.

4. Proof read your press release.

5. Print the press release out on your laser printer and attach a high quality black and white photo of your product, if applicable. Write a short covering letter and send it to the editor of the publication.

Tips:

> **1.** Whenever you send a press release, always call the magazine first and identify, and get the proper spelling of the name of the person the press release/article should be sent to.
>
> **2.** If you are promoting a product i.e. a book or video, then tell the editor that "A review copy is available."
>
> **3.** Send the press release in a good envelope and do not fold the press release, you could also use some cardboard to keep it from being bent.
>
> **4.** Many editors will give you a call before printing your press release to ask you a few questions, so be ready to answer them in a polite and efficient manner. (Have a copy of the press release handy.) Some time ago I was telephoned by an editor of a national newspaper and because of my enthusiasm and politeness, she wrote a great half page write up on me.

You'll see a few samples of press releases which will

give you an idea of what they look like. One is a traditional press release and one is a typeset article.

Summary

Everyone can use a press release, whether it's a new product, a book or you are a consultant providing a service, you can plug yourself for FREE by using a press release.

NOTE: I've concentrated on newspapers here, but press releases can also be sent to radio or TV stations and now internet sites. Many authors have their books featured on the radio and TV, and many radio stations will ask you to go in for a live on air chat about your product or book. This is great FREE advertising.

Whatever service or product you are offering, I urge you to use press releases. I've listed a good book on the subject called "Be your own PR MAN," in the reference section and I suggest you either buy a copy or take this book out from the library. This book also has excellent tips on public speaking, holding a press conference and dealing with radio and television interviews.

☺

Two lions were walking down the supermarket aisle doing their weekly shopping, one lion said to the other, "It's quiet in here for a Saturday!"

Press release typeset to look like a magazine article

Photo Shown Here

Bill Myers has put together his own 'Desktop Video' production studio so that he can produce what he calls 'Guerilla' video from his home in Hot Springs, Arkansas.

Guerilla Video from Arkansas?

By Jojo Gann
'On Assignment' Business Writer

Hot Springs, Arkansas - The Guerilla Video Network is not a reality yet, but if Bill Myers has his way, it may be sooner than you think. Myers, an Arkansas businessman, says people are fed up with American network TV. "It seems the networks try to create programming that appeals to the lowest elements of our society. Which means most of middle America has to stoop to their level of entertainment or do without."

His concept is 'guerilla' video. Videos and TV programming produced by the people and for the people. Programming that could be created by anybody, and made available to those that wanted it via satellite or videocassettes. Programming produced in the home video studio.

Of course there was the problem of technology. Myers lives in the backwoods of Arkansas, a long way from the nearest TV studio. And Myers had no experience with TV production, other than "30 years as a viewer", as he tells it. And a modern TV studio can be very expensive to put together, even if one knows what he is doing.

But Myers, who has a background in computers, felt sure that somehow a personal computer could be used to create the graphics and animation necessary for modern videos, and this could be

combined with video footage shot and edited with camcorders and VCRs.

A Desktop Video Solution

After six months of research, Myers discovered ways to tackle broadcast quality video productions in a studio that cost him less than $5,000 to set up. About half the cost was for the computer, the rest was for the camera, VCR, lights and studio props. "The key to my success was that the technology I needed just happened to be available at the right time. The most important device, the genlock for the computer, just hit the market a few months ago."

With his desktop video studio up and running, Myers has found he can produce animation, graphics and special effects that rival those of the major networks at a fraction of the cost in time and equipment. Since putting together his studio, Myers has produced 11 different video documentaries and 'how-to' tapes that are targeted for "the Americans that Hollywood forgot." Those who have above average intelligence and want to do more with their lives than just watch TV."

Myers said he feels that this new technology will open doors for people who have found they couldn't get their ideas aired on mainstream TV. "People are interested in this technology. They know how powerful TV can be, and people see desktop video as an opportunity to change the world, or at least let

the world know how they feel. Anybody with their own desktop video system can put together a quality video production in a few hours with the cost limited to personal time and the blank tape."

Call Them 'Guerilla' Videos

Myers says he isn't trying to compete with Hollywood. His videos, and others like them, are for people fed up with the plastic images produced by Hollywood. "We don't use actors. We use real people and that's a major difference most people see right away. Viewers of guerilla video are people they can relate to, people like themselves, not fancy pants Hollywood actors."

While most guerilla video productions are not broadcast quality, most are well received by their audiences. Because the major studios have such tremendous overhead when undertaking any project, they can't touch the subjects that are available on guerilla videos. And this is the key to their success.

The TV Revolution Has Finally Reached The People

Many people are discovering that grass roots videos from real people have become a way to reach out and affect other people's lives with information not available in the mainstream media. Myers has found that his own guerilla videos on subjects such as pirate TV and desktop video technology have been very well accepted. "We've gotten hundreds of letters thanking us for making this information available."

One thing is certain. People are beginning to use some of the latest communications technology, including satellite transmission, to create alternate programming. Guerilla productions are showing up in the form of documentaries, news broadcasts and even satellite delivered home shopping shows, and maybe someday the Guerilla Video Network will be a reality.

Bill Myers is the editor of The Video Marketing Letter and the founder of Group M Video, which markets several videos on how to set up your own desktop video system. Group M also offers a free desktop video hotline to help other people using this technology. For additional information or to order tapes on desktop video technology call 1-501-321-1845 or write Group M at 100 Bridge St. #27, Hot Springs, AR 71901.

Traditional press release

Loose inserts

I have used loose inserts very successfully, mainly in other people's newsletters. A loose insert is a leaflet or small brochure that is inserted with another product, such as a bank/credit card statement or a newsletter. In my case I carried my loose inserts in various financial and business newsletters. The advantages of a loose insert are the speed and the cost.

For example, I could have my loose insert put in with 50,000 newsletters for far less than actually posting out a salesletter to 50,000 people.

On the whole I would not sell directly from a loose insert, I would just give an overview and offer a free information pack by phoning in or returning the coupon.

How to circulate your loose insert

Firstly you write, design and print your insert and then you send it to the newsletter's mailing house, they then put your insert in with the rest of the mailing.

Most list brokers can help you with loose inserts and you can also contact the publication directly. The typical costs for a loose insert are around £50 to £60 per thousand.

CHAPTER 24

Back-end selling & good business practices

Let me make an important statement to you "A one off sale will make you some money, however, a lifetime customer will make you very rich!"

Here's the mistake that many businesses make, both large and small:

Joe Smith buys a book, video tape or fishing rod from a company via mail-order, most companies fulfil that order and then that's it, they forget about the customer, BIG MISTAKE!

You see, the chances are that as long as you have supplied a good product and you fulfilled Joe Smith's order promptly, he will be happy with your company and in most cases would be happy to spend money with you again and again. In fact you have now overcome the resistance of the first sale, he trusts you because you have previously delivered goods or a service to him.

How to correctly back-end sell

When you ship the client's first order, send a letter thanking him for his order and enclose a catalogue or details of another product that you think he will be interested in. I would also suggest that you send him a special discount voucher if he orders from you again in the next 21 days.

If you don't hear from him for awhile, then send another letter stating that "You recently ordered the XYZ video from us and I would like to tell you about our new ZZZ video."

And this is how you keep in contact with customers, alternatively you could offer a newsletter, as we have previously mentioned.

Some customers will buy everything that you send them details of, in a previous business I have mailed 20 to 30 different product offers out to the same customer and they have bought everything, in fact it got to the point where I just couldn't find anything else to sell them! Now imagine if I had just mailed out that client's first order and then forgotten about them.

Don't wait until the golden goose has died before you find another one!

Let's say that you have either developed or found a great mail-order product, the orders are pouring in, everything's on the up and up and things are going great. Now most products don't sell forever, trends change, a competitor may start price cutting etc. and before you know it, the Golden Goose is laying less eggs! The key is to have another product/service ready to roll out, it's rare that you will be able to sell the same product or service forever. As previously mentioned, you will need back-end products to make real money.

I do however, want to warn you about a mistake that I have made in the past and that is dropping a product or pulling out of a business too early. It is important to let the winning products keep going until they start to become economically un-viable, but make sure that you have something else up your sleeve or you have planned for a slow down.

Resting a product

If you have constantly been advertising a product, it can sometimes pay to put that project aside for awhile and then bring it back again, film makers do this, recently the Star Wars film has been brought back again and has been very successful all over again. Pop groups also do this, they go away for a a year or two and then they come back with a new record or a greatest hits compilation.

Learn to watch trends

However big or busy you become, never allow yourself to get out of touch with what's going on, both in your industry, with technology and any other up and coming businesses. You need to know what's going on in the world, what people are thinking, what they are buying and what they are concerned about etc.

It is pointless burying your head in the sand when it comes to changes and new developments, you need to be ready to ride the wave of any new trend, because if you simply ignore it, the chances are you'll get washed up!

I have always liked to keep up to date with technology and the latest trends, and although it is impossible to know about every new product that comes on the market, you do need to have a good general overview.

Thanks to watching trends and taking advantage of new changes I have benefited greatly, some of the trends include:

> **1.** I have made a great deal of money in the cellular phone industry, thanks to watching the trends. I was also the first person to realise that a cellular phone could be given away free and you would still make a profit.
>
> **2.** I made extra income by using a premium rate number (0898, 1-900) in one of my businesses, it was great, people were paying me money to listen to my sales message.
>
> **3.** I made money in the CD-ROM industry, both

directly and by investing in other companies.

4. Because of finding out about software like QuickAddress as previously mentioned, I have managed to make my life easier and key data into the computer with better accuracy.

Who knows how much I will gain in the future from new technology and trend watching, as I write I am watching some new trends on the internet very carefully.

Now many of you might say "You're lucky, you always seem to be in the right place at the right time," that is total rubbish! I am certainly no luckier than anyone else and the only reason that I am in the right place at the right time, is because I made sure that I was there! By watching trends I position myself in the right place, you can and you should do exactly the same and then no doubt people will say to you that you are lucky and you're in the right place at the right time, but we know differently, don't we!

The dangers of having too much money

If you're starting out with plenty of money to invest, you'd better watch out! Having too much money to begin with in business is worse than having a limited starting budget. Let me explain:

Many big companies and government bodies throw money at problems, rather than finding an intelligent and non-costly way to avoid the problem in the first place.

Large amounts of start-up capital make you lazy, complacent and comfortable. I started out with very little capital and many other successful mail-order millionaires also started out with tiny amounts. This is the best way to start any business. Not having much money to spend will force you to investigate and research all the possibilities, before you let go of that limited cash.

Even if you do have a substantial amount of start-up capital, put it away where you can't get to it and force yourself to work within a tight budget, where every penny is crucial. You will make fewer mistakes by working like this than if you had an unlimited budget. Take for example advertising agencies and their so called wonderful adverts that they produce and place for big clients, like motor car manufactures. I'm sure you've seen the double page spreads which are a total waste of space. Anyone with half a brain could have produced a better advert in 1/2 a page or less! The reason the agency takes 2 pages is because it's the client's money and they have a big budget. FACT!

If you are starting out with a limited budget or are living in poverty, you should consider yourself lucky! Being poor is perhaps the best motivation for success. You'll have a real reason to make your project work. When you are broke you really don't have anything to lose, but you have everything to gain.

Immigrants are 4 times more likely to become self-made millionaires

I am the son of an immigrant, my father arrived in the U.K. from Italy with a battered up suitcase, a few clothes and a few pounds in his pocket. As if that wasn't bad enough, his two words of English were "Hello" and "Thank you." By working as a hairdresser (his profession) during the day and a waiter during the evening, he saved up enough money to open his first hairdressing salon. After 25 years he recently retired a very rich man and over the years he set up a chain of successful hairdressing salons.

I know that there are thousands of other success stories all over the world and no doubt there are thousands more to come. I recently heard about Sam Yeoung, a young immigrant from China. He started working at McDonalds on minimum wages and within 6 months he was assistant manager, he then became manager and on to district manager. A few months ago he opened his own McDonalds and is now on the way to becoming a millionaire.

Nearly everything can start in a small way

Most people say that they need capital so they can start big and get ahead, well I can tell you from experience that you are better off starting in a small way and building up. Here's a staggering fact, Richard Branson of the Virgin Group owns around 120 different companies including, the airline, the cola and the record stores, but did you know that apart from a few companies, each one was started up from scratch? They never buy an existing big business, they build them up themselves. His airline business was started on a very small budget with a couple of very old leased planes, it was then built up gradually and newer planes and routes were added.

So the next time you think to yourself, if only I had more start-up capital, think again. You must stay **LEAN** and **HUNGRY.**

The Big Boss

Even when you are self-employed you still have a boss, the BIG BOSS is the CUSTOMER.

> **There is only one boss. The customer. And he can fire everybody in the company from the chairman on down, simply by spending his money somewhere else.**
>
> Sam Walton, Walmart
> One of America's most successful retailers

Remember that for most products and services the customer has a choice, no law states that he or she has to spend money with you or your company, it is your job to make the customer want to give their hard earned cash to you.

Too many of the big companies fail to recognise that if enough customers get fed up with their service and decide to stop using them, then it will only be a matter of time before a big company becomes a very small company! As I write there are a few airlines around the world who are upsetting far too many customers and I strongly believe that there is trouble ahead for them.

Sam Walton's Pledge

If you or I went to work in a Walmart store we would be taught this important pledge:

> From this day forward, every customer that comes within ten feet of me, regardless of what I'm doing, in this house, I'm going to look him in the eye, I'm going to smile, I'm going to greet him with a "Good morning" or a "Good afternoon," or a "What can I do for you?" - so help me Sam!

I suggest you copy out a slogan based on Sam Walton's for your business and stick it up on the wall and read it at least once a day.

Don't be an octopus

I already mentioned in the first section about spreading yourself too thinly. Here are my 4 rules to remember when you start making it big:

1. Don't become complacent, that's how market leaders become 2nd, 3rd or even worse.

2. Don't think that you know it all and that you are bullet proof.

3. Don't put it all back in, remember what I said about the slot machines in Las Vegas, lots of people win, but most don't walk out with any money!

4. Don't think that you can do everything, you can't.

I've seen the octopus scenario so many times and I really want you to avoid making the same mistakes. I want you to be ambitious and to work to your full potential, however, I don't want you to become a gambler and be reckless.

You and I are not bullet proof, if your business is a success and there is no reason why not, then of course you may wish to expand and try other businesses etc., however, don't start trying to run 20 companies all at once, it just doesn't work. Now some people may say, "But what about the companies that are conglomerates or people like Richard Branson," well many conglomerates like Hanson Trust have recently demerged, they've gone back to being lots of smaller companies. As for Richard Branson, he mainly works on licensing his brands, for example, Virgin Cola is not made by him, it's made by another company and Virgin just brand the product. I also think that in time Virgin will go the Hanson Trust route and start demerging in the future.

Good ways to expand

Goods ways to expand are with agents, licensing, joint ventures and subcontracting.

Agents

I have recruited many agents both in the U.K. and overseas to sell products for me. It is a great way to have a large sales force with no fixed costs, the agent only makes money when they make a sale, that way I was always delighted to write out big commission cheques, because if the agent was earning, I was earning.

Licensing

Virgin and Disney are very good at this, they allow their name to be used on various products and in turn they get a cut. You can licence or sell the rights to one of your products overseas.

Joint ventures

Sometimes you don't want to take a big risk on your own or you may have expertise in one area, but you are lacking in another, that's where a joint venture can be a good idea, obviously you have to pick your partner carefully.

On a smaller scale I have done deals with "loose competitors," where we have sent out their sales material with our orders and vice versa.

At the moment many companies on the internet offer links/adverts to other web sites and in return they reciprocate.

Subcontracting/using a bureau

When I wanted to start using premium rate telephone numbers, I could have gone out and leased my own lines, set up my own equipment and received a higher percentage per minute, but instead I opted for a bureau. I subleased the line, I used their machines and expertise etc., and yes, I did receive a lower percentage per minute, but I didn't have any start-up costs or long-term contracts.

Sometimes it is better to take a smaller cut and not deal direct, especially if it's a sideline. Using an outside order taking service is also a good example of subcontracting.

Are you ready for success?

Sounds like a crazy question, but most people don't know how to handle success, money and orders. Do you know that many companies go broke after they have received a big order? Well it's true, what usually happens is that they're just not prepared for the order, they have problems funding the stock, getting the staff to make up the orders and source the raw materials. They then can't get the order out on time, they lose the order and the company is left in a mess.

I am a big mail-order gadget buyer, but lately every time I've phoned up for something it has been out of stock, as I write I have been waiting 6 weeks for something, which I ordered from a big company.

Let me give you some more problems that success in business can bring:

Stock problems

There will be times when you just can't meet the demand, in my cellular phone business in the early days, I had terrible stock problems. I had thousands of orders but it was getting harder and harder to source the stock, in some cases I was paying more for the phones than what I was selling them for, just to keep customers happy! Another big problem was installations, you see in those days it was mainly car phones that needed to be fitted and getting people to install them was a nightmare.

My tips on dealing with stock problems are firstly, don't charge the customer's credit card or cash their cheque until you can deliver the stock. Secondly, tell the customer the TRUTH, explain the problem, and what you are doing about it, explain that you really appreciate their business and patience and offer them a gift/small token as a thank you.

Administration

My biggest saviour was that I had set up a simple yet effective computer system (I still use it today), so I had all the details on my computer and within seconds of a call I could tell if the goods had been shipped, where they were shipped to and on what date. Every time a customer called or something happened, a note would be put on the computer, i.e. courier sent goods back.

Bad administration means that you are out of control, if a customer phones you up to place an order or to check up on an order and you can't trace it within 30 seconds, then you're in big trouble.

Good filing

In most businesses even with computers, you will still have some paper records, make sure these are filed away in a good logical order. If you are using a computer, then make sure that you co-ordinate the records on the computer with the paper records, for instance, account number 7450 on the computer should be the same as 7450 in the paper system. Don't let filing mount up, do it the same day as it's easier this way.

Good banking, accounting and security

Whether you are a Sole Trader or a Public Limited Company, you must get into the habit of good banking, accounting and security.

The first rule is to always make sure you deposit your cheques etc. every single day. Some people wait until the end of the week which is stupid, you should get the money into your account as quickly as possible. If you accept credit cards, then make sure that you go through their reconciliation procedure every single business day.

The second rule is accounting, you need to know exactly how much money you have in your bank account, how much is outstanding to you, if applicable, and how much you owe to others. Most people think that accounts, cash books, and projections are not needed, but they are real management tools and they help you to spot problems quickly.

FACT: When I started as a small company you could ask me at any time of the day how much we had in the bank and how much was outstanding in bills, I could tell you down to the penny! Now even when the company became very large and hundreds of thousands of pounds were going through the business, with two bank accounts and a credit card terminal etc., I could still tell you the same, you see it was a habit.

Let me also tell you that not one bank has ever ripped me off, I look at every single entry on a bank statement and every bank charge. Just to let you know, the banks have made plenty of mistakes on my accounts, let me tell you a few so you can watch out for them:

> Cheques being cashed twice. The same cheque number let's say 3456, for £3,900 appeared twice on the bank statements, now if I hadn't spotted it, that would have been a big loss!

> Bank charges. I use a few special services for instance, I always have a weekly bank statement, which you get charged for. I also make various international payments which are charged for and I use electronic banking services which are charged for, watch these charges carefully, look out for duplication and overcharging.

The best way to deal with any bank mistakes is INSTANTLY, not a year later. That's why being on the ball pays and that's why a weekly bank statement is important and I suggest you have one on your business account.

That's one thing I did learn from working for a bank, they are totally unreliable and they will scream and shout when there is a mistake against them, i.e. they get short changed or something is paid a day late, yet if they make a mistake with a customer or another bank, they don't worry too much!

Accounting

I will confess that I don't have the patience to sit there writing up columns etc., that is why I've had a bookkeeper since the day I started in business, however, let me make this clear, I still know what's going on, I still look at those books and if there's something in there which I'm not sure of, I'll query it. You see, employing someone doesn't take the end responsibility away from you.

I make sure that I understand the bookkeeping and accounting procedures, I know the key dates of when taxes should be paid etc. For certain things I will do part of the return and my accountant will finish it off.

A good accountant will help you set up a bookkeeping and accounting system. The key to good accounting is to do it as you go along, not wait until the last minute.

VAT (U.K.) and Sales Tax (USA)

It will be very likely that you will have to register for VAT if you are trading in the U.K. and your turnover (not profit) is going to be over £48,000 (see note) per annum. By registering you will have to add 17.5% (see note) on to the price of your goods, which is then passed on to HM. Customs & Excise normally every quarter, so basically you are collecting taxes on behalf of the government, which isn't really on, but you don't have a choice! The good news about being registered for VAT is that you can claim back the VAT which you pay on legitimate expenses in relation to your business. For example, you can go out and buy a computer for the business, which costs £1,000 + VAT and you will be able to claim back the VAT.

Completing VAT returns can sound daunting, however, as long as you ensure that you keep good up to date records, then you'll find it quite easy after awhile. Your local VAT office will help you and provides information for people who are new to VAT, your accountant will also be able to help you set up either a manual or computerised system for dealing with VAT.

The main thing to remember is that the VAT money is not yours, even though it will be in your bank account for awhile, so if you sell something for £117.50 including VAT, make sure you don't count the £17.50 because it isn't yours.

Note:

This is the current VAT rate for the U.K. but it could change by the time you read this, as could the minimum threshold.

Security

Let me ask you a question, "If your computer was stolen or caught fire during the night, would you still be able to run your business?" Most people don't think about this until it actually happens to them. You see, you need to have back-up procedures such as, another computer in a different location with the same date stored on it and regular computer back- ups on to a tape or disk.

You see, if your computer is stolen it's not the computer that is the real loss, it's the data stored on the hard drive, all your names and addresses etc., which if you have backed up, can be restored on to a new computer and you can be up and running within minutes.

Fraud

It is important to keep your cheque books and other financial documents locked away, even if you trust your staff, you have to think about visitors such as, couriers, delivery men, potential customers and sales reps etc.

Beware that both small and large companies are victims of fraud, and don't fall for any scam letters from Nigeria telling you that if you give them your bank account details, a letterheaded piece of paper and your signature, they will transfer millions into your bank account, what will actually happen is that they will drain your bank account dry!

Beware of your rubbish

Ask any good investigative journalist how to find out anything about a person or a company and they will tell you to go through their rubbish. Make sure that you shred or rip up your rubbish, people throw bank statements, phone bills, utility bills and other letters away without even thinking. All these documents can be used against you in a fraudulent manner.

I remember there was a big story about the Duchess of York some years ago, she had written a note, thrown it away and the press had picked it out of the rubbish and printed it on the front page of the newspaper!

Bugging and espionage

Now you may be thinking, "This guy is paranoid, why is 007 going to spy on me?" Well if you are in a competitive and sensitive business like software, finance, advertising or mail-order, your competitor could be watching you, here are some points to watch:

1. Can your computer screen be seen by someone from the outside, at night computer screens stand out. I have walked past many offices and I could see everything that was on their PC, with a long lens camera you could get clear photos of what's on your desk, wall or screen.

2. Are your telephones or offices bugged. It is possible that the free calculator gift that came through the post or the temporary girl that was helping you out, may not be what you think!

3. Watch out for post interception, especially in offices where the post doesn't come right to your door. I could pick up your post, steam it open, copy it and seal it back up again and you wouldn't even notice. Just think if you have just received a large contract or an order etc., I now know all about it!

I have featured these tips because I want you to be aware of what can happen, like me you will no doubt work very hard to achieve success and I would hate for something stupid to cause you unnecessary problems and possibly large financial losses. You're going to find out that business is challenging enough, without any extra complications. JUST BE AWARE.

Doing business overseas

There's a BIG WORLD out there and the chances are that your winning product, video tape or book can be sold successfully outside your home country. It is a narrow view just to sell your product in the U.K. or USA because that's where your company is based. Today with the Internet, World Wide Web, reliable overseas couriers and cheap international fax and telephone rates, there is no reason not to do business in other countries.

If your product is a HOW TO manual, you could quite easily write a European edition and a US edition, some products will not even need to be changed.

I have previously mentioned that many of the videos that I sold successfully were primarily written for the US market, but I managed to sell them in the U.K. and Europe.

If you need help in selling overseas, you can possibly find an overseas agent or find a mail-order company who will carry your product in their catalogue.

Credit cards are the global currency

I have sold products to customers in Belgium, Spain, USA and Germany to mention a few and because I can accept credit cards, there is no currency problem. A Visa Card issued by a Spanish bank goes through your terminal just as easily as a card issued locally, there are no currency problems because you get paid the amount you asked for, i.e. you still key in £35.00.

Do think about overseas markets, if you advertise your products in an airline magazine or national newspaper, you will always receive enquiries from overseas, don't turn them away. When I've advertised in English Sunday papers, I've had enquiries from Australia, Russia, USA and Africa.

> **NOTE:** Overseas freight and postage should be charged to the customer, as this can really eat into your profit margins, you may want to get a price list from the post office or your courier for various countries.

☺

Doctor: There's not much hope. You are very ill. Is there anything you'd like me to do for you?

Sick patient: Yes please! Go and find me a better doctor!

CHAPTER 25

Learning to invest in your business and keeping costs down

When you start making money in business you will no doubt start focusing on things that you may want to buy for your business and I would like to share some of my experiences:

1. I believe in investing in computers and machinery etc. that will be of benefit to your business, however, I believe that anything you buy for your business must earn its keep, I am not into buying something just to look good.

2. If you need to buy a machine, think out the possibilities of maybe renting one first, or taking it on a trial basis, also would it be cheaper to subcontract the task out to another company or to use a bureau?

3. If you are tempted to move into business premises just because you are doing OK, then think again, save your money, work from home and use a business centre.

4. Try to always buy a slightly used/ex-demo or even a slightly older model. (See saving money section for more tips.)

5. Always keep your costs down to a minimum, many people who start to make money get complacent, they buy items that they don't need, they start taking expensive business lunches, take out vanity advertising or features about their business and generally buy office items at inflated prices. Remember, it is easier to save £1 than it is to earn £1.

I read that Henry Ford offered $25,000 (and that was a very big sum in those days), to anyone who could show him how to save a single nut and bolt on each automobile he made.

It was thanks to Henry Ford's penny saving schemes that cars were able to be produced at a price where nearly everyone could afford to buy one. Think about this example when you are running your own business, I have been able to save thousands of pounds in my business, which in turn meant extra profits for me just by saving small amounts here and there. Costs such as envelopes, postage and paper etc. which most companies don't even think about, can lead to massive savings.

> **NOTE:** If you work for a company or you shop/do business with someone and you spot something that they could be doing to save money, then write to them giving them a rough idea and then if they are interested, which everyone will be, get a solicitor to draw up an agreement and sell them the idea. Something simple that you spot, could be worth thousands of pounds to you.

The saving money section will give you more ideas on keeping your business costs down. When people start out in business they tend to be very resourceful because in most cases they have very little capital, then when they start making money, they become complacent and wasteful, don't make this mistake.

Now at the same time don't be a total miser, ensure that you are comfortable when you are working, have a nice chair, a few pictures and maybe some plants etc. A happy work place makes you more productive.

Investing wisely in business is essential, I have already mentioned that I invested in a computer and a laser printer as soon as I had my first profits. Companies who don't invest in machinery and technology get left behind. I've seen companies that have clapped out old machinery which breaks down all the time, yet the directors have brand new company cars! You need to get your investment priorities right.

Why do companies go broke?

First of all, if you follow everything that I have told you up till now, you will avoid all of these problems. It is quite amazing that I had addressed all of these problems before I read the following research. The researchers at the Imperial College of Science, Technology and Medicine have been looking at why many small and medium sized businesses fail, they sampled 486 businesses which had failed and concluded as follows:

1. Failure to clearly target the product or service at the right customer was often a contributory factor of failure. (Remember what I was saying about sending direct mail to the wrong people.)

2. Under-pricing, with businesses not realising that their market would have been prepared to pay more for their product or service, this was more of a problem than over-pricing. (Remember what I said earlier about it is always better to over-price than under-price, and new businesses normally under-price.)

3. Lack of planning was a frequent cause of failure, especially for new businesses. (I would guess that they were not ready for success.)

4. Poor management was also common, along with poor financial systems, failure to manage debt and poor planning. (Again, you may have thought I was crazy when I said earlier that I always knew how much money was in the bank and how much was outstanding etc.) I also doubt that they had written any personal or business goals.

The survey also concluded that many business owners didn't see that their business was getting into trouble, until it was too late, they were also reluctant to seek any outside help.

Learn from these business failures and you can avoid these deadly mistakes, ignore them and you'll be another statistic!

Attending trade shows, public events and large shopping centres

I have attended many trade shows and shows aimed at consumers such as, the Ideal Home Exhibition and it is always a good place to look for new contacts and ideas. It was thanks to the first computer trade shows that I was able to make money from software.

Now although most of the products that I have been involved with in the past have never been sold directly at a trade or public show, you should be aware that you can make large amounts of money by selling products this way, especially if your product has a general appeal. This is also a good way to test products and get instant market reactions.

One of my heroes in sales and business is Ron Popeil, who is now a multimillionaire thanks to his business, Ronco. He started his career by working on market stalls and then by selling his products at exhibitions and shows. Ronco's products included, pasta making machines, food slicers, the "Food Dehydrator" and the "Pocket Fisherman" to name a few. Now when Ronco went on to television, he used many of the techniques that had been tried and tested from his live demonstration days.

Tips on making a trade/public show work for you

1. Identify the target audience, will they be interested in your product. It is pointless attending the Clothes Show Live Exhibition if you are selling a product relating to cars!

2. How many people attended the show last year/last time?

3. When booking a stand try and get the best position you can, even if it means paying a bit extra because location is important, not the size of your booth. Good locations are near to toilets/restrooms and snack areas.

4. Have a practice run at home, set up the booth to the exact space that you will have at the show, this will give you an idea of how you can set up the booth with the maximum effect.

5. Make sure that at least one or two other people are there to help you run your booth.

6. Make your booth look as professional as possible, use posters and display your product clearly etc. People need to know exactly what you are selling, if your product can be demonstrated, then make sure you do so, have a microphone and make as much noise as you can, you need to attract the audience's attention, don't just sit there like a dummy, try and build up a crowd, people are like sheep and will soon flock around you.

7. Keep the price of your product at a round figure when you're at a show, this makes it easier for people to pay in cash without giving any change, i.e. £10 or £20. Shows are one of the only places where you can make money with lower profit margins, because the volume is big and you don't have any direct mail or postage costs.

8. Have a jar where people can drop their business cards in, or fill in a slip with their name and address on to receive further details. You can build up great mailing lists at shows. You could hold some sort of free draw/raffle to encourage people to give their details.

9. Have plenty of bottled water and a few snacks on your stand, it will be a very long day and you need to drink, also the chances are that you are going to be on your feet all day, so wear comfortable shoes.

10. Be ready for anything, bring sticky tape, scissors, pens, markers, paper and cardboard, so that you can make up any last minute signs. Also remember to have a cash box to put all the money in!

Summary

Selling products directly at a trade show or public exhibition can be a great way to make large amounts of money in a few days. Your main cost is the stand, but if you have the right product for the market, then you will make money.

If you are new to trade shows you will want to start off by testing a few of the smaller shows before you go for the big ones.

Making trade shows/exhibitions work, without paying to exhibit there

The key to this is to bring lots of business cards and leaflets about your product or service and give them out to as many of the exhibitors as possible. Let's say that you sell to engineering companies, now for you to visit 400 different companies, possibly all over the world would be very expensive, yet by attending a major trade show where these companies will be exhibiting, you can go from stand to stand. Try to pick the quietest day of the show, normally the morning of the last day, this way you will get more time.

CHAPTER 26

Summary to making money

I want to use the next few pages to summarise and recap. The keys to making money are:

1. Be in business for yourself

Whether it is part time to start with, or by acting as an agent, or consulting a few customers alongside your existing job, <u>start your own business.</u>

2. Put the customer first

The aim in business is of course to make money, however, if you just focus on the money without taking any time and effort to look after your customers and to find out what the market wants, then it is going to be very hard to make money. You must also genuinely enjoy your work, be proud of your business and be happy to serve your customers. Some of the world's most successful entrepreneurs such as, Henry Ford, Conrad Hilton and Hoichiro Honda always believed that money was just a by-product of their business.

Realise that a one off sale/order will not make you rich, it is repeat business that will make you rich.

3. Be market driven, not product driven

Find out what the market wants or who you can sell the product to, before you start to spend time and effort on making/buying in a product.

4. A one man/woman company must still give a professional image

Using good letterheaded paper, a good telephone manner, computers, a business centre and a fax line etc. will put you on a level footing with the big boys, even though you are a tiny company.

5. Learn not to waste money

Don't get suckered into wasting money in business, negotiate everything and run a tight ship, even when things are going well. At the same time realise that money invested wisely to improve the business, money spent on training, books and seminars etc. is money well spent, it's pointless using Stone Age equipment and not investing in new skills.

6. Be ready for change and be prepared

One thing is certain in business and that's nothing is certain in business, things change, today's big seller is tomorrow's totally unfashionable item. Keep your eyes open, watch out for new trends and markets. Also be ready for problems such as, computer failures etc.

7. Don't quit, believe in yourself, work hard and give everything your very best effort

You must realise that stress, problems, new challenges, frustration and let-downs are part of everyday business life and if you are going to start sulking and hide in a corner when something goes wrong, then you won't survive in business for very long. Understand this, you will get knocked down, it happens and it's acceptable, the question is do you keep bouncing back up again? You must bounce back, learn from your mistakes and keep going. Stay on the ground for too long and that's where you'll be forever, get up, fight back and you'll be a winner.

8. Realise that marketing is the key

> **"No enquiries means no orders, no orders means
> no money, no money means no business, no
> business means you're out on the street!"**
>
> Vince Stanzione

I know this sounds harsh but that's the reality, good marketing makes or breaks you. You must advertise, use press releases, use direct mail, use the internet and use any other method you can that will effectively spread the word about your product or service.

My closing advice on making money

In short, "Be in business for yourself," it can be lonely at times and the hours can be long, especially when you are starting out, but the benefits both financially and personally of owning your own business, far outweigh the few disadvantages. The sense of pride that you get is hard to describe until you feel it for yourself, starting a business from nothing and building it up with your own efforts, blood, sweat and tears is a sensational experience. You can never get the same satisfaction from working for someone else.

Remember that this section is just the beginning, to succeed in business you will need to become a good student, as you will need to continually learn new skills and information. This book will get you started, however, there's a long road ahead, but it's one worth travelling on.

The information I have revealed in this section will allow anyone with little or no previous business experience, to start making money the smart way. I've given you tips that will save you making the mistakes that most business start-ups make and by using this information, together with your own hard work and perseverance you will be a winner in business.

In the next section we will talk about saving money and how to get "the maximum bang for your buck." Being a smart buyer and making your money go as far as possible is an important factor which is often overlooked in business.

☺

Nervous passenger: Every time you go round a sharp bend, I get very nervous!

Driver: Don't worry, do what I do then. Close your eyes!

CHAPTER 27

Section 3

Saving Money

So far we have talked about self-development in the first section and making money in the previous section, now I want to reveal to you the power of saving money and being a SMART BUYER.

When I say to people that shopping and buying is difficult they think I'm mad, after all, when you see something that you or your business needs/likes you buy it. Yes, you can do that, but if you want to hold on to your money and maximise your spending power, then you need to be a smart buyer.

I've seen many people struggling to live on £100,000 a year and then I've seen people who have everything they want on £100,000 a year, so what makes the difference? It's the way the money is spent.

Making every £1 equal at least 150 pence

Once you learn to get "the maximum bang for your buck," you will realise that instead of having to work harder to make more money, you can simply spend wiser and still achieve the same results.

Now, I'm not saying that we should go and live rent free on a park bench to save money! That's not a life-style that you or I would aspire to have, however, I am talking about how simple actions that most people don't think of or are too embarrassed to ask for, can make a massive difference.

So let's get started on the real ways to save money...

Airlines

I often get asked how I fly around the world for such small fares and the simple answer is, I go looking for the best deals. Now I have been told that I'm not allowed to name any airlines, but I will give you some examples and ideas.

Don't buy the ticket direct

The biggest mistake you can ever make is to phone an airline's free-phone central reservations number, only fools do this. You'll never get a discount dealing direct, why? Because most airlines don't want to be seen offering discounted flights, instead they sell their leftovers or x amount of seats to travel consolidators who then sell the fares at a discount. The only time you should ever phone the airline direct is to use them for information, flight times and to get a starting price.

> NOTE: I have been able to get a discount on every major airline, even when I have been told by the airline that they do not discount!

I recently went to Canada with a large airline and I travelled First Class for the price of an economy ticket! It's amazing, I paid £500 for this ticket, yet on the ticket it said £2,800 and no doubt people on the same flight were paying this amount. I booked the ticket through a consolidator, not direct.

Now of course, when I was on the plane I was treated as a full fare customer, the cabin crew didn't know what price I paid for the ticket. I'm a smart shopper and this is how I make my money go further.

Getting upgrades

On many occasions I pay the lowest economy fare and again, I do this through a consolidator. The key to getting an upgrade is to look presentable, be friendly, confident and generally be a nice person to do business with. Remember what I told you at the start of the book about "Taking an interest in the little people," well here's where to do it.

The main reason I get an upgrade is because "I ask for one," it's simple isn't it? If you don't ask for an upgrade, you can't expect the booking clerk to say, "Here, have a First Class seat!"

Tips for upgrades:

1. Join their frequent flyer programme, it's normally free and it shows that you are a loyal flyer. I've got about 20 cards!

2. Look smart, many airlines will not upgrade you if you are wearing jeans etc. You need to look the part if you want to travel in business or first class, don't look like a tourist wearing a T-shirt with a camera round your neck!

3. Say that you would be grateful for a "courtesy upgrade." If it's your birthday, honeymoon, partner's birthday or a special occasion, make sure that you tell the check-in clerk this, people like to help out if it's a special occasion. Even if you don't get an upgrade, most airlines will give you a bottle of Champagne or a gift.

4. Buy a few shares in various airlines. This way you can say that you're a shareholder and in turn you actually own part of the airline. It might only be 10 shares, but you are still a legal voting shareholder. Some airlines offer special rates for shareholders.

Good consolidators

Here is a list of consolidators that I use for both business and economy class, now before I go any further, I want to state that I receive no commission or have any incentive to recommend these companies, I have used them myself and I found that they offer a good service at good rates. Like all things in life companies and offers change, so you will still need to do your own research and seek out your own consolidators.

> NOTE: Don't confuse a consolidator with a high street travel agent, most travel agents are not much better than direct airlines.

Travelbug
597 Cheetham Hill Road
Manchester
M8 5EJ
Tel: 0161 740 8998

Travelbug
125a Gloucester Road
London
SW7 4SF
Tel: 0171 835 1111

Airline Network
Network House
Navigation Village
Riversway, Preston
PRO 2YP
Tel: 01772 72 72 72
Fax: 01772 760287
ITV Teletext: Page 275

Flightbookers
177/178 Tottenham Court Road
London, W1P 0LX
Tel: 0171 757 2500
Internet: WWW.flightbookers.co.uk

Booking and paying for your flight

I always pay using a credit card, this way should anything go wrong, then it's the credit card company's problem and not yours! 99% of agents and consolidators are reputable, however, there are a few rogues who will try to sell you a worthless ticket.

> Note: A debit card or charge card is not the same as a credit card and does not give you the same rights.

Hotels

At some time or the other we all stay in hotels, both for business and pleasure, and believe me I've stayed in my fair share. Again, the aim is to stay in the best room or suite, for the minimum amount of money.

My number one tip is not to phone the free-phone central reservation number unless you really have too. Wherever possible, telephone the hotel direct as they will always deal on rates unless they are very busy (which is rare). Most hotels are lucky if their occupancy is 60 or 70% so there are always spare rooms.

Why hotel rooms get discounted

If you are the owner/manager of a hotel and let's say you have 200 spare rooms for tomorrow, if I phone you up for a room for tomorrow and make a sensible offer (I call sensible about 50% to 60% less than their asking price), what would you do? It's better to take a reduced rate than leave the room empty.

Don't feel embarrassed to haggle for a good rate and room, I do it all the time and after a while it becomes habit.

Some hotels now offer free rooms during off-peak times, subject to you paying for breakfast and an evening meal. I think this is very good value because you were going to eat anyway!

Upgrades on rooms

Hotels are very sly and I find that on the whole they never give you a really nice room unless you haggle. When checking into a hotel, never do anything until you see the room first. If you say, "Can I inspect the room first?" in most cases you will get a better room than if you had just checked in.

When you inspect the room, check for things like:

1. Is the room close to a lift/elevator that is likely to be noisy?

2. Is the standard of cleanliness to your satisfaction?

3. Is the bathroom clean and tidy?

4. Is the decor, furniture and room layout to your satisfaction?

5. If you're a non-smoker, is it a non-smoking room? Is there a stale smell of smoke in the air? (One hotel tried to convince me that a room was a non-smoking room, when I clearly knew it wasn't, I then asked them to explain why there were cigarette burns on the furniture and carpet!)

Hotels have different rooms and configurations, so you and I could both be staying in the same 5 star hotel, yet my room could be totally different to yours, so be aware of this.

If you are happy after your inspection then that's great, go ahead and sign up. Your rate of tolerance should be offset by the amount of money you are paying and the standard of hotel, for example, if you're staying in a motorway motel, don't expect a royal suite for £25 a night, at the same time it should be clean, tidy and fit to stay in etc.

The problems start when you spend large amounts of money in 5 star hotels and they try to palm you off with substandard rooms.

If you're not happy with the room

After your inspection if you're not happy with the room, then say so, express your disappointment and point out the problems, you should then ask to see a better room and/or the HOTEL MANAGER. With a bit of haggling you'll end up with a nice room/suite for an economy price.

Loyalty programmes

Just like airlines, hotels now have loyalty programmes as well and again, I would join as many as possible, some hotels do charge a fee, but if you are travelling a lot and you intend to use that chain quite often, then it's worth it.

Benefits vary from scheme to scheme, but common benefits are:

1. An upgrade to a junior suite when you book a standard room.

2. Free newspaper.

3. Fruit, gift and wine on arrival.

4. Complementary breakfast, evening snacks and drinks on the club-floor.

5. Complementary use of boardroom and office facilities.

Hotel consolidators

Just like airlines, hotels consolidate as well and here is one that I use quite often:

Corporate Reservations Services
30-32 Staines Road
Hounslow, Middlesex
TW3 3JS

Hotel Reservations: Tel: 0181 577 2424
Conferences: Tel: 0181 570 1188

This company can also get very good rates on conference room facilities.

Buying a few shares in hotels

I own shares in 2 hotel groups and I receive a special discount card which entitles me to discount room rates, discounts on food in their restaurants (which I can use even when I'm not staying at the hotel) and discounts on health club facilities.

As a shareholder you have more power if anything goes wrong, after all, you're a part owner of the hotel!

Where to find the best hotels in the world

Let's say that it is a special occasion and you want to stay in real luxury, then I would suggest you obtain a copy of "The Leading Hotels of the World" book which is available free from:

U.K.

The Leading Hotels of the World
15 New Bridge Street
London
EC4V 6AU
England
Tel: 0171 936 5000
Fax: 0171 353 1904

U.S.A.

The Leading Hotels of the World
747 Third Avenue
New York, NY 10017-2803 USA
Tel: 212 838 7874
Fax: 212 758 7367

This book also contains the telephone/fax numbers, the hotel manager's name and lots of additional information on all the hotels listed.

Hotels that are listed in this book have to work very hard and each member receives frequent rigorous inspections by a team of professional hoteliers. Hotels that are members of "The Leading Hotels of the World" are very proud to be members and will do anything to keep this title.

If a hotel listed in this book does not meet or exceed your expectations for excellence (which I doubt), then I encourage you to complain. Don't forget, even the world's leading hotels have quiet periods and will discount, many of them have special weekend packages as well.

Summary to getting a good hotel deal

If you take the first thing that is offered to you, which is what most people do, then you deserve what you get, however, if you are willing to politely negotiate and stand up for yourself, then you will be treated with respect and you will end up with a nice room or suite. Don't forget, a hotelier would rather sell a room at a discount than leave the room empty and get nothing, so you've got the upper-hand.

How to keep up to date with airlines and hotels

There is a great magazine called Executive Travel, which is available through subscription only, but if you are a regular traveller and own a business, which most of you will or will be, you should be able to subscribe free of charge by filling in a questionnaire about your travelling habits, for more details write to:

Executive Travel
Reed Business Publishing
Oakfield House
Perrymount Road
Haywards Heath, West Sussex
RH16 3DH

How to hold a meeting or get-together at a hotel for FREE

Few people realise that you can use hotel facilities even if you are not staying there. I have conducted many business negotiations in a plush hotel lobby and in hotel bars. All you pay for are a few bottles of mineral water or a few cups of coffee from the bar. As long as you look smart no one ever troubles you. You can make phone calls in a better environment than a phonebox, send faxes (and receive them), read their newspapers and make use of their many other services. Always choose a fairly large business hotel, that way you blend in.

Discount car-hire

You'll be amazed at the difference in prices available from one company to another, or buy quoting the right discount code/scheme reference.

On the whole I have always found it cheaper to book car-hire before you arrive at your destination, it seems that if you just turn up at the airport unannounced, they just charge you the full going rate.

The airline consolidators previously mentioned can get quite good deals on car-hire, you can also contact the various firms directly, however, the key is to ask "Is this the lowest rate available?" and also look out for promotions that may be offered through your credit card, American Express or an airline. They normally quote a discount code number which will reduce the quote dramatically, i.e. Hertz has CDP 706770 etc. If you don't have a code, ask the person on the other end nicely and they will normally key one in for you.

Corporate discounts

Whether you're a one man/woman business or a multinational, you will get a corporate discount if you mention that you own a business and you are a regular user. Car-hire firms also have loyalty programmes and if you are a regular hirer, it could be worth getting a card.

NOTE: I personally stick to the larger well known car-hire firms because I've had bad experiences with some of the local one-off hire companies, their cars and the service can be very poor and even if they are a bit cheaper, it's not worth it.

Buying electrical goods

I love hi-tech electrical goods such as, video, TV and satellite systems etc. but I never buy at RRP. (Recommended Retail Price), this is what Joe Public pays when he walks into a store, not knowing what he's looking for.

The key to discount shopping is to do your research, if for example you are buying a video, you should read a few magazines such as, What Video etc. and become knowledgeable of what's on the market, an informed shopper is a smart shopper, try to know more about the product than the salesman does. Once you know what you want, your task is to find the product at the best price.

Manager's offers/returned goods/ex-display

Nearly all big electrical retailers offer money back guarantees and many people do take the stores up on their offer and return the goods. Now the stores have to sell these goods on and normally offer a 25% to 30% reduction.

I recently bought a top of the range video, it was an exchanged product, the instructions had been lost and there was no remote control. Now I knew from my research that the video was very good and retailed for around £450, the store had marked it down to £300 and I made them an offer of £250, which they accepted.

The video recorder was fine, it still had 12 month's guarantee and even carried a 7 day money back guarantee. As for the instructions, I managed to set it up without them and I wrote a nice letter to the manufacturer who sent me a new set free of charge. I got hold of a brand new remote control for £30, so for £280 I had a £450 video recorder, not bad hey! Anyone else can do the same, just keep your eyes open for ex-demonstration or returned goods, they offer excellent value and you still have peace of mind with a guarantee.

Shop soiled goods

I have bought items that were slight seconds and furniture which had a few scratches at greatly reduced prices. The way I see it is, you'll get scratches on your furniture in due course anyway, so what's the difference! Look out for stores that are closing down or having a refit.

How to get money off anything

The easiest way to buy anything at the best price is to research the market. There is always a store somewhere willing to offer you a discount just to get your business, even if it's £10, it's better in your pocket than the stores.

The simple thing that people just don't ask is "Is this your lowest price?" or "Could you knock something off the price if I buy it today?"

Try it, you'll be surprised how many small and large stores will take something off for you, who dares wins!

Buying a nearly new car at a discount

How would you like a nearly new car, normally no older than 6 to 8 months, which still carries all the manufacturer's guarantees and is in excellent condition, for around 30% to 40% off the normal retail price?

Well it's possible and the dealers listed on the next page specialise in dealing in these type of vehicles, the only disadvantage is that some of the cars may have a higher than normal mileage.

Where do these cars come from? Many are ex-hire cars because big companies like Hertz and Avis only keep their cars for 6 to 8 months and then they sell them on, some cars are also ex-demonstration, ex-lease cars or repossessions.

These dealers stock all major brands including, Ford, Rover, Vauxhall, Nissan, Fiat and many others.

Nearly New Cars/Trade Centre Car Supermarket
44-45 Hythe Road (off Scrubs Lane)
White City
London
NW10
Tel: 0181 969 5511 (open 7 days a week)

MJA
Staines Road West
Sunbury, Middlesex
Tel: 0500 499 599

Look in Exchange & Mart magazine, available every Thursday for their adverts.

Buying and selling a car

As mentioned above, buying a nearly new car is a smart way to buy, however, you may wish to buy a car elsewhere and you probably have a car to sell.

Selling your car

If you are looking for the highest price for your car, then in nearly all circumstances, sell it privately through a newspaper or Exchange & Mart, dealers always offer a trade-book price, which is substantially less than the value you could get.

Keys to selling:

    1. Make sure the car is clean, both inside and out.

    2. Make sure you can prove a full service history and keep receipts of any work you have undertaken, i.e. new tyres.

    3. Try to sell the car from spring to September, especially if it's a convertible.

4. If someone makes you an offer below your asking price which you are not willing to take, then keep their number and say you'll get back to them.

5. Answer any questions that the buyer may have truthfully, but don't talk too much, i.e. "I had an accident a while ago, but it looks as good as new!"

Keys to buying:

These are almost exactly the reverse of selling.

1. Don't get fooled by how clean the car looks, check closely for damage and rust etc.

2. Ask for the full service history.

3. Try to buy your car around December or January, no one apart from me buys cars at these times and dealers are desperate. A great time to buy a convertible is when the weather is really bad.

4. Always get a qualified mechanic, AA or RAC to carry out a full inspection, before you part with your cash.

5. Get the car checked with HPI. this tells you if there is any outstanding finance, the car was a write-off/made up of two cars stuck together or is stolen.

6. Buy with your head and not only your heart, if you smell a rat or something just doesn't sound right, then walk away, your instincts are normally right.

7. Think about the insurance group, the engine size and model such as GTI, can make a big difference to the premium.

There's a saying in the motor trade "What do you think about XXX car? The answer depends if you're buying or selling!" If the motor trader is buying the car in they'll say, "Oh, this is bad model, high insurance and prone to rust," now if they are selling the same car to you they would say, "Great, popular model, economical, sporty engine!"

Try to research the market before you buy or sell a car. Get hold of a few of the latest car magazines and read up, an informed and knowledgeable consumer is a smart buyer.

Buying, selling and exchanging

There are now a few legitimate companies who buy, sell and exchange all sorts of electrical goods, household goods, computers, jewellery, records, tapes, CD's and videos etc.

When I recently moved house I had quite a few items that I didn't really want and instead of throwing them out, I took them to one of these stores and got cash for them. As well as making you money, it is also environmentally friendly, I think we throw away far too much.

Before I go any further, these stores are legitimate, they will only buy goods from you that are yours, i.e. NO STOLEN GOODS. You will be required to provide ID. and the stores have video surveillance.

These are the 2 main ones I know of, however, I'm sure there are others.

CASH CONVERTERS
286-292 Camberwell Road, London, SE5
Tel: 0171 277 4424

352 Holloway Road, London, N7
Tel: 0171 609 2022

37 High Street, Dunstable, Bedfordshire
Tel: 01582 667376

NOTTING HILL EXCHANGE
64 Notting Hill Gate
London
Tel: 0171 792 3474

As well as selling your unwanted goods, you can also see what other goods they have which may be of interest to you.

CHAPTER 28

Choosing where to live, buying/ selling a property and mortgages

For most people their biggest living expense is their rent or mortgage, the cost of housing varies dramatically from one part of the country to the other. For example, an average 1 bedroom flat in London buys you a nice 5 bedroom house with some land in many other parts of the country.

For many people work dictates where they live, yet with the types of businesses that I have outlined in the making money section, this is no longer a problem, you can work on a remote farm, as long as you have a phone/fax and a post-box fairly nearby.

Do think about moving out of highly priced cities, I have lived in London and in country locations and on the whole, I find that the country does offer a better standard of living. If you miss the city you can always go on day trips or stay a few nights in a hotel.

As well as lower rent and property prices, you'll also find that insurance premiums, both for your car and home, are slashed when you move out of cities and big towns.

The decision of where you want to live is yours, but do think about it because this could be a big money saver. For

many, they prefer a main residence in the country and a
small flat in London or a city, this way you get the best of
both worlds.

Renting

First of all, renting a property is a mugs game! You are
basically paying someone else's mortgage for them, some
people rent for years and at the end of it they have nothing
to show for their money.

Renting is a good temporary solution, but is foolish in the
long-term. It is better for you to be the landlord or landlady,
take in a lodger or two and get them to pay your mortgage
for you.

A good friend of mine does this, he has 3 lodgers and he
also lives there as well. The lodgers pay enough rent to
cover his mortgage, electricity, gas and his food bill, so he's
basically living there RENT FREE with no living expenses.
Now the great benefit of this is that he's building up an
asset, his property has increased in value and his mortgage
is going down, so one day he will own the property outright
and it will have been paid for by the lodgers.

Buying a property at the right price

For many, buying a house/flat will be the biggest investment
and decision that they will ever make, yet I have seen
individuals buy a house or flat with little care, concern or
research. They see a property, their heart rules their head
and before you know it, they have bought themselves a pile
of trouble. As if this isn't bad enough they then go and get
bad mortgage advice and end up with a terrible mortgage to
add to their problems. Now you may have had some
problems with property ownership in the past or you know
someone who has, but by using some common sense
pointers, you can avoid costly mistakes.

Let me tell you what type of properties sell well and
those that don't. You see, when you buy a property you
should be thinking about the resale potential. The chances

are that you won't want to live there forever, and although I cannot guarantee that you'll make a profit from your property, I would hope that you can at least get back the money you paid for it, so today you are the buyer, but one day you will be the seller.

Properties that SELL WELL

1. Houses with 4 bedrooms.

2. Houses with a reasonable amount of garden, but not too much land as this can put many people off.

3. Houses with a bedroom that has an "en-suite" bathroom.

4. Houses in a cul-de-sac.

5. Houses that have good open countryside views.

6. New houses or houses that are a few years old.

7. Detached homes.

8. Houses in a good location and close to amenities.

9. Houses with good central heating, preferably gas.

Properties that are HARD TO SELL

1. Older houses (some older 1970's styles are very out of fashion).

2. Purchased council estate houses.

3. 3 bedroom houses.

4. Small houses in remote villages (larger houses sell better).

5. Houses on a main road.

6. Small flats.

7. Flats over shops.

8. Large houses on small plots (houses that are overlooked are bad news).

9. Houses that don't have good central heating.

10. Houses with old electrics and plumbing.

11. Flats with high management/maintenance fees (I've had trouble with this in London in the past).

Now let's say that you've found a property you like, let me tell you what I would want to know:

1. Are you buying the property with your head and not your heart?

2. Why are the current owners truthfully selling? How long have they been there? And how much did they pay? (You can find this out if they won't tell you through Land Registry.)

3. Are there many houses for sale in that area?

4. Is there anything you should know about, i.e. a new airport, motorway or fire station across the road?

5. Take a walk around the area at different times and also walk past or drive past the house at different times, is there anything strange happening? Pop into a local shop or pub and while buying something, casually mention that you are thinking of moving into the area and buying a house in XXX road, you'll be amazed at what you can find out, i.e. "He's just lost his job" or "Their business is going through a rough time."

6. Are the current owners desperate to sell, how long has the property been on the market? Find out how many different agents are trying to sell the property. (If a house is being offered by many different estate agents, then I guarantee you that they are desperate to sell.)

7. Think hard about why you want the house and how long you plan to be there for.

8. Try and find a comparative property to get a guide price from, this means a similar property in a nearby area that has sold in the last 6 to 12 months.

9. If you are buying a flat, check the management fees and ask for the last 3 years accounts of the management company and find out what the annual rate of increase in management fees has been. Also are there any possible large expenditures coming up such as, a new roof or redecoration of the hallway? If you buy a flat, you are liable for a percentage of these costs.

Making an offer

Let's say that you're now happy with the property and subject to the survey/searches, you need to make an offer which is a good deal to you, yet not ridiculously low that the vendor will think you are a total joker. My view is that there should be at least 10% off the asking price in it. Whatever offer you make don't ever make your final offer straight away for example, if the most you can afford is £125,000 don't make this offer first, offer £120,000 and hopefully you'll settle at £122,000.

> **NOTE:** Try and not show your true feelings, either with the estate agent or the vendors, say you are interested, but never show that you are desperate to buy the property. If an agent says that they have had other offers, then call their bluff and walk away, and ask the agent to show you another property.

Summary to buying a property

I could probably write a whole book on this subject, however, I hope you will find my pointers useful. You have to live somewhere and as long as you buy with your head, you should be able to make a profit on the property or at least break even. Remember to go against the flow, people tend to move house in the spring or summer, but if you are willing to buy and move in during the winter months, you'll normally be able to get an extra few thousand pounds off the price.

When everyone is talking about property and there is a property boom like 1988 and 1989 in the U.K. then that's the time you should be a SELLER, you should be a buyer when everyone else is SELLING, for instance in 1991 to

1993 there were some excellent bargains in the property market in the U.K. because so many property companies were going broke and people were panic selling.

Paying your mortgage off quicker/ getting a better deal

Most people take out a mortgage over 25 years, however, if you have to take out a mortgage, I suggest you take one out for 15 to 20 years maximum. You see, although your payments will be slightly higher, you will be paying back less accrued interest. If you have a current mortgage you could contact your lender and ask them to adjust the term.

The key to a mortgage is getting it paid off as quickly as possible, if you have some spare cash you can always pay off a bit extra on your mortgage, some people pay a few extra payments a year to reduce their balance quicker. Contact your lender for further details on how to make extra payments towards your mortgage.

Getting a better deal

If it was along time ago that you took your mortgage out, you could find that another bank or building society could provide you with a better deal, and even though there may be some fees and hassle in changing over to a new mortgage lender, for many it's worth it. You could also find that just by phoning your existing lender up and telling them that you've seen a lower rate elsewhere, they will renegotiate your mortgage interest rate. You see, if you have been a good customer they will not want to lose you.

A guide to getting a good mortgage or re-mortgage

Firstly, remember that you are buying a product, borrowing money is just like buying anything else, take the first offer that is given to you and you'll be paying too much, however, with some research and a bit of haggling you can cut your monthly mortgage quite dramatically. Here are my points to follow:

1. Check the small print. Can you pay off or change the mortgage without a penalty? If there is a penalty, how much is it? Are there any other conditions such as, compulsory insurance requirements etc.?

2. The best deals are available to those who have at least a 25% deposit to put down, or if you are switching mortgages and you are only asking for 75% or less of your current property's value.

3. If you are a First Time Buyer, then make sure that you get an extra discount.

4. In most cases you can buy your buildings and contents insurance cheaper through another source than your building society, however, sometimes it is best to play dumb and take theirs if you will benefit from a much better mortgage deal. Also, some lenders say that you only have to take the first year's buildings and contents insurance through them, thereafter you can go elsewhere.

5. Do make it a priority to ensure that your mortgage is paid on time because a bad mortgage reference will mess up your chances of getting a good deal in the future. If you hit problems, then tell the building society/bank immediately and make whatever payments you can.

6. Don't deal through a Mortgage Broker unless you really have too.

7. If you need to know where you stand, then a fixed rate mortgage could be for you, either for part or the entire term of the mortgage. For example: A fixed rate mortgage of 7% for 10 years means, regardless of whatever happens to interest rates, you only pay that rate.

Finally, I want to talk about the biggest and most misunderstood part of a mortgage, which is whether to have an endowment or repayment mortgage.

Repayment mortgage

This is the straightforward method where you pay the

interest and capital off. At the end of the term that's it, you've paid everything off.

Endowment mortgage

This is where you pay interest only on the mortgage, this means in 5,10 or 20 years time you will still owe the lender the same amount you initially took out, all you have been paying off is the interest.

Now at the same time you take out an Endowment, which is basically a savings plan that is managed by a bank/fund manager, who invests your money for you and hopefully, in 20 or 25 years time the fund will have enough money for you to pay off your mortgage. Now the problem is that there's no guarantee that the endowment will have grown enough to cover the final mortgage payment, and any shortfall will have to be paid by you.

Getting the right endowment is the key and I will talk more about savings and investments shortly, but if you go down the endowment route then do your homework, also do be aware that salesmen earn big commissions from endowments and that's why you will be told that they are a good idea.

Summary

Because a mortgage will probably be the largest amount of money you will ever borrow in your life, take your time and do your research, there are many good magazines on the market such as, What Mortgage, Which Mortgage and Moneywise.

CHAPTER 29

Shares, investing, pensions and savings

The easiest way for you to become wealthy is to start putting money away on a regular basis, whatever your position, even if it's only £50 a month, get into the habit of saving and investing. As you start making more money I would suggest that you put away at least 30% of your annual income, if you can discipline yourself to put away more, then that's even better. You may say that it's hard to save money and yes I agree, especially when you're earning a small income, however, it must be done. You need to face up to the fact that one day you won't be able to work, even if you want to. Don't expect the Government to look after you because the way things are going, I doubt if there will be a state pension by the time many of us retire.

You need to look after yourself and you need to start saving today. If you have a good income coming in when you're older, your standard of living will be much better, you will be able to afford private medical care, you can have a private nurse, a maid or a chauffeur etc. The last thing you want to have is money worries when you're older.

Why you should be a saver and investor

The old saying is "Money makes money." If you start building up some extra capital, with time and by making smart investments, you could be increasing that capital by around 15% to 20% per annum. These figures are realistic and some investment companies return a lot more than this.

Let me show you how £1,000 can grow over 10 years

Year 1 £1,200

Year 2 £1,440

Year 3 £1,728

Year 4 £2,073

Year 5 £2,487

Year 6 £2,984

Year 7 £3,580

Year 8 £4,296

Year 9 £5,155

Year 10 £6,186

So put in simple terms, £1,000 now turns into over £6,000 in 10 years, which isn't as long as you think. Now here's the best point about investing, on the whole you don't need to do much, you just wait. Some people may be thinking that a bar of chocolate will cost more in ten years time, so £6,000 won't be worth much, and it's true you do have to think about inflation, but I assure you that unless you are living in Russia or some other unstable economy, inflation does not run at 20%.

Once you build up enough capital, you will never have to work again if you don't want to, you can simply live off the interest and investment income. As I've already mentioned, in your old age you may not be able to work even if you want to.

How to invest your hard earned money

First of all I want to tell you that investing money is FUN, can you honestly tell me that you don't find turning £1,000 into £2,000 interesting and fun?

The keys to good investing:

1. Taking a medium to long-term view. Quick results are nice, but the real way to make big returns is by being patient, consistent and by keeping your head. Work on a 5 to 10 year time frame.

2. Spread your money around and never put all your eggs in one basket. I'll talk about asset allocations later, but you basically need a mixture of investments and you always need some liquid cash which can be withdrawn on instant access or 7 day's notice for emergencies.

3. Be sharp and don't fall for any scams like 500% returns from ostrich farming or a guaranteed 10,000% increase in pennyshares within 6 months! Yes, there are some wonder stocks and I'll talk more about them later, but they are the exception and not the norm.

4. Think hard about who you invest your money with, do lots of research, read books, attend courses and learn as much as you can about smart investing.

A pension plan

For most people a private pension plan should be their first investment. A pension plan has tax advantages that are worth taking. Carry out your own research into top performing pension companies, Sunday newspapers such as the Sunday Times and the Telegraph carry a lot of information on pension companies and also read the Investors Chronicle. Your monthly contribution i.e. £50 or £200 will depend on how much you want to achieve at the end of the pension.

Note: Take the time to choose the right company to use for your pension plan, don't just walk into your high street bank and buy theirs because there is a chance you'll be short changed, many of the top performers are specialist pension fund managers that are not necessarily household names.

Unit trusts, mutual funds, pooled investments and Individual Savings Accounts (ISAs)

I have always liked these type of investments because there is a fairly low entry level and you get a balanced investment in lots of different shares, instead of buying one share directly.

Let me explain how a Unit Trust/Mutual Fund works. A bank/fund manager sets up a fund, let's call it the ABC American Growth Fund, when they set up the fund they lay out objectives such as, to invest in American companies who offer medium growth. They then market the fund to individuals like yourself and with the money that you and other individuals send them, they then invest this on your behalf to obtain maximum returns, now they make their money by charging a management fee.

Now let's say that you invest £2,000 in this fund, you will be buying units in the fund and let's say each unit costs £1, so you now have 2,000 units which you can buy or sell. The unit will go up or down depending on how the fund is doing, let's say your fund owns XYZ shares and they get taken over at a much higher price than the fund manager bought them for, then the fund has made a profit and in turn your unit will increase, at the same time if your fund manager makes bad investments then your units will go down.

How to choose a good unit trust

Again research the market, most Sunday newspapers carry league tables of the best and worst performing trusts, now I must warn you that "PAST PERFORMANCE IS NO GUARANTEE FOR FUTURE PERFORMANCE," but if a fund has been doing well consistently for over 5 or 10 years, then the chances are it will continue to do so.

A good source of information in the U.K. is the Investors Chronicle which I've been buying for years, it comes out every Friday and is available from most big newsagents. You'll see many adverts for unit trusts in the Sunday papers, send off for information and make your decisions based on your own research.

Don't forget that you can invest in as many different funds as you wish, so you could invest in a steady growth fund with one company and then invest in a more speculative technology fund with another company.

The pros and cons of a unit trust

Pros

1. It gives you the chance to invest in markets which are difficult for you to trade in as a private investor, for instance Latin America, Poland or Taiwan etc.

2. It works on the don't put your eggs all in one basket principle, your fund will be divided into lots of stocks, therefore one bad investment will not sink the whole fund.

3. You don't need to monitor your investments on a daily basis as your fund manager does this for you. The fund manager also has the expertise and better access to information and resources than a private investor has.

Cons

1. You don't have a say in how your money is invested.

2. You can feel out of control.

3. There are some terrible fund managers out there and some funds under perform the market dramatically. I recently met someone who invested £5,000 over 5 years with a large household name and ended up after costs with about £4,900. He would have been better off leaving his money in a building society.

On the whole the pros outweigh the cons and you can keep an eye on your unit prices by either phoning the company up for a quote, or by checking the Financial Times.

Most fund managers will also send you a regular update on how the funds are doing. If your fund manager is constantly under performing the market and is at the bottom of the league tables, then take your money elsewhere, every fund has its ups and downs but there is a limit.

Individual Savings Accounts (ISAs) U.K. only

This is a new tax free investment account which has replaced the Personal Equity Plan (PEP). You can invest a maximum of £5,000 per tax year in any one tax year. In the 1999/2000 tax year you can invest £7,000. On the whole a ISA. works like a unit trust and there are some self-select ISA's that allow you to choose some of the shares in your ISA.

Should I take financial advice?

You may have noticed that so far I haven't told you to take any financial advice and on the whole I think you should steer clear of Financial Advisors and learn to deal with your own affairs, only seek financial advice if you are desperate and even then, take it as an opinion and not a fact.

This statement will upset a lot of people who make their money from charging fees and commissions, however, I think it is only fair that I reveal to you why your best interests are not always in the mind of most financial advisors.

Firstly, most financial advisors aren't independent, they're not really even allowed to call themselves that, because they are employed by big financial fund managers or insurance companies and they are only allowed to sell their company's products, so they are SALESMEN. Many are ex-car salesmen, estate agents or double glazing salesmen etc., so do you really want to invest your hard earned cash based on their advice?

What about those wonderful Independent Financial Advisors? Well they are a bit better, but they're still salesmen and they need to earn commissions to live. You see, many of the best funds to invest in are the one's that DON'T PAY any commission to salesmen/IFA's and the chances are that you won't be recommend any of these!

> **Note:** There are a few financial advisors who you pay by the hour for advice, they will not sell you anything and they will not take any commission, if there is any commission earned they will give it back to you. This is quite a fair way to do business.

The best financial advisor you'll ever meet is YOU, after all, no one cares more about your money than you do.

Risk + Reward

The easiest way to put this is, if you leave all your money in a bank or building society your risk will be minimal, however, so will your reward.

Now unless you are a thrill seeker I don't suggest you plough your life savings into a new technology pennyshare, however, at the same time you shouldn't leave your money just sitting in a building society.

Savings accounts and banks/building societies

As previously mentioned, you always need to have some cash that you can have access to either very quickly or immediately. The key to getting the highest return is to shop around because the rates of interest on savings can vary dramatically from one institution to another, the smaller societies tend to offer better interest rates, however, you may not have a local branch so it would mean dealing by post.

Investing in shares

As I stated earlier, I was a stockbroker for some years and I have dealt with hundreds of private and corporate investors. Dealing in shares has become cheaper and easier in the last few years. Today almost anyone can open a telephone account with a stockbroker like Charles Schwab and trade immediately.

What you need to know about shares

Firstly, shares go up as well as down and because of new technology, shares are traded more aggressively than they were in the old days of the Stock Exchange floor, this means that even a relatively safe share can move sharply higher or lower in a matter of 30 minutes.

Now although there have been some stock-market crashes mainly 1929, and 1987 which I witnessed first hand and possibly by the time you read this there may have been a 1999/2000 crash, on the whole shares over a long period are good investments. I also want to point out that whether we are in a BULL MARKET, which means that shares on the whole are in an upward trend or in a BEAR MARKET, which means that shares on the whole are in a downward trend, there are always opportunities and you can still lose lots of money in a bull market and make lots of money in a bear market.

What shares should you buy?

Well firstly, we've mentioned that many hotels and airlines give discounts to shareholders, so depending on your circumstances you may want to buy shares in a company that you use regularly, especially if they offer a discount.

On the whole for most investors they will be looking for shares of medium sized companies, normally listed in the bottom half of the FTSE 100 or the FTSE 250. These are companies that provide growth, but do not have the risk factor associated with the smaller stocks. I don't tend to invest in the top big companies in the FTSE 30, as they have already made it and on the whole provide little growth potential.

Research and furthering your knowledge

The Investors Chronicle is a good source of information on companies and they also give regular share tips, however, be warned that Investors Chronicle also gets it wrong at times! Investors Chronicle is very respected and is heavily read in the city.

A excellent TV station that I strongly advise you to watch regularly, is CNBC, this station is available on Satellite and Cable throughout the U.K. and Europe, I watch this channel regularly and you can learn so much from watching. Most stockbrokers and fund managers have TV's in their offices with CNBC on. Up till around 2pm this channel covers the U.K. and European markets, then from 2pm till 11pm it covers the US market, then throughout the night it covers the Asian markets and at weekends they have excellent business and computer programmes.

I would also suggest that you learn more about why companies go up and down, what dividends and price/ earning ratios are etc. There are many good books and courses on this subject and I suggest you take a trip to the library or a good business bookshop. There are also various seminars on investing and tax planning.

If you would like to know more about investment courses then write to me care of First Success Publishing and I will point you in the right direction.

Space does not permit me to write about everything there is to know on shares, however, I hope you will look into this further. Shares can make you extremely wealthy, for instance if you had only bought 20 or 30 shares in Microsoft or Coca-Cola 10 or 15 years ago, you would now be extremely wealthy!

The random method of picking shares

This may sound totally mad but it's a fact that if you were to open up the Financial Times at the share price listings in the back, close your eyes and point to 10 different shares at random, the chances are that you will out perform many city brokers and fund managers over 5 years!

Making money from pennyshares

It is everyone's dream to pick a share that's worth a few pence and for it to sky rocket into pounds and before you know it, your few hundred pounds investment has turned into thousands. Well it does happen and I've picked my fair share of them, however, I must warn you that you can also lose your complete investment therefore, if you do want to try your hand at pennyshares, then only invest what you can afford to lose.

What you need to know

Firstly, a pennyshare is normally a company who's shares trade at anything from 1p to 60p, now let's get this clear, it doesn't mean that the company is cheap because it is trading at a few pence. Without getting too technical, a company can change its share price by issuing more shares (a script issue) which gives the impression of a share price going down or a (consolidation) which gives the impression of the share price going up.

The key to valuing a company is its market Capitalisation, this is the amount of shares in issue x the current market price.

You see, a script issue puts more shares into the market and a consolidation takes shares out of the market and although the share price will change, the capitalisation will not, it's just how you divide the cake.

Why shares trade in pennies

The two main reasons are that, either it's a small company and new to the market, therefore it's trading at a low share price, or it was a pound share at some stage and the company has hit bad times and the share price has crashed.

How to make money with pennyshares

The two basic scenarios of making money are:

A) It's a small company, possibly a new company that has little track record but does have prospects, for example a new product, a new wonder drug or a new piece of computer software etc. I have invested in small oil exploration companies in the past, which have done very well when they have struck oil. The other way you make money with a pennyshare is a take-over bid, this is when a bigger company wants to buy out the company you have shares in and they offer you a higher share price to sell. Two of my oil exploration companies have been taken over and resulted in large profits this way.

B) This scenario takes the view that a big company who was successful, hits rough times and the share price crashes. Now this doesn't always happen, but it's possible that with some time and new management etc., the company can start to rebuild, and even if the company does not go back to where they were before, you can still make large profits. Let me give you a true example:

Some years ago a British retailer called Next Plc, which had done very well through the 80's, hit bad times in the early 90's, the shares had been trading at around £3.00 a share and because of problems and losses etc. they became a pennyshare. I bought Next Plc at 11p. My view was this:

> **1)** The worst that could happen would be if they were to go broke and I would lose all of my money, which was a relatively small investment at 11p a share.

> **2)** Someone would take them over and pay more than 11p a share for them.

> **3)** They would recover.

Anyway as some of you will know Next didn't go broke, in

fact the last time I saw the share price it was over £6.00 a share! That's not a bad return, it took around 5 years for the price to go from 11p to £6.00.

Another advantage of a pennyshare is that you can buy more of them for your money. For example, 10,000 Next shares cost me £1,100 when I bought them and today they would cost me over £60,000.

How to buy and sell shares

The easiest and cheapest way is to open an account with a stockbroker like Charles Schwab Europe, if you are in the U.K. or Charles Schwab in the US. For details on opening an account with Charles Schwab Europe phone 0121 200 4802. Schwab can buy and sell all U.K. traded companies and they are also able to trade US companies. Schwab do not provide any advice or recommendations, they are execution only brokers, which means that you call the shots. A full list of stockbrokers can be found in the Investors Chronicle.

Tax planning and claiming benefits

Most people don't claim what they are entitled to, they either don't know what they are entitled to or don't bother.

The chances are that there is a grant or benefit that either you or your business could be entitled to. If you have been unemployed and you are now starting your own business, then you will definitely be entitled to a grant. If you're going back to work after having a baby, you should also be entitled to some benefits, including free training in computers etc.

Again, space does not permit me to go into depth on this subject, however, you can start to research what you may be entitled to. The other point with grants and benefits is that they are always changing, but with your own research you should be able to track down what you are entitled to.

NOTE: Watch out for companies who promise to get you a grant or benefit for your business in return for a large up front fee, in many cases they'll take your fee and run, or provide you with worthless information.

Tax planning

One of the biggest savings that you can make is by finding ways to pay less tax, there are many legal tax loopholes that are used by wealthy individuals, to reduce or even eliminate their tax liabilities.

As an employed person you have less possibilities open to you than if you were self-employed or a company director, however, you can still ensure that your employer is deducting tax and national insurance at the correct rate. Ensure that your Tax Code is correct because you may find that you have been overpaying for years.

As for the self-employed and company owners, I suggest that you get hold of a book called "The Green Book," which was written by lawyers, chartered accountants and former tax inspectors. The book will give you a true understanding of offshore companies, trusts, avoiding Capital Gains Tax, protecting your assets and much more.

Even if you are not super rich, as long as you are making a fairly good income you should be able to offset setting up fees and management fees against tax savings.

More details about the book are available from: SCF Group, Scorpio House, 102 Sydney Street, London, SW3 6NJ.

Cheaper motor insurance and home insurance

Motor insurance

The main areas that can make a difference to your motor insurance is where you live, your occupation, your driving records and of course, the value of your car, here are a few tips to follow:

1. Make sure that you are using the right post-code, it can make a big difference to your premium.

2. If you are willing to meet the first £250 of a claim (excess) instead of the normal £50, you will find that you can reduce your premium.

3. If you are a low mileage motorist, then you should be able to get a lower premium. Ask insurance companies for low mileage discount schemes.

4. Deal direct with the insurance company and not through a broker, as this cuts out commission.

5. Do phone around as the difference can be incredible and don't just accept your current insurer's renewal quote, check the premium every year. Just because XYZ was dearer last year, it doesn't mean they won't be cheaper this year.

6. Make sure the insurance company has you grouped in the right occupation band.

7. Never lie on an insurance form or over the phone, if you need to claim and the insurance company finds out, they are legally entitled to not pay out.

8. Make sure the insurance is legitimate, they say that you only know how good the company is when you come to claim. Also make sure that your insurance company offers a FREE hire car, if your car is in a garage for 2 weeks you'll need a car and hiring is expensive.

Household insurance

Many of the tips are as above except:

1. Some insurance companies now offer "no claims" on household insurance as well, and if you have a good record this can make a difference.

2. Make sure that you are fully insured but are not paying for insurance that you don't need. Some companies offer block insurance of say £25,000 for

contents and if you only have £10,000 worth of contents, then you could be paying for too much cover.

3. Shop around and beware of taking buildings and contents insurance from your bank or mortgage lender as they tend to be expensive.

4. Some insurers now offer an "excess" on home contents, so if you are willing to pay the first £100 of the claim you can reduce the annual premium.

5. Just like motor insurance, make a note to review your insurance as things change and don't accept your current insurer's renewal quote without comparing it to others at the time.

☺

Why shouldn't you play cards in the jungle?
Because it's full of cheetahs!

CHAPTER 30

Buying designer clothes for less

For most of us we cannot justify spending hundreds if not thousands on one suit or dress, however, there is a way to get designer fashions at around 50% off the store prices and that's by using a dress agency or buying through designer sales.

Designer sales, slight seconds, samples and leftovers

Nearly all designers including, Versace, Armani, MaxMara and Moschino etc. offer end-of-line items or end of season fashions at reduced prices, however, don't expect to find them in their stores because you won't. These designers sell the leftovers to companies who specialise in having clothing sales or selling to smaller boutiques. Many companies hold special one day sales in hotels, so look out for the adverts in local newspapers and on the radio.

Here's a list of some of the permanent discount outlets:

London area

Labels for Less
50 South Molton Street, London W1
Tel: 0171 409 3011

Stock mainly comprises of leftovers from previous seasons, including Issey Miyake, Genny, Donna Karan. DKNY, MaxMara and Moschino.

The Salvage Shop
34-36 Watling Avenue, Edgware, Middlesex
Tel: 0181 952 4353

Stock is mainly from loss adjusters from premises that have been flooded or suffered fire damage. Lots of well known brands.

Bradleys
85 Knightsbridge, London, SW1X 7RB
Tel: 0171 235 2903

There is a permanent half-price sale of La Perla lingerie, swimwear and nightwear. Stock is mostly end-of-line.

Discount Dressing
39 Paddington Street, London, W1M 3RN
Tel: 0171 486 7230

Offers literally hundreds of new designer fashions normally obtained from bankrupt businesses, cancelled orders or over-makes.

The rest of the U.K.

The Designer Warehouse
Paradise Mill, Park Lane, Macclesfield, Cheshire
Tel: 01625 511169

They stock mainly samples, over-cuts and seconds.

Change of A Dress
294 Broxtowe Lane, Nottingham
Tel: 01602 291531

Very upmarket stock, including many of the big fashion names.

Seconds Out
10-14 The Arcade, High Street, Cookham, Berkshire
Tel: 01628 850371

Offers middle to upper range designer labels, including Karl Lagerfeld, Versace and Chanel.

Sands
18 Castle Arcade, Cardiff
Tel: 01222 230020

Stocks many top names, including Escada, Betty Barclay and Louis Ferraro.

Designer sales

These are not permanent outlets and you should contact them to find out the date of the next sale and the location.

The Kensington Fashion Fair
Organised by Blenhiem Exhibitions, Tel: 0171 323 3302

The fair offers a good selection of designer names for both men and women. The fair also offers jewellery and accessories.

The London Designers' Sale
94 Thurlow Park Road, London SE21
Francesca Eggeling Tel: 0181 670 4745

The sale takes place 4 to 5 times a year in Chelsea and 2 to 3 times in Docklands. Attendance is usually by invitation so make a point of asking to be placed on the mailing list.

Serina's Sale, organiser: Lady Serina Bridgeman
Flat 1, 3 Westgate Terrace, London SW10
Tel: 0171 373 9345

2 to 3 sales are held each year, usually of nearly-new designer clothing and accessories. Write asking for your name to be placed on the mailing list.

Dress agencies

Up till now we have concentrated on new and nearly-new clothing, however, there are a number of excellent dress agencies that buy, sell and exchange designer clothing. Most of the clothing has hardly been worn and offers excellent value for money.

If you have quality designer items that you no longer wear, then trade them in, you can receive cash or exchange them for something else and you can of course just buy if you have nothing to sell.

London Area

Pandora
16-22 Cheval Place
Knightsbridge, London, SW7
Tel: 0171 589 5289

This is one of London's best dress agencies and is packed with excellent designer wear, well worth a visit and it's only a few minutes walk from Harrods.

The rest of the U.K.

Touch of Class
8 Mark Lane, Eastbourne, Sussex
Tel: 01323 639890

Offers designer label clothing for men and women, including Jaeger, Windsmoor, Aquascutum, Burrberry and Daks.

Lynne Sim & Daughter
86 Cadzow Street, Hamilton, Strathclyde, Scotland
Tel: 01698 422265

Sells quality nearly-new designer clothing, including Chanel, Yves St. Laurent and Mondi.

The Frock Exchange
9 Seaway Road, Preston, Paignton, Devon
Tel: 01803 522951

Includes women's and men's wear with a selection of designer labels.

For a full listing of dress agencies check in the back of Vogue magazine.

Men's agencies and discount outlets

Although the market is mainly geared towards ladies, there are a few men's discount outlets. The Kensington Fashion Fair mentioned in the ladies section also carries a good stock of men's designer items.

Permanent discount outlets

Cavenagh Shirts
659 Fulham Road, London, SW6 5PY
Tel: 0171 371 0528

Offers a mail-order service and sales through normal shop outlet. Stocks Jermyn Street quality men's and women's shirts at around half the price.

Goldsmith & Company
101-105 Goswell Road, London, EC1
Tel: 0171 377 5770

Top quality men's clothing available at discounted rates.

Men's dress agencies

Penguin Society
189 West End Lane, London W6
Tel: 0171 625 7778

Gently worn clothing, includes designers such as Armani, Boss, and many others.

Mansworld
177 High Street, Berkhamsted, Hertfordshire
Tel: 01442 864740

Sells new and nearly-new, with some big fashion names including, Boss and Christian Dior.

☺

A police motor-bike patrol officer couldn't believe his eyes when an old lady sped past him, swerving from side to side.

As he got closer he could see the old lady was knitting and steering the car at the same time, the officer shouted "Pull over, pull over" and the old lady replied "No it's a scarf, but thanks for asking!"

CHAPTER **31**

Buying from auctions & wholesale

Most people have never been to a legitimate auction and are really missing out. Before I go any further, I stress legitimate auctions because there are some companies who call themselves auctioneers, but are really just sales companies.

Contrary to popular belief anyone can go to most auctions and they don't just sell deceased estates, house clearances and general junk, although there are some auctions like this, there are also auctions who offer the following:

Lost/stolen unclaimed property and seized goods

These are the government auctions with many items coming from the Police, Customs & Excise and British Rail etc. These auctions tend to offer a wide range of goods.

Bankruptcy and liquidation stock

These auctions consist of brand new stock, raw materials like cloth or screws, and office equipment/manufacturing equipment. I was at a recent auction for a sportswear company that had gone broke, all the clothing was brand new and still had price tags on them, the clothing was being sold for around 30% of the retail value.

Job lots and end-of-line products

This is where big name manufacturers clear out their warehouses of seconds, end-of-line products and mail-order returns etc.

What you need to know about auctions

The best type of auction is one that has no reserves, this is common with government auctions and it means that if there is an item and no one else is interested in it, you can bid £1 and walk away with it. You see, big auction companies don't have the time or space to hold stock, they just want to get rid of it.

Finding good auctions

First of all some of the better auctions tend to be held on weekdays and not weekends, as this stops the casual bargain hunter going. Look in your local Yellow Pages for a full listing of auctioneers and try to get on their mailing list. I have listed a few auctioneers here:

Southgate Auction Rooms
55 High Street, Southgate, London, N14 6LD

Centaur Auctions
Centaur House, Lea Valley Est. Harbet Rd, London, N18

Eatons Auction Rooms
24-25 Baron Street, Rochdale, OL16 1SJ

Swindon Auction Rooms
The Planks, Old Town, Swindon, Wilts. SN3 1QP

Kerr and McAlister
Queens Park Auction Halls, 140 Niddrie Rd,
Glasgow, G42

Look in your local Yellow Pages for a full listing of auctioneers in your area.

If you are serious about auctions, then I suggest you subscribe to a newsletter such as the Government Auction News. This will make it easy for you to find out when there are auctions going on in your area:

Government Auction News
17 Fleet Street
London, EC4Y 1AA

How an auction works

Once you know the time and date of the auction you will be able to attend the viewing session, this could be the day before the auction or a few hours before. This gives you the chance to have a good look at the items, which are known as LOTS. Each Lot will be marked with a number and make sure that you write this down as most auctioneers lump items together for example, 20 assorted video tapes = Lot 10.

After the viewing you will normally need to get a Bidding Card, this is obtained by putting money on account, normally £50 or £100. If you don't buy anything, then you get your money back at the end of the auction and if you spend more than your deposit, you pay the difference.

Bidding at auctions

First of all do make sure you are bidding for the right item, listen to the Lot number and the description. The auctioneer will then open with something like "Do I have a bid of £50?" and if there is no answer, he will come down until a price is accepted by someone, then the price starts moving upwards again.

> TIP: Set a maximum price in your mind that you are
> willing to pay for the Lot and do not go over that,
> I've seen many people at auctions getting carried
> away and they end up paying far too much.

Unlike what you see on TV, to bid you don't scratch your nose or raise your eyebrows, the main way is to raise your hand with your ticket number, the auctioneer is well trained to spot bids even in a crowded room and will look your way.

If yours is the winning bid the auctioneer will say "Sold to the gentleman/lady on the right" and he will normally ask you for your bidding card number, that's how they know it's you.

Gaining experience at auctions

My advice is to go to a few auctions and watch other people, most people at auctions are quite friendly and will often help you out with any questions you have.

NOTE: Most auction houses want their money straight away, preferably in cash. In some cases they will hold the goods for 1 day, so you can come back, but usually no longer than this. They also expect you to take the goods away within a day as they need the space. Some auctions can arrange for delivery of big items, but there is a charge for this.

Summary

Auctions can be a very good way to buy new and used goods at low prices. Keep your head when bidding as it's easy to get carried away. Auctions can be very lucrative if you are interested in buying and selling, many items bought at auctions can be sold on at a profit through local adverts or to your friends and family.

Office products, stationery and envelopes etc.

If you are running your own business which most of you will be, then I strongly recommend that you get an account with Viking Direct if you're in the U.K., including Ireland and the Channel Islands.

They deliver to your door normally the next day and their

prices are very competitive. Viking Direct sell nearly everything you can possibly think of that your business will need including, photocopier paper, envelopes, pens, packing materials, office furniture, fax machines, photocopiers, toner cartridges for your laser printer and even coffee.

To open an account call them on 0800 424444 or 0800 622211. Their address is Viking Direct Ltd, Bursom Industrial Park, Tollwell Road Leicester, LE4 1BR.

I guarantee that you'll be happy with this company and you will save money by using them, I have dealt with them for many years.

Buying at wholesalers

One of the big advantages of owning your own business is that you can get membership to wholesalers and buy goods at greatly reduced prices. Now contrary to what most people think, you don't have to buy a minimum of 2,000 tins of baked beans or 1 ton of sugar at a time, most wholesalers sell in packs of 6 or 12, as for electrical goods and many other items, you only have to buy 1.

The two wholesalers that I have listed sell almost everything at substantially reduced prices. Items include, food, drink, electrical goods, household goods, toys, DIY items, gardening goods, CD's, computers and many other items.

Access to these warehouses is by membership only, there is no fee for Makro, however, there is a fee at Costco, but it's well worth it.

To join you'll need some proof that you are in business i.e. a business bank statement, telephone bill or letterhead etc.

For more details contact your local Makro branch:

Aberdeen 01224 896896

Belfast 01232 611022

Bristol 01179 591262

Cardiff 01443 841010

Charlton 0181 293 0011

Eccles 0161 789 6911

Edinburgh 0131 458 5151

Fareham 01489 885131

Glasgow 0141 882 9051

Birmingham 0121 550 7341

Hull 01482 229900

Leeds 0113 263 3341

Leicester 0116 263 0730

Liverpool 0151 546 9211

Newcastle U Lyme 01782 566212

North Acton 0181 965 6655

Nottingham 0115 986 6888

Poole 01202 659100

Preston 01772 769944

Rayleigh 01268 785 578

Reading 01734 313633

Sheffield 0114 275 3830

Swansea 01792 644000

Teesside 01642 634234

Washington 0191 416 4001

Costco

Costco are an American wholesaler who have recently opened outlets in the U.K. They sell food, electrical goods, clothes, alcohol and many household goods at extremely competitive prices. To find your nearest branch call the Costco branch in Watford on Tel: 01923 213113.

Matalan

These are excellent discount warehouses that mainly sell clothes, however, they do stock some household items. Their prices on items such as jeans, shirts and sweaters are remarkable, most items sell at 50% off the recommended retail price.

Matalan have a network of warehouses throughout the U.K. and to find your nearest one contact:

Matalan Discount Club (Cash & Carry) Ltd
Head Office, Gillibrands Road
Skelmersdale, WN8 9TB
Tel: 01695 552400

CHAPTER 32

Banking and credit cards

In the making money section I warned you about banks overcharging on business accounts and cheques being cashed twice and bank charges etc., I want to remind you again to watch out on your personal bank accounts.

The main item to watch out for on personal accounts are Direct Debits. Is the same direct debit being taken out of your account twice and is it the correct amount?

Also if you cancel something, make sure that the direct debit/standing order is cancelled on the correct date as many companies will sneak an extra month through!

No fee credit cards

In this day and age we all need a credit card, have you ever tried to book a hotel or hire a car without one? It's almost impossible.

I have noticed in the last few years that various banks have started to charge a card fee, which is crazy. There is no need for you to pay a fee to carry a credit card. The only fee that I currently pay is the American Express card fee.

A good no fee credit card is provided by:

MBNA International Bank
P.O. BOX 1004
Chester Business Park
Wrexham Road
Chester
CH4 9WW

This bank provides a 24hour service, a gold Visa card, a free additional card for your spouse or family member, a credit card cheque book, competitive rates of interest on cash and credit card purchases, access to cash world-wide through ATM's (cash machines) and cards are available to employed and self-employed.

If you have an outstanding credit balance and you transfer it to MBNA, they will normally offer you a special reduced interest rate for the first 6 months.

Robert Fleming
Banking Services
16-22 Western Road
Romford
RM1 3SP

This bank provides a no fee visa card and many of the same benefits as above. They also offer good general banking facilities and competitive interest rates on current account credit balances.

There are many other no fee credit cards and you should look in the national press for details. If you are happy with your current credit card and they charge a fee, then drop them a line or phone them up before the next renewal and tell them that you don't want to pay the fee, you'll be surprised how many card issuers will drop the fee rather than lose a customer.

The same goes for interest rates charged on credit cards, haggle because you have nothing to lose and everything to gain!

Cut the cost of international calls

Call charges have dropped dramatically both in the U.K. and US, however, you can still save money by using calling cards and independent telecom companies.

At the time of writing I can call or fax the USA from the U.K. at any time of the day for only 6p per minute, now even with the B.T. and Mercury discount schemes, they cannot match these rates. So what's the catch? None really, you have to pay for your calls up front by buying an electronic phone-card of normally £25 of units, then as you use the units up you call a number and the card can be topped up over the phone.

To use the service you call a special number first which is a free-phone number, type in a PIN number on your phone and then you make the call as usual. A new company that I have started to use is One.Tel and they do not require upfront payment. They simply bill you monthly.

Calling cards offer great discounts to many countries, including the US, Europe, South Africa, India and Japan to name a few.

Calling home from aboard

Another good reason to have a calling card is that it's much cheaper to phone home when you're away, you also don't have to worry about hotel telephone surcharges or finding lots of change to put in a phone-box.

There are many discount calling companies and here are a few that I have used:

One Tel, London Tel:0171 331 9777 (No up front payment)

First Telecom plc, London Tel: 0171 572 7700

World Telecom, London Tel: 0171 384 5000

Worldcall Tel: 0800 0747 000

There are many new companies entering this market so look in airline and business magazines for their adverts.

CHAPTER **33**

Summary on saving money

I would like to sum up this section by saying that learning to spend and invest wisely is the key to holding on to your wealth and it's the key to making your money last. Many people say to me that because I'm rich I don't need to haggle or get discounts, yet the truth is that it's partly because of my careful spending that I ever accumulated any wealth in the first place.

As I have previously stated, I am not a miser, I enjoy spending my hard earned money, but I also ensure that I get the best deal I can, this way I can have my cake and eat it! Even after all these years I still get tremendous satisfaction when I get a discount, upgrade or a special bargain.

Do learn to take charge of your financial life and learn to invest your money wisely, money does make money and as I have previously outlined, a relatively small sum can grow into a considerable amount over time.

Use the information in this section to your advantage and you too can make your hard earned money go further. It has taken me years to learn these secrets and this is the first time that I have ever shared them.

I am always happy to learn about new money saving schemes and discount outlets, so if you either own a business or you have a favourite discount outlet, then drop me a line and I will add it to the next reprint.

Where do we go from here?

Well we have come along way and if you've worked your way to the end of this book, then pat yourself on the back and congratulate yourself. If you genuinely use the information that I have revealed to you in this book, then you will be on the road to an incredible journey, but please remember that achieving the success you deserve is a journey and you have a long way to go yet. The next and final section is the reference section where I have listed various addresses, telephone numbers and books etc. which will be of value to you.

Is it over?

I hope not! Firstly, I would love to hear from you and you will find a questionnaire at the end so you can air your views about this book. Please TAKE THE TIME TO COMPLETE THIS FORM. I'd love to hear your success stories and with your permission I could even incorporate them into the next reprint of the book and if I do, I'll send you a personal copy.

The next step

I have put everything that I could print into this book, however, there are many things that I cannot describe in printed words, I need to show you visually, you need to hear my voice and see my facial expressions.

I cannot guarantee when or where, but I will be holding 2 to 3 seminars a year and as a reader of this book, I would like to invite you to attend. The seminar will be full of action packed information where I will go through many of the points outlined in this book, together with many new concepts and ideas, I will also be happy to answer your questions and give advice.

I intend to keep the seminar numbers fairly small and I want them to be as private as possible. If you are interested in attending, then please drop me a line and I will put you on the mailing list, I will then send you further details as and when they are available. I know that there will be more people who will want to attend than I can take, however, I will work on a first come first serve basis.

Register today FREE of charge and receive regular updates and a free audio cassette

By simply completing and returning the form at the end of this book by post or fax, I will keep you up to date with all the latest news and any changes. I will also send you a free audio tape called "How to programme your mind for success" which you will find invaluable.

Keep in touch using the Internet

I have formed an official Web Site for the readers of this book and I encourage you to make use of this free service, simply log on to the World Wide Web and go to WWW.Firstsuccess.Com

Personal Power II by Anthony Robbins

One of the best self improvement packages that I have ever used and continue to use is Personal Power II by Anthony Robbins. It is a 30 day programme which you go through on CD or audio cassette. The package is unique and I strongly recommend it. Some of the topics covered include:

The key to Personal power, taking control, the power of focus, values and beliefs, anchoring yourself to success, eliminating self-sabotage, how to solve problems quickly and effectively and much more that will complement what you have learned in this book.

The complete package is around £170 but it is worth it. If you would like more details about Personal Power II, Email me or write to First Success Publishing. This is a great investment that you can make in yourself.

My final summary

I would like to close this book with the same line that I started with, which is "As far as I am aware we only live once, at least on this planet, therefore, don't you think that you should reach out and get everything that you really want out of life?"

When I asked you this question many pages ago, you didn't know how to go about changing your life for the better, but now you have the knowledge the million dollar question is, will you start putting it into action? I urge you to take action and use your new knowledge, you truly have everything to gain and nothing to lose.

Finally, this book has taken many years to write and I would urge you to read it at least 10 times over and use it for reference as often as you need to, there is no way that you can gain the full benefit from this book by reading it only once.

Let me take this opportunity to wish you all the success and happiness in the world because you truly deserve it and I thank you for reading this book.

Vince Stanzione

Reference section

Here's a list of my favourite books which I have found very useful in both my business and personal life.

Motivation and personal success books

The Lazy Man's Way To Riches- Joe Karbo
ISBN 1-884337-22-8

Trump The Art Of The Comeback -Donald Trump
ISBN-0-8129-2964-0

The Millionare Next Door - T.J. Stanley & W.D. Danko ISBN 1-56352-330-2

Think Like A Tycoon - W.G. Hill
ISBN 0-906619-27-0 Scope International

Success Secrets - Mark H. McCormack
ISBN 0 00 215186 3 Collins

Personal relationship guidance
Are You The One For Me? - Knowing Who's Right & Avoiding Who's Wrong - Barbara De Angelis
ISBN 0-440-21575-7 Dell Publishing

Books related to business

The Salesman Of The Century - Ron Popeil
ISBN 0-385-31378-0 Delacorte Press

Tested Advertising Methods - John Caples
Prentice-Hall

Ogilvy On Advertising - David Ogilvy
ISBN 0-471-79831-5 Multimedia Publications

Be Your Own PR MAN - Michael Bland
ISBN 1-850910365-X Kogan Page

Good magazines

Computer Shopper
Investors Chronicle (U.K.)
Entrepreneur International
Business Week
Income Opportunities (USA)
Marketing Week
Exchange & Mart (U.K.)
The Trader (U.K.)

Internet access

Here are a few internet access providers who offer free trial software:

Dial Pipex
P.O. BOX 64
Stevenage
Hertfordshire
SG1 2YX
Tel: 0500 474739

Global Internet
113-123 Upper Richmond Road, London
SW15 2TL
Tel: 0181 957 1042
Fax: 0181 957 1100

Don't forget that you will need to buy a modem, I have found that the US Robotics Sportster is a good reliable modem which sells for around £130. Check in Computer Shopper magazine for the best price.

For free internet check cover disks on magazines such as Internet Magazine. You can get a free Freeserve internet disk by walking into any Dixons store in the UK.

Shopper magazine for the best price. You can also keep up with the latest Internet news by reading magazines like Computer Shopper, Internet magazine and others.

Interesting web sites

WWW.Firstsuccess.com
This is my excellent site, here you'll find the latest information on topics relating to this book, you can leave messages for me and E-mail any comments and suggestions.

WWW.bloomberg.co.uk/com
This is a great place to check all your U.K and US share prices.

WWW.Yahoo.com
This is a good general search engine, however, I mainly use it for the Yahoo quote service which gives all the American and Canadian share prices, charts, announcements and much more. Click on Stock Quotes from the search page.

WWW.EntrepreneurMag.com
This is the electronic version of my favourite business opportunity magazine. Although it is mainly aimed at the US market, you will still find lots of useful business information that can be used regardless of where you live.

WWW.hilitedms.co.uk
My listbrokers site. Good place to research mailing lists.

WWW.Ask.com/.co.uk
Ask Jeeves is a good place to search the net for anything in easy language for example: "who is Vince Stanzione" or "Where can I buy cheap cars from."

WWW.Networksolutions.com
Good site to register your your domain names or check who owns a domain name.

WWW.Amazon.com

The world's biggest on-line bookshop carrying over 2.5 million books, including many hard to find and old books.

Office stationery and business supplies

Viking Direct Limited
Bursom Industrial Park
Towell Road
Leicester
LE4 1BR
Tel: 0800 424444 Customer services: 0800 424445
Fax: 0800 622211

Mailing list broker

Hilite Limited
Ash House, Ash Road, New Ash Green
Longfield, Kent
DA3 8SA
Tel: 01474 874848
Fax: 01474 879292

Other list brokers are listed in BRAD Direct Marketing.

Videos

How to Earn £20,000 a month with low budget direct mail projects

Secret Weapons of Direct Mail

How to Earn £100,000 a year with a newsletter

To obtain details on these videos, write to: First Success Publishing, Video Dept. Exchange House, 494 Midsummer Boulevard, Central Milton Keynes, MK9 2EA.

Help me to help you and receive a FREE audio cassette and regular updates

However good myself and others think this book is, I am always ready to improve and listen to reader's suggestions, I also love to read letters from readers who have changed their life by putting the information in this book into practice, so if you have anything to say then please drop me a line.

Please take a few minutes to complete and return this form. Once completed you should post it to First Success Publishing, Comments Dept. Exchange House, 494 Midsummer Boulevard, Milton Keynes, MK9 2EA. Once received we will post you your free audio cassette "How to programme your mind for success" and we will send you regular updates as and when. **If you have already received the tape with the book then please tick here** ☐

Name _____

Address _____

_____

Postcode _____

Tel: _____

Fax: _____ E-mail: _____

What did you think about the first section of this book?
(Personal development, self-confidence, positive thinking etc.)

Excellent ☐   Very Good ☐   Good/Fair ☐   Poor ☐ (please tick one)

Have you found that the information in this section:

A) Helped to build your self-confidence   YES ☐   NO ☐
B) Improved your general outlook on life   YES ☐   NO ☐
C) Helped you to get things done   YES ☐   NO ☐
D) Helped set goals and map out your future YES ☐   NO ☐
E) Help you to get on better with others   YES ☐   NO ☐
F) Helped to make more right decisions   YES ☐   NO ☐
G) Improved your energy level   YES ☐   NO ☐

Please feel free to write any other comments about this section:

_____

_____

What did you think about the second section? (Making money, business secrets, increasing your pay etc.)

Excellent ☐ Very Good ☐ Good/Fair ☐ Poor ☐ (please tick one)

A) Helped me to start my own business	YES ☐	NO ☐
B) Helped me to increase my pay	YES ☐	NO ☐
C) Helped me to decide that I was working in the wrong job	YES ☐	NO ☐
D) Helped me to increase my current business profits	YES ☐	NO ☐

Please feel free to write any other comments about this section:

_____

_____

What did you think about the saving money section?

Excellent ☐ Very Good ☐ Good/Fair ☐ Poor ☐ (please tick one)

Have you used any or all of the methods to buy goods or services at discounted rates? YES ☐ NO ☐

If yes, did you use the information to save on (tick all relevant):

Airlines ☐ Hotels ☐ Car Hire ☐ Clothing ☐ General Goods ☐ Car Purchase ☐ House Purchase ☐ Insurance ☐ Telephone Calls ☐ Stationery ☐ Others ☐ (please specify):

Please feel free to write any other comments about this section:

_____

Final summary

Please write a few words on what you thought about this book as a whole.

_____

_____

Would you be interested in future details on (tick all relevant):

Seminars ☐ Videos and audio tapes on self-development ☐ Videos & audio tapes on business ☐ Other books ☐ Consultations ☐

THANK YOU. I APPRECIATE THE TIME THAT YOU HAVE SPENT COMPLETING THIS QUESTIONNAIRE AND IT WILL BE READ BY ME PERSONALLY. YOUR FREE AUDIO TAPE WILL BE POSTED TO YOU.